Historic
Canada

CHATHAM

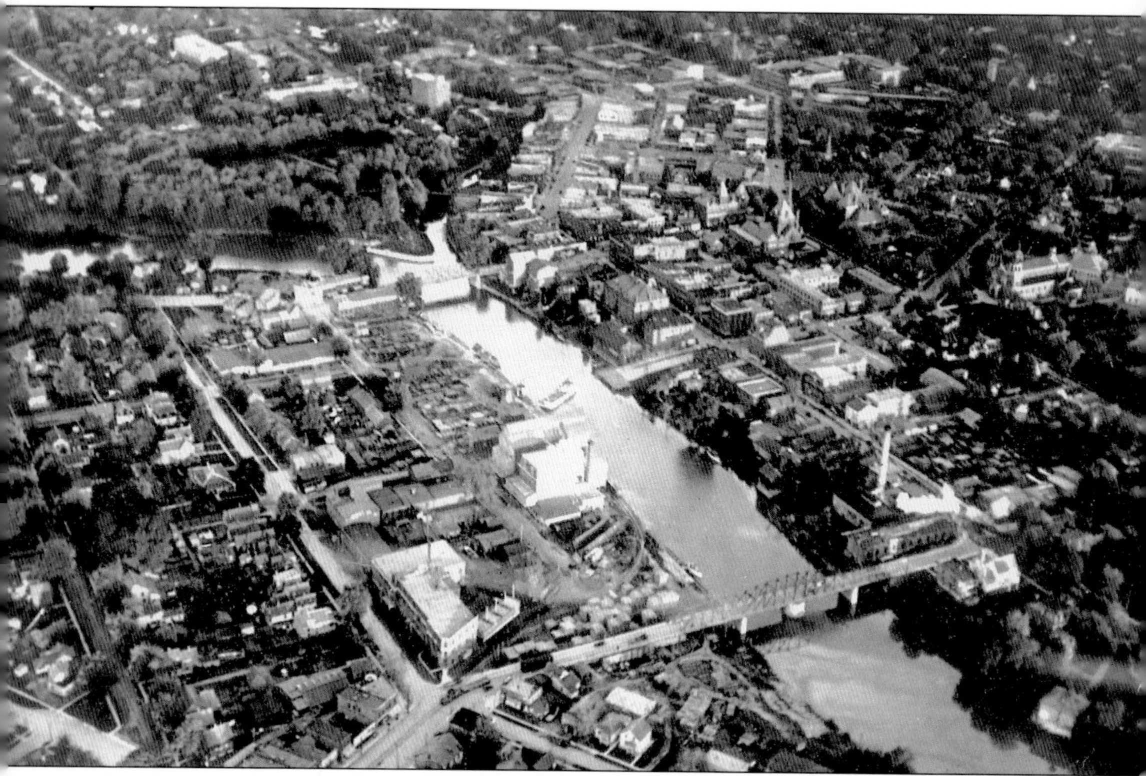

In what must be the earliest aerial view of Chatham (*c.* 1909), a vibrant downtown area and a busy Thames River between the Third Street Bridge and the Fifth Street Bridge are shown. Careful examination of this bird's-eye view of the city reveals many downtown structures that no longer exist. Among these buildings are the Chatham Power House, Harrison Hall, the Central School, the Rankin Hotel, St. Joseph's School, the Chatham Post Office, and the Kent Mills. (Courtesy National Archives of Canada.)

Historic Canada

CHATHAM

Jim and Lisa Gilbert

ARCADIA PUBLISHING

ISBN 978-0-7385-1150-4

Published by Arcadia Publishing
Charleston, South Carolina

Printed in the United States of America

Library of Congress Catalog Card Number: 2002113042

For all general information contact Arcadia Publishing at:
Telephone 843-853-2070
Fax 843-853-0044
E-mail sales@arcadiapublishing.com
For customer service and orders:
Toll-Free 1-888-313-2665

Visit us on the Internet at www.arcadiapublishing.com

On the Cover: Seen is the Central School yard *c.* 1938. (Courtesy Glen Wood.)

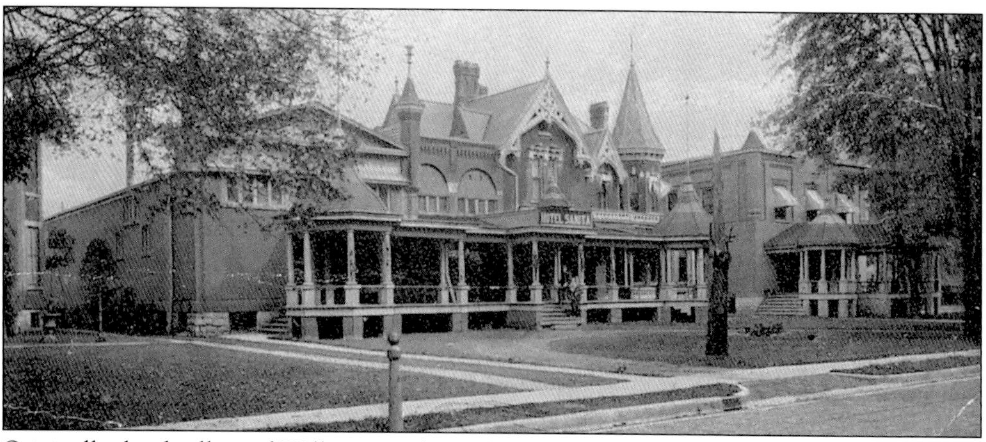

Originally the dwelling of William Northwood (1879), this building subsequently became the home of T.H. Taylor, and then, in 1902, it became the Chatham Mineral Baths and Sanitarium. When the mineral water supply from McGregor's Creek dried up *c.* 1908, it was transformed into the Hotel Sanita. After this venture closed *c.* 1924, the building housed the Chatham Vocational School, and in the 1960s, it became what it is today—the Chatham Cultural Centre. This *c.* 1908 photograph shows the building in its mineral bath stage. (Authors' collection.)

Contents

ACKNOWLEDGMENTS

We would like to gratefully acknowledge the following people, organizations, businesses, and institutions for allowing us to use their photographic collections and for sharing their time, expertise, and historical knowledge: Helen Blackburn; Dr. Dick Charteris; the *Chatham Daily News*; the Chatham Kent Museum; Bill Coltart; Darren Crow; Mollie French; W.G. Glassco; Doug and Dienne Howard; Mary Jane Hunter; Mr. and Mrs. Jack Jamieson; Dale Legary; Al Mann; Mr. and Mrs. Milt Mardling; Marg Mills; Lloyd Mitton; the National Archives of Canada; Tanya Neaves; Jane Parry; Roy Poulter; Loretta Roberts; Joanne Gail Sewell; Peter Stanojevic; Joe, Stan, and Jean Uher; the Union Gas Archives; Austin Wright; and Jane Brokenshire Wright.

A special debt of gratitude goes out to the area's local historians, who continue to have a sincere love and passion for our area's past. Without their excellent and painstaking research, we could not have completed this book. We would like to personally thank the premier local historian, Victor Lauriston, for his pioneering efforts in the field; Win Miller for her tireless and energetic pursuit of local history; Peter Stanojevic for his perseverance, good advice, and intimate knowledge of local history; and John Rhodes for his excellent research skills and eclectic interests. In our eyes, these people are true heroes, and we salute them.

We would also like to thank Tanya Neaves for her cheery, positive, and tireless efforts in helping us put this book together under, at times, some difficult situations.

A special thank-you also goes to the coordinator of the Central Library in Chatham, Sheila Gibbs, and the excellent staff of the Chatham Kent Central Library for their willingness to go out of the way to help us in our research. Their positive approach and helpful manner is one that all Chatham Kent municipal services would do well to emulate. They exemplify the importance of knowing who their clients are and catering to their needs. It is much appreciated.

INTRODUCTION

Lt. Gov. John Graves Simcoe gave Chatham its name, just as he did many other place names in Ontario. Simcoe travelled on foot up La Tranche, which he had just rechristened the Thames River, in February 1793. When he reached the forks of this river and a tributary "of major proportions" (McGregor's Creek), he surveyed the land and decided that this location would be a good spot for a defensive port and a shipbuilding centre.

A year and a half later, Abraham Iredell was dispatched to the Forks (the informal name for Chatham) to survey the town site. William Baker also arrived to begin building gunboats and a blockhouse in preparation for the conflict that then appeared imminent with the young American republic to the south. Unfortunately for Chatham, Simcoe was recalled to England shortly after this, and many of his dreams and plans departed with him. As a result, Chatham languished for many years, a settlement and defensive centre in name only.

This is not to say that our developing settlement took a back seat to history during this time period. In June 1812, war with the United States did come to Upper Canada, and the next year, in October 1813, it found its way to our doorstep. After the Americans won the Battle of Lake Erie on September 10, 1813, Maj. Gen. Henry Procter, then in command at Fort Malden, decided to retreat to Burlington. His path of retreat took him and his army, as well as the large group of native allies with him, up the Thames River and quickly through the small developing village of Chatham.

Before leaving Fort Malden, Procter had promised the leader of the native contingent, Chief Tecumseh, that he would make a stand at the Forks (Chatham). Tecumseh and his Indian Confederacy were dismayed at the prospect of moving from Fort Malden and farther from the lands that they regarded as their home. They were only persuaded to come along because of this promise to take a stand and fight the invading U.S. forces.

Therefore, when Tecumseh arrived at the Forks and saw that nothing had been done to prepare the site for battle, he and his native allies were furious, and nearly half of them deserted the British army immediately. A brief rearguard action was fought at the Forks, on the site of present-day Tecumseh Park, on October 4, 1813, but the main battle took place farther upstream the next day. In this famous skirmish known to Americans as the Battle of the Thames and to the British as the Battle of Moraviantown, the great native leader was killed, ending for all time the hopes of a native homeland in the Ohio Valley.

The battle also devastated the settlers in the area. A few stalwart pioneers had, by this time, settled on the site of what is now Chatham. The best known of these settlers were John and

Martha McGregor, who kept a gristmill and a farm. The mill was destroyed by the natives and the British during their retreat to prevent it from falling into the hands of the invading American forces. Other settlers (such as the Dolsens, Fields, Pecks, and Chryslers) were similarly set back when this area became temporarily American.

For these and other reasons, Chatham did not become a settlement in anything more than name until the latter 1820s. Before that time, the major settlement on the lower Thames was located about four miles downstream at Dolsens, which today is not much more than a farmer's field. However, as mentioned, in the late 1820s, Chatham began to eclipse Dolsens as the major centre in the area.

Chatham's growth was given a further boost when, as a result of the Rebellion of 1837, the long-promised military presence became a reality with the construction of a military barracks and the posting of a regiment. This military presence lasted into the 1840s, cementing Chatham's hold on the title of commercial centre for the lower Thames and resulting in Chatham officially becoming a village in 1850. What finally sealed Chatham's establishment as a town of some importance was the coming of the Great Western Railroad in January 1854. As it did with so many other communities across Canada, the railroad's arrival led to a period of economic growth and prosperity for many Chatham residents, and as a result, Chatham became a town in 1855.

During the 1850s, Chatham became the centre for another kind of railroad as well. This was a very different kind of endeavour, one that was undertaken not for economic gain but for humanitarian reasons. It was, of course, the Underground Railroad. With the passing of the Fugitive Slave Law in 1849, fugitive slaves and free black men alike no longer felt safe in the northern United States. As a result, they began streaming across the border, and Chatham became a mecca for many blacks at this time. Among the many blacks who came to the community were Mary Shadd Carey, who became the first black woman in North America to edit a newspaper, and Martin Delaney, who, among other things, became a leader in the movement to reestablish a black homeland for former slaves in Africa.

Another man who followed the blacks to Chatham was John Brown, the radical abolitionist who planned to overthrow the government and establish a new, slavery-free United States of America. Brown's plan for what he hoped would become the first step in this coup d'état centred around the takeover of the U.S. arsenal at Harper's Ferry, Virginia (now West Virginia). A good portion of this raid was prepared in Chatham in May 1858.

Brown's scheme, of course, was doomed from the start, but his failed attempt and his death on the scaffold as a result are generally considered to be a major catalyst for the American Civil War. An outcome of the Civil War, the freeing of the slaves, led to an eventual exodus of black citizens from the Chatham area back to the southern United States. Fortunately for the town of Chatham, not all those who sought freedom here returned to the United States, and as a result, Chatham still retains its rich repository of black heritage.

After the 1860s, Chatham was firmly established as a centre of Kent County, and the town could turn its eyes outward. While it did not remain immune to the economic fluctuations that every community in North America experienced then and now, Chatham positioned itself on a course toward increased economic growth that led, in 1895, to its achievement of city status.

Through the early years of the 20th century, Chatham continued its economic climb, given further impetus by World War I and, of course, coming to a screeching stop in the 1930s with the Great Depression. To provide a complete picture of Chatham's development in the 20th century is far beyond the scope of these introductory notes, but a few specific examples of the people and events of the time will provide some insights.

A good illustration is the Gray Carriage Works, which was one of the industries that contributed to Chatham's prosperity in the 1880s and 1890s. Then, in 1915, Robert Gray began manufacturing an automobile in partnership with Dallas Dort of Flint, Michigan. The car they made became known as the Gray-Dort and proved to be a very popular vehicle, especially in western Canada. Dallas Dort decided to pull out of the partnership in 1923, and the Grays did not bear the finances to take over sole ownership of the company; therefore, the Gray-Dort died. It certainly was a remarkable car, and it helped establish Chatham as a centre for automotive-related industry. Another reason for this was the Chatham Wagon Works, which eventually became a branch plant of International Harvester, today called International Trucks, still located there.

Chatham had its share of problems as well. For example, in 1937, 1947, and 1968, Chatham experienced disastrous flooding of the Thames and its tributaries. Today, the Lower Thames Valley Conservation Authority works to control and regulate water flow, but flood damage is still a possibility for many Chatham residents.

Chatham has also seen a number of its sons and daughters become famous in such endeavours as writing, politics, sports, and entertainment. Arthur Stringer moved away and became a well-known writer in New York in the first half of the 20th century; Lester Pearson, who became Canada's prime minister, lived in Chatham during his teenage years; Judy Lamarsh, a former federal cabinet minister, spent many of her formative years in the city; Darcy McKeough, a former Ontario cabinet member, continues to reside in Chatham Kent; baseball Hall of Famer Fergie Jenkins was born and raised here; and singer Sylvia Tyson remains committed to enhancing Chatham's cultural scene.

As Chatham entered the new millennium, it also entered, amid much debate and consternation, the new world of amalgamation. The city of Chatham, which had existed as a city since 1895 and as a settlement since the 1790s, became the municipality of Chatham Kent.

As we embark upon this new phase of our existence, a great deal of fear, trepidation, and skepticism drifts among the populous; however, the reality of the situation is that we will most likely survive by doing what we have always done—relying on the strength, ingenuity, and tenacity of our citizens to see us through any problems that we may encounter. Foreign invasions, downturns in the economy, and natural disasters have tested but not broken us, and therefore why should we not be able to withstand the onslaught of present and future trials and tribulations?

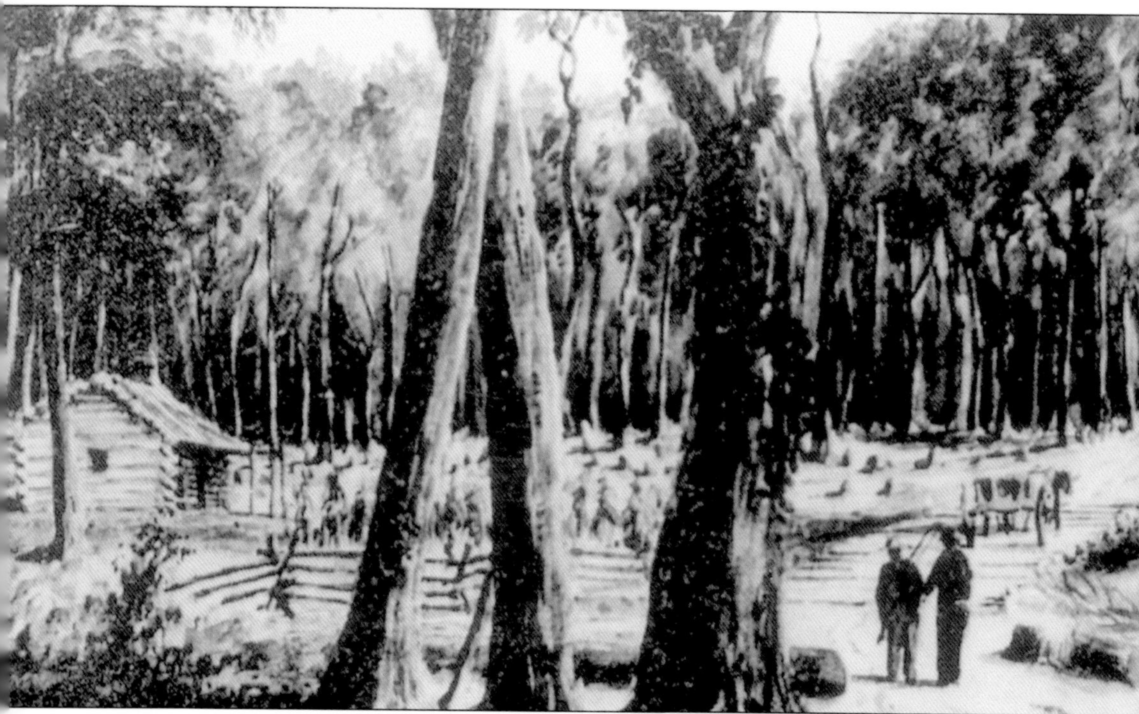

This sketch, entitled *Bush Home near Chatham*, was drawn by Lt. Col. P. Brainbrigge *c.* 1838. It shows the large number and size of the trees that early settlers to the area had to conquer in order to build a settlement. Trees, mud, and malaria were only a few of the obstacles they needed to overcome in the earliest of days. (Courtesy Chatham Kent Museum.)

One

Public Buildings and Public Houses

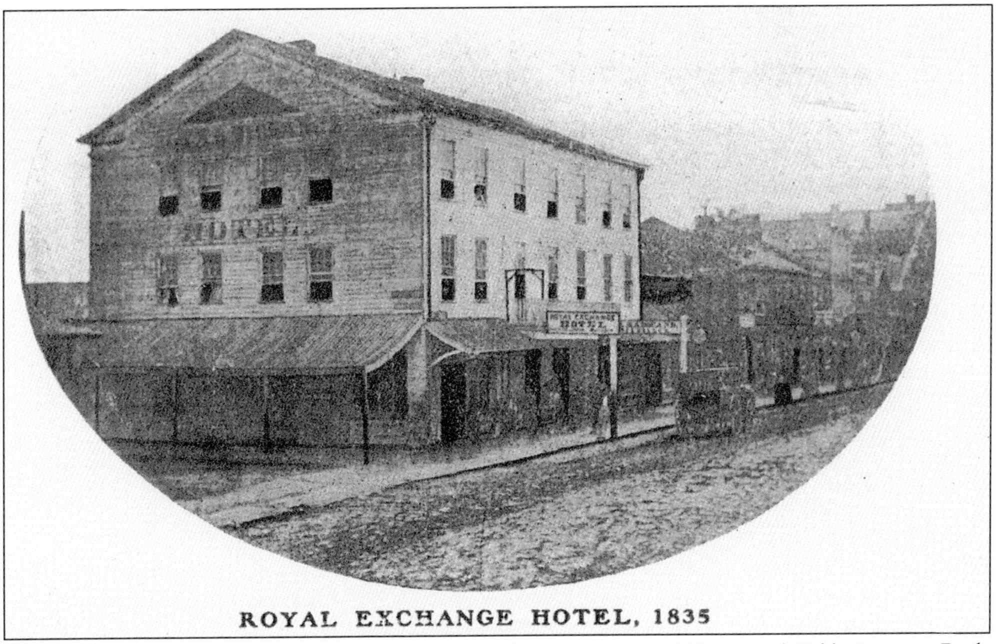

The Royal Exchange Hotel existed on the southwest corner of King and Fifth Streets. Built in the 1830s, this classy hotel was destroyed by a spectacular fire in February 1898. (Courtesy Chatham Kent Museum.)

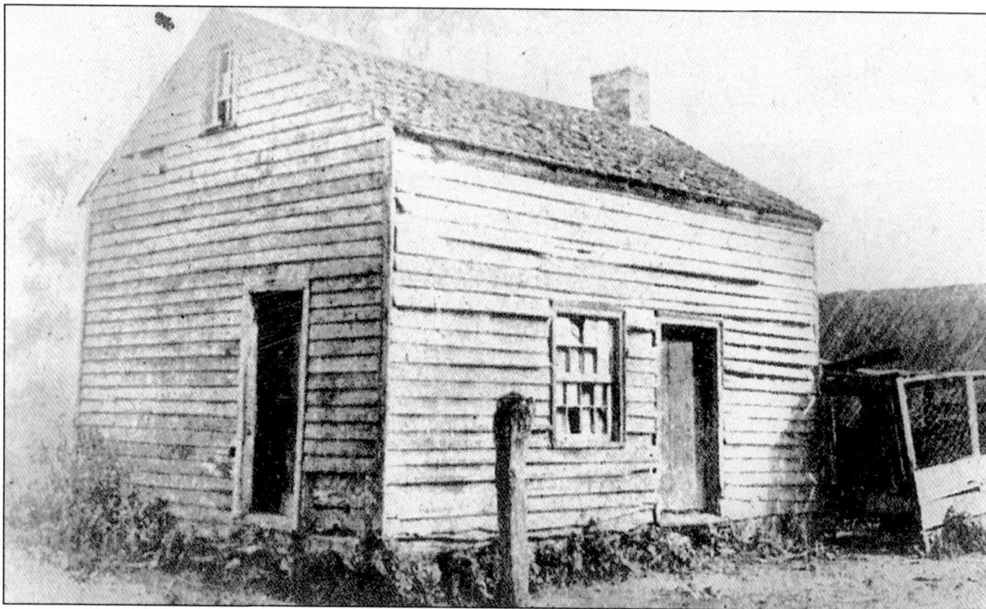

Chatham's first post office, established *c.* the 1830s, was on the McGregor Farm, situated on McGregor's Creek beyond the end of King Street East. Originally, a mill owned by John and Martha McGregor existed here as the heart of the settlement in its early years. The post office was operated by John McGregor's son Duncan, who also became Chatham's first postmaster. (Courtesy Chatham Kent Museum.)

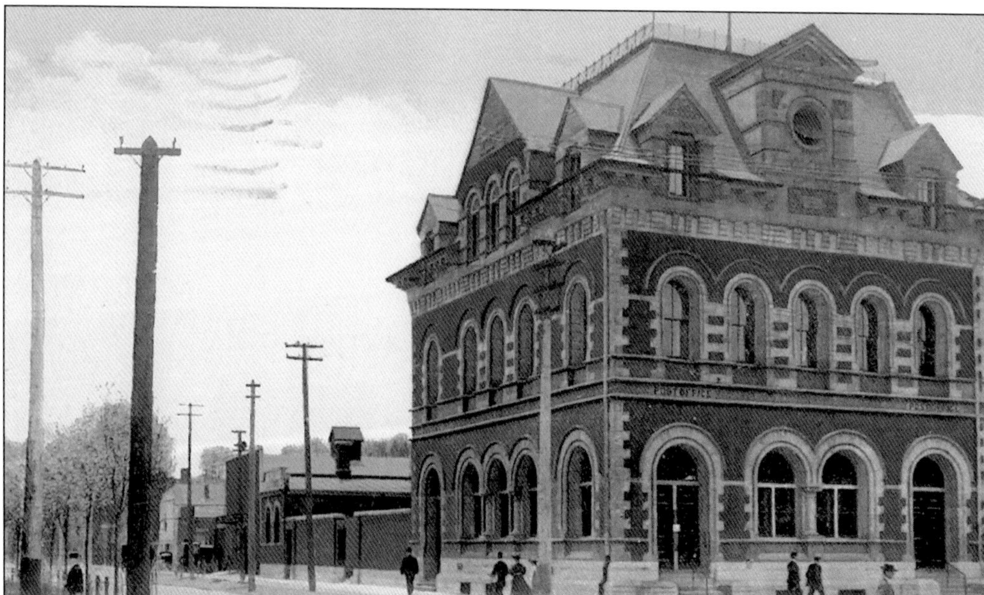

Situated on the southwest corner of King and Fourth Streets, the three-storey Chatham Post Office, shown here *c.* 1913, was built in 1884 for $35,000. At the time of its construction, the building was described as a "very substantial and handsome structure." It was constructed of brick and liberally faced with cut stone. Along with the post office, customs, inland revenues, and other departmental offices were located in it. It was torn down in 1957 to make way for the Woolworth department store. It is now the site of the Royal Bank. (Authors' collection.)

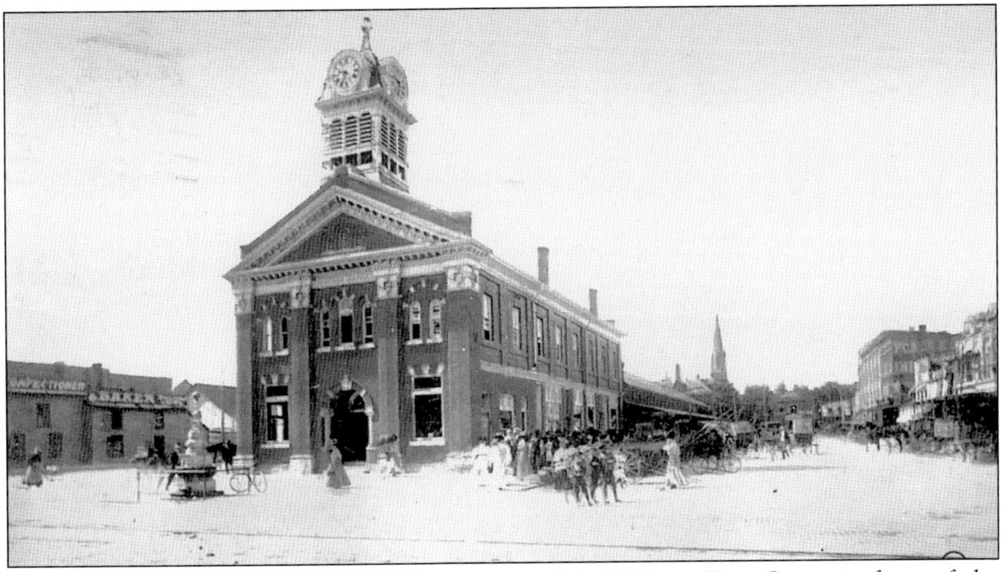

The original Chatham Town Hall was constructed in 1856 on King Street in front of the Chatham Market Shed at a cost of $6,000. The building housed an upstairs council chamber where the police court was held, and police cells were located in the basement. In addition, No. 1 Fire Company's headquarters were situated here as well. This regal-looking structure was noted for its impressive clock tower and water fountain. It remained, in one form or another, until the late 1970s. Its last use was as the home of Canada Trust. This photograph was taken c. 1910. (Authors' collection.)

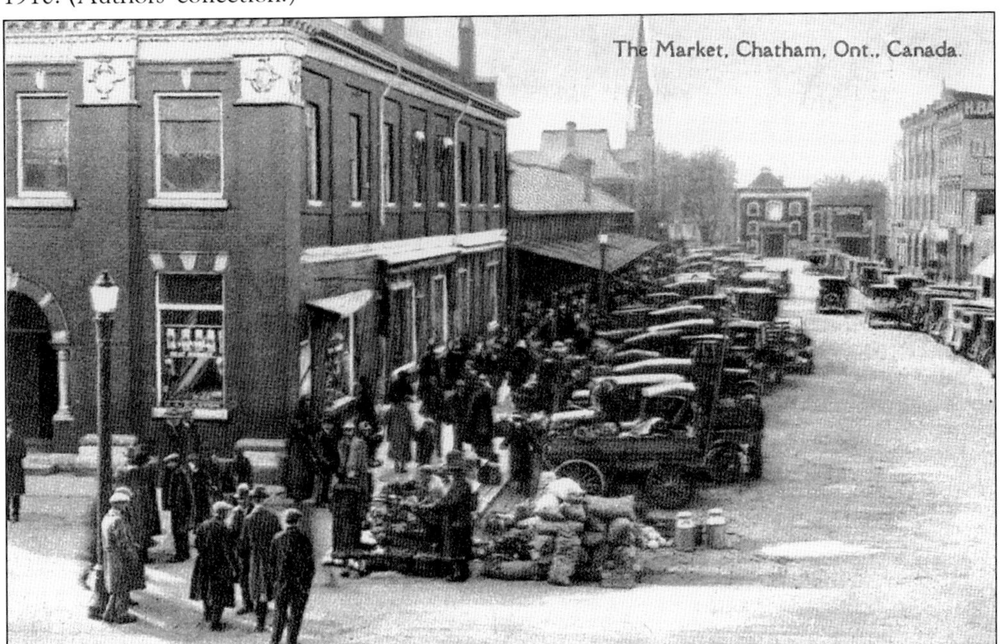

Although the Chatham Market Shed was attached to the original town hall, stores were on the first floor of the town hall, and merchandise was sold on the sidewalk outside of the structure. This c. 1918 postcard view, looking south on Market Street West, shows the steeple of Christ Church on Wellington Street East in the background. (Authors' collection.)

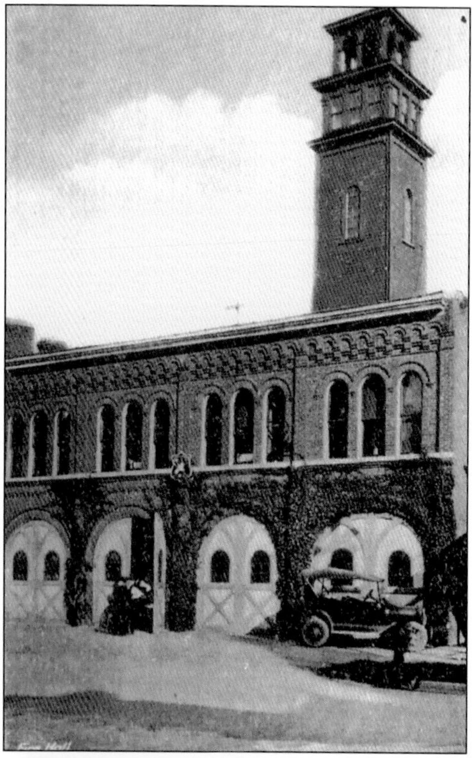

Fire Hall No. 1, on Sixth Street, was built in 1881 to house Chatham's first paid fire department. Its central location allowed Chatham's early fire department to respond to fires in remarkably quick times. The fire tower, pictured here *c.* 1910, was used as a fire-observation post and allowed firefighters to spot blazes before they got out of control. (Courtesy Doug and Dienne Howard.)

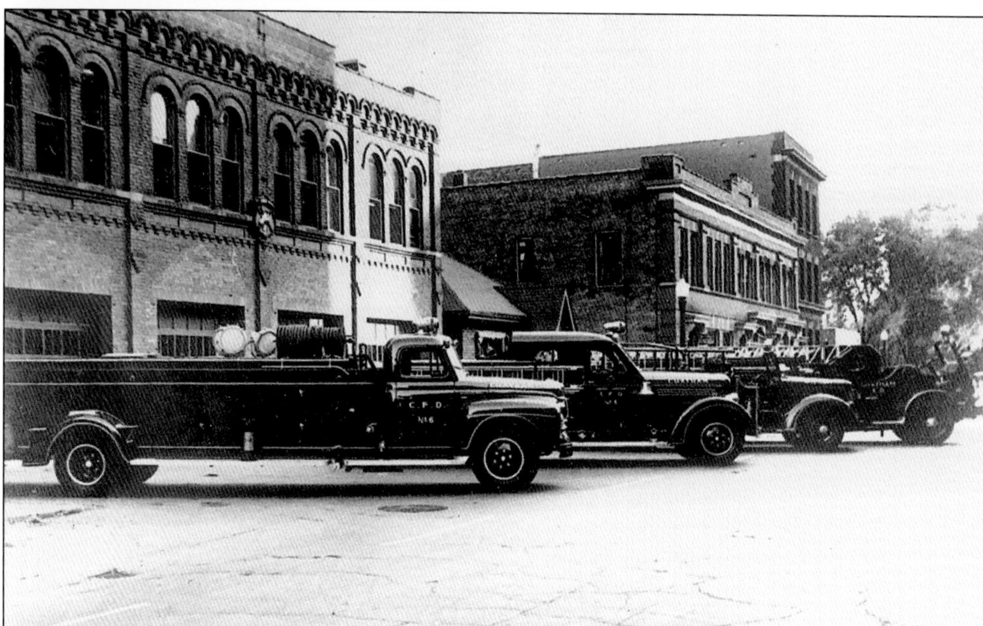

This *c.* 1940s photograph of Fire Hall No. 1 on Sixth Street in downtown Chatham depicts the same fire hall, now with new doors and from a slightly different angle. This view, looking south on Sixth Street, shows the grounds at Chatham's Central School at the trees beyond the last fire truck. This fire station existed until the 1980s, when it was torn down in order to build the Downtown Chatham Centre. (Courtesy Doug and Dienne Howard.)

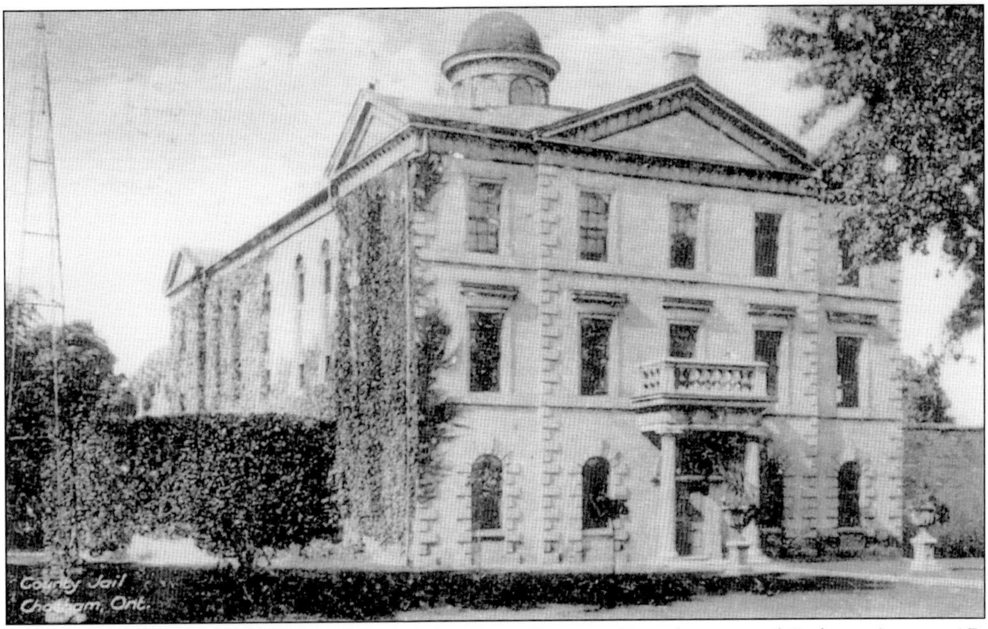

Ground was broken for the building of the Kent County Courthouse and Jail on August 17, 1848, on a pie-shaped plot of land situated between Seventh and Eighth Streets. The spot had been designated as a site for a courthouse by Chatham's first surveyor, Abraham Iredell, in 1795. The new courthouse was finished in January 1851 and was formally declared open on May 29. This photograph was taken *c.* 1918. (Courtesy Doug and Dienne Howard.)

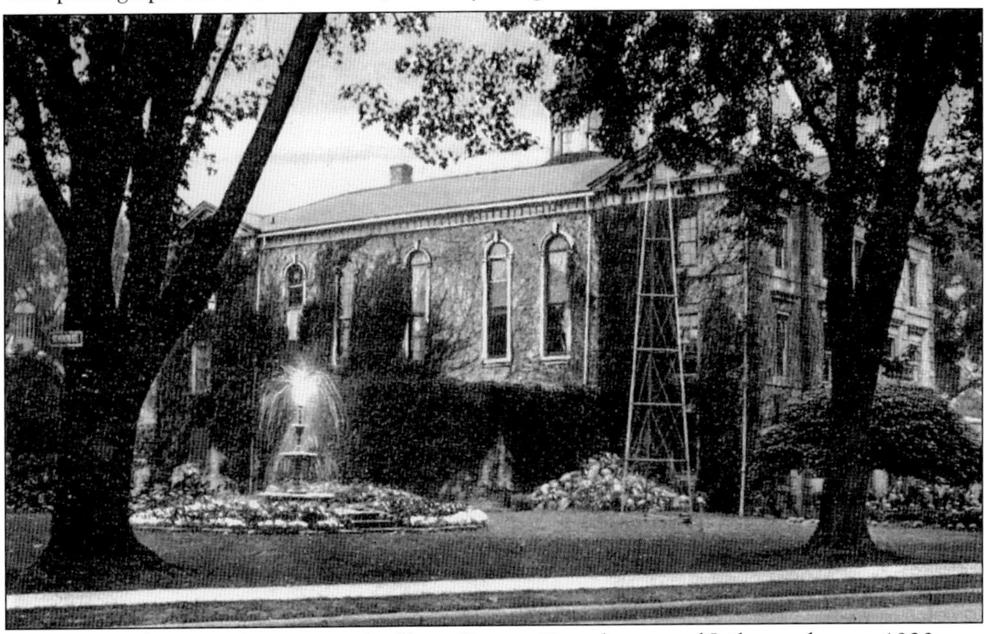

During its early years of existence, the Kent County Courthouse and Jail, seen here *c.* 1920, was affectionately called "Old Tin Top," as its first roof was made of tin and was conspicuous from a considerable distance. A young Scottish stonemason and future prime minister of Canada, Alexander Mackenzie, is reputed to have worked on the construction of the rear wall of the jail in 1848. (Authors' collection.)

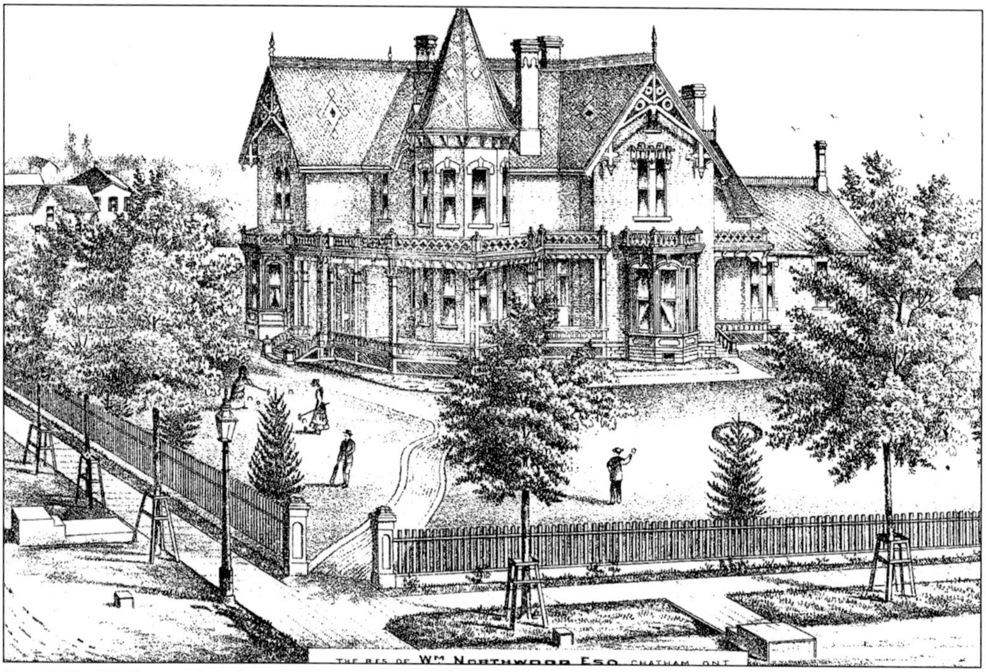

In 1879, William Northwood, the mayor of Chatham in 1879 and 1880, built a high-Victorian house for his family at the northeast corner of Murray and William Streets. The ginkgo tree, still standing on the site today, was purchased on a trip to the Orient. In the late 1880s, Northwood sold the home to T.H. Taylor of Taylor Mills, who lived there until his death in the 1890s. The house is seen here *c.* 1881. (Authors' collection, from the *Historical Atlas*.)

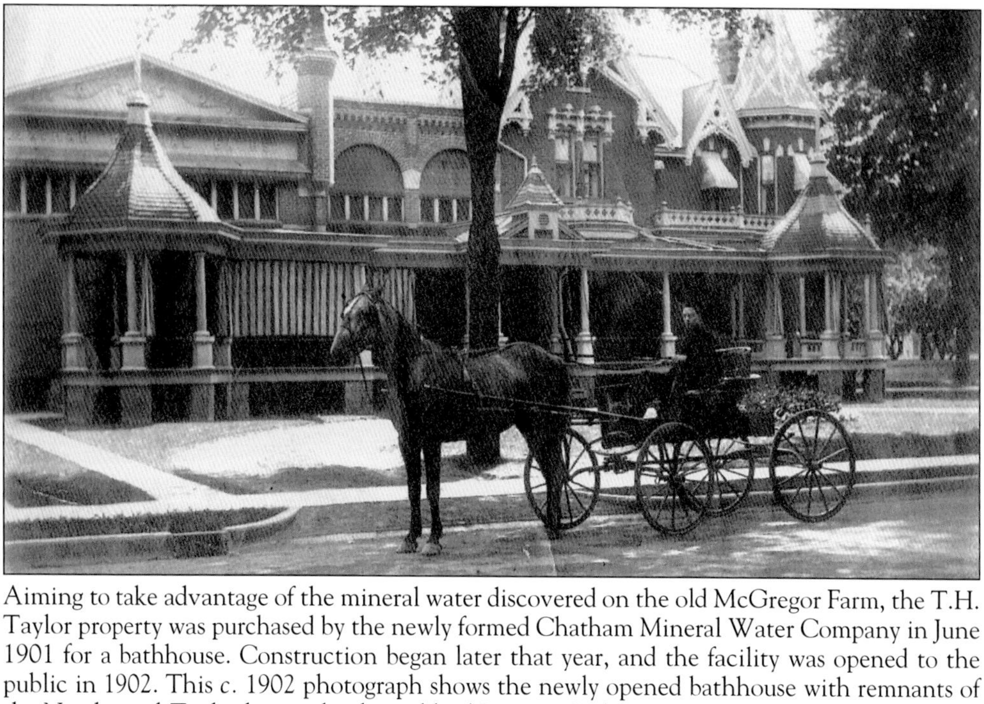

Aiming to take advantage of the mineral water discovered on the old McGregor Farm, the T.H. Taylor property was purchased by the newly formed Chatham Mineral Water Company in June 1901 for a bathhouse. Construction began later that year, and the facility was opened to the public in 1902. This *c.* 1902 photograph shows the newly opened bathhouse with remnants of the Northwood-Taylor home clearly visible. (Courtesy Jack Jamieson.)

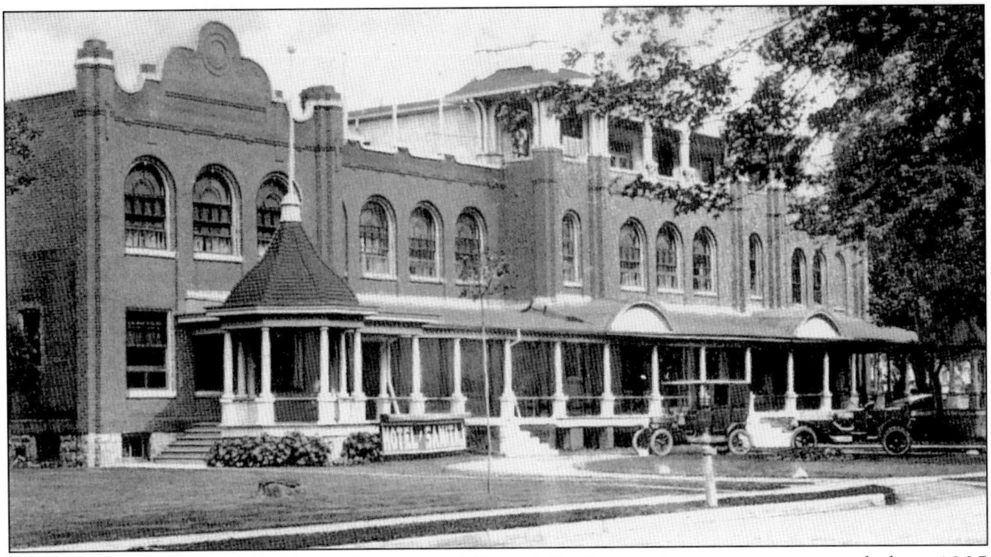

Filled with bright promise, the Chatham Mineral Baths' sanitarium was expanded in 1905 to include an enlarged dining room, 26 new bedrooms, sitting rooms, and sunbaths, a large ballroom, and a basement. The owners also renamed it the Hotel Sanita, and it was now capable of accommodating 300 bathers a day. Unfortunately, the mineral springs dried up, Prohibition arrived, and by 1924, the Chatham Board of Education had purchased the school. The site then became Chatham Vocational School. In the 1960s, the site became the home of the Chatham Cultural Centre. This photograph was taken *c.* 1906. (Courtesy Mollie French.)

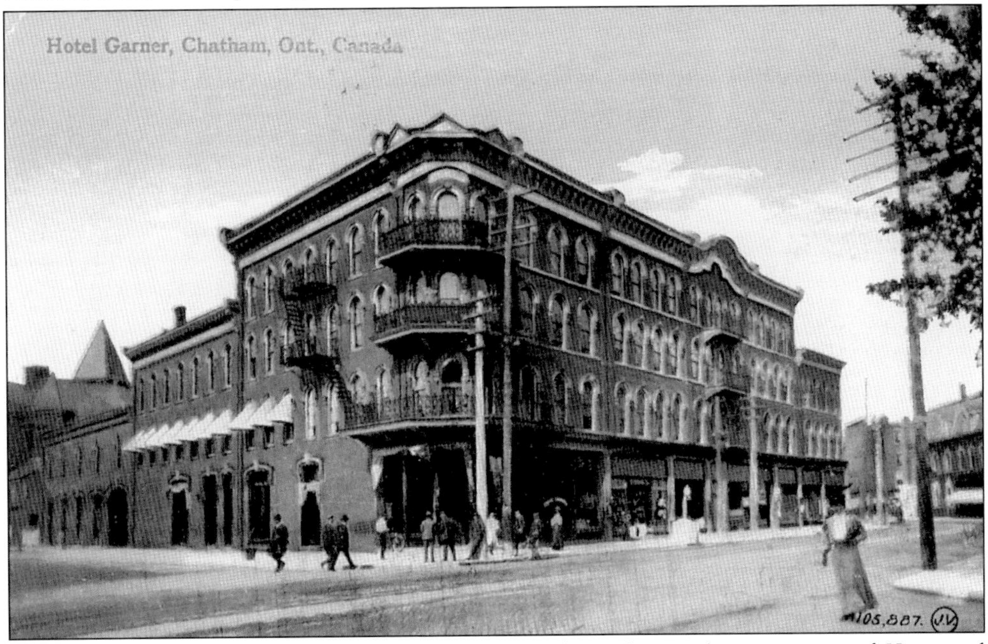

The Garner Hotel, seen here *c.* 1912, was situated on the southwest corner of King and Sixth Streets. Built in 1873, it was considered to be one of the finest hotels in southwestern Ontario. In a spectacular 1929 fire, this 80-room, four-storey structure was totally demolished. However, by 1930, the Garner had been replaced by a larger, 140-room hotel, the William Pitt. (Authors' collection.)

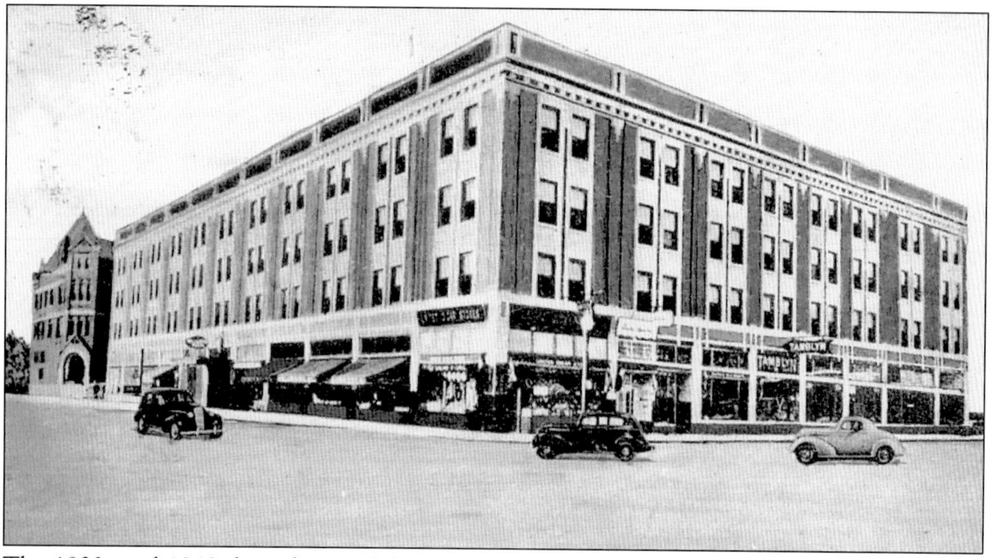

The 1930s and 1940s brought new life to Chatham's downtown area, and cars lined the main thoroughfare to frequent such establishments as the newly built William Pitt Hotel and the stores that occupied its street level. Stores located in the William Pitt Hotel were Tamblyn's Drug Store, Laura Secord Candy Store, and the United Cigar Store. This photograph was taken *c.* the 1930s. (Authors' collection.)

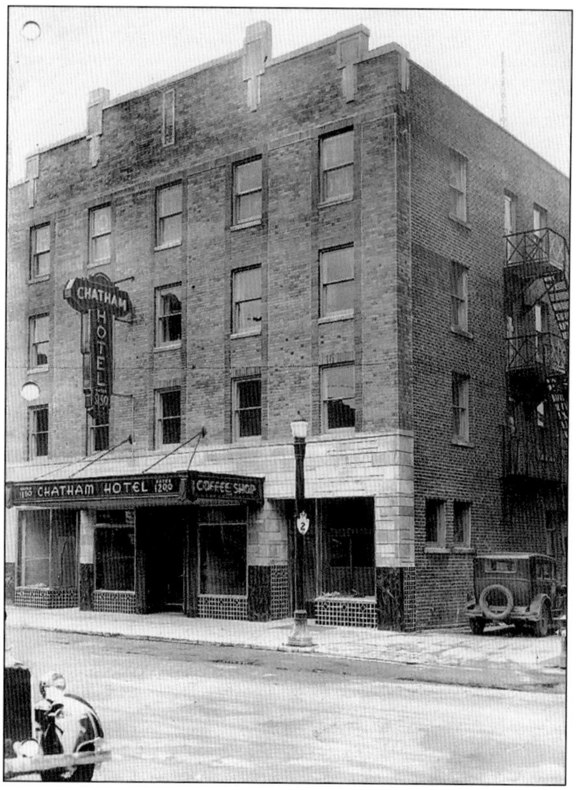

Soon after the opening of the William Pitt Hotel came the January 13, 1934 opening of the Chatham Hotel on Fifth Street. When it opened, it was considered to be the very latest in hotels. No rooms exceeded $2 a night, and each one had a private bath. The Chatham Hotel, shown here *c.* 1935, was owned by J. Beverly Kerr. (Courtesy Union Gas Archives.)

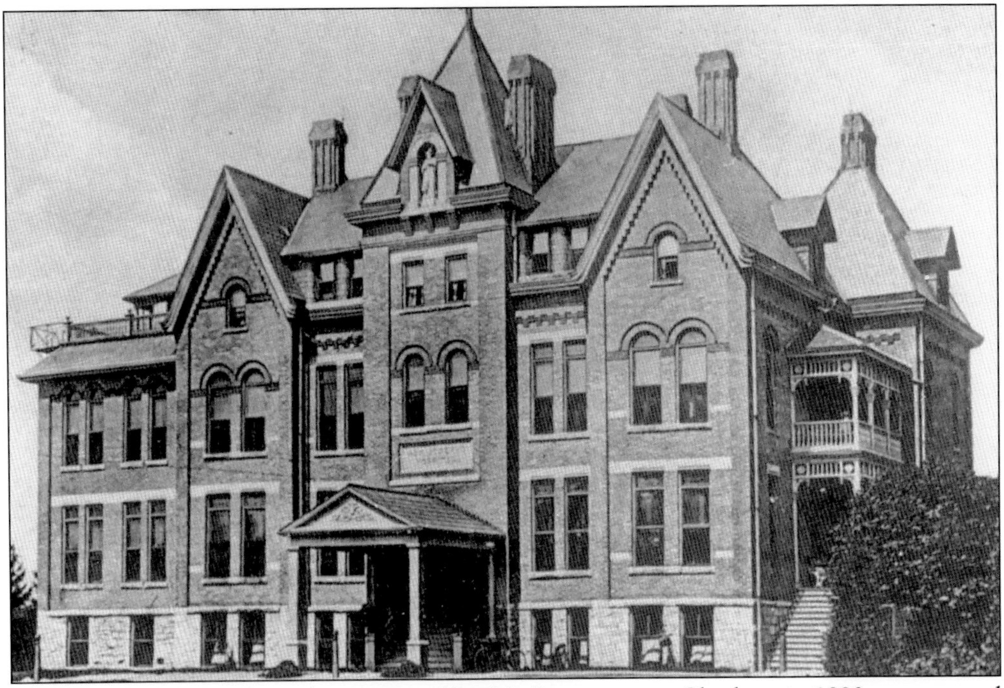

The Sisters of St. Joseph, at the request of Dr. J.L. Bray, came to Chatham in 1890 to set up and operate St. Joseph's Hospital. The original 1890 hospital was situated on Centre Street in the former Salvation Army barracks; however, by January 1892, the new hospital on King Street was ready, and patients were transferred there by sleigh. St. Joseph's Hospital was one of several hospitals started throughout the world by this nursing order. This *c.* 1902 photograph shows the hospital after the first west wing additions were made in the early 1900s. (Courtesy Chatham Kent Museum.)

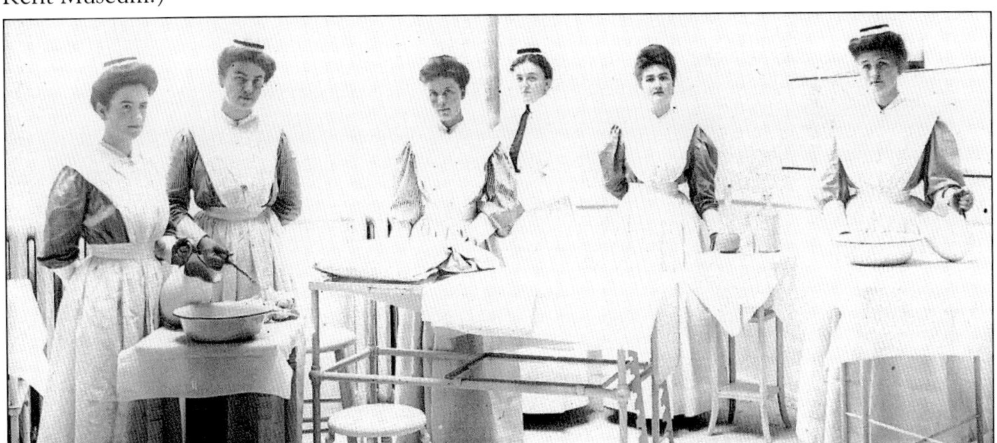

In this undated photograph, probably *c.* 1905, a dedicated and pristine team of nurses at St. Joseph's Hospital prepares for the next patient. By modern standards, this operating room may seem rather primitive. For the first three years, there was no system for heating water on the floors, and all water had to be heated on the kitchen stove and carried to the operating room. The pitchers and basins in this picture were probably used for that purpose. This photograph hung for many years in the office of Dr. Dick Charteris as a reminder of how far medicine had progressed. (Courtesy Dr. Dick Charteris.)

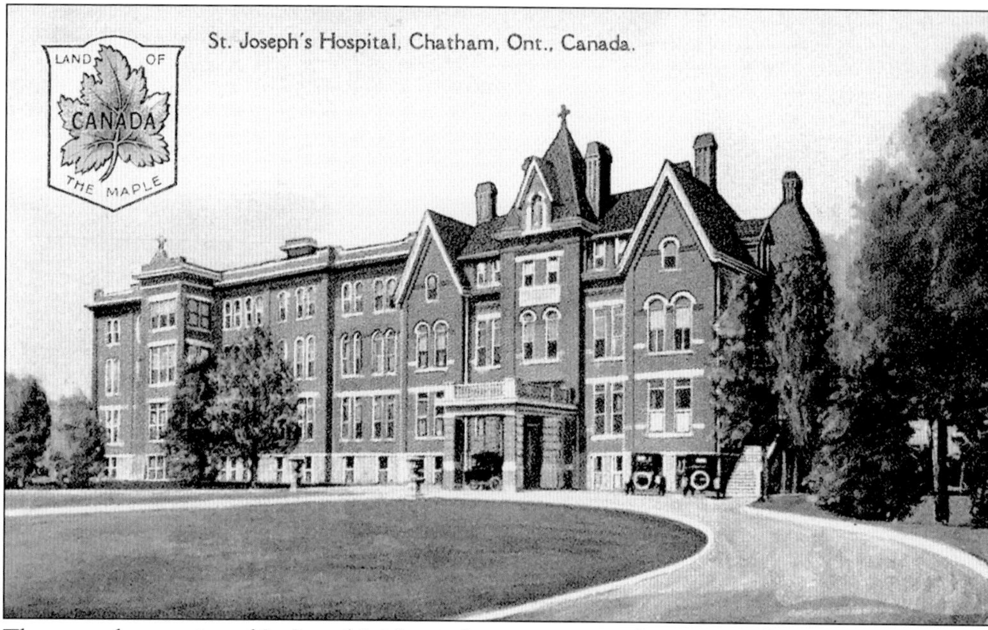

The second west wing of St. Joseph's Hospital was constructed in 1912 and was officially opened by Reverend Father James on December 1, 1913. The wing, seen here *c.* 1913, was constructed by the Blonde Lumber Company and was designed to fit seamlessly into the existing structure. (Authors' collection.)

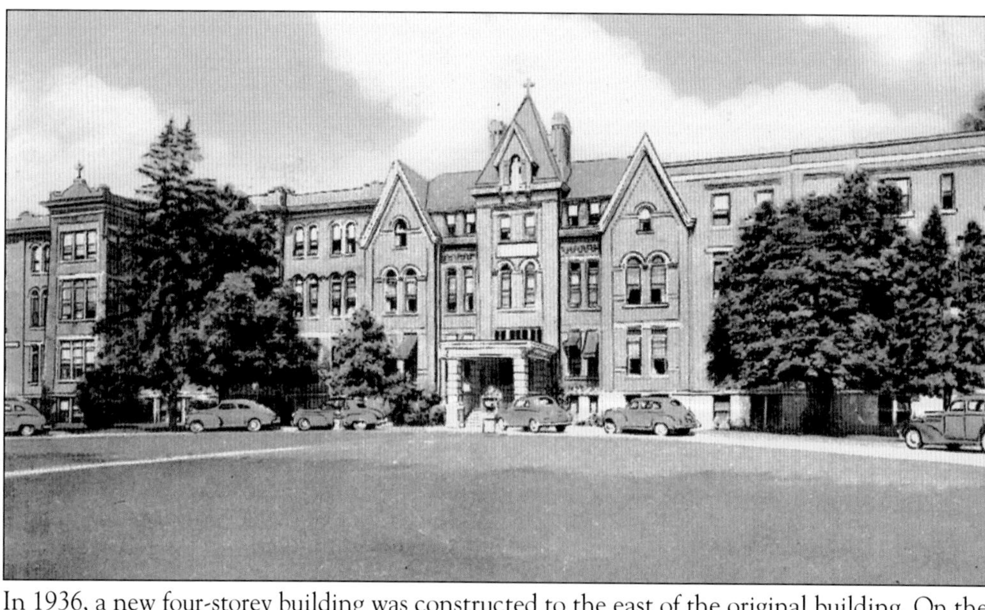

In 1936, a new four-storey building was constructed to the east of the original building. On the first floor of this new east wing were private and semiprivate rooms and a four-bed ward, fracture room, chart room, and waiting room. Once again, the addition was designed to fit in with the rest of St. Joseph's Hospital in an architecturally pleasing manner. This photograph was taken *c.* 1940. (Authors' collection.)

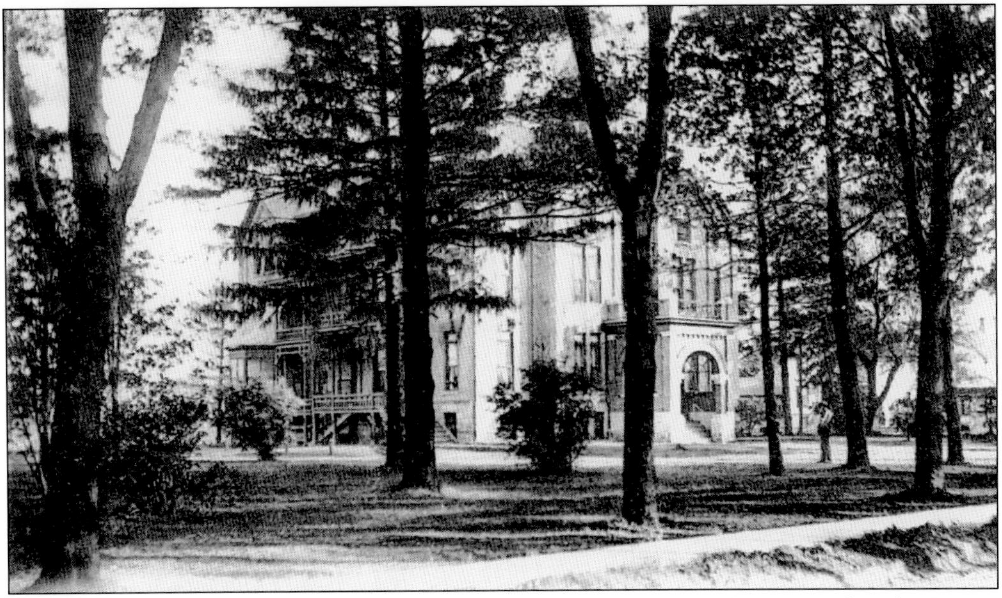

Public General Hospital began its existence on the southeast corner of Emma and Violet Streets on the site of Chatham lawyer C.E. Pegley's home, the Cedars. The cornerstone was laid on October 21, 1891, with the first patient admitted on April 11, 1893. This view shows how the hospital looked in the late 1890s and early 1900s. (Courtesy Mollie French.)

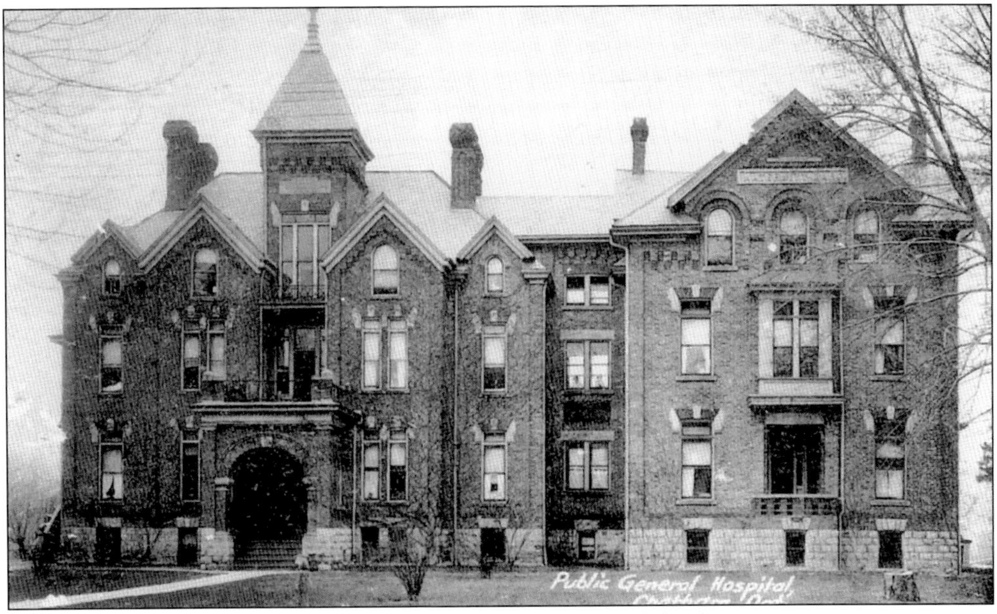

In 1907, the Ladies Assisting Society staged a very successful fundraising campaign, procuring enough money to build a much needed addition to Public General Hospital. On February 26, 1908, the new maternity ward was opened. In this c. 1910 picture, the original building can be seen on the left, and the 1908 maternity ward addition is on the right. (Authors' collection.)

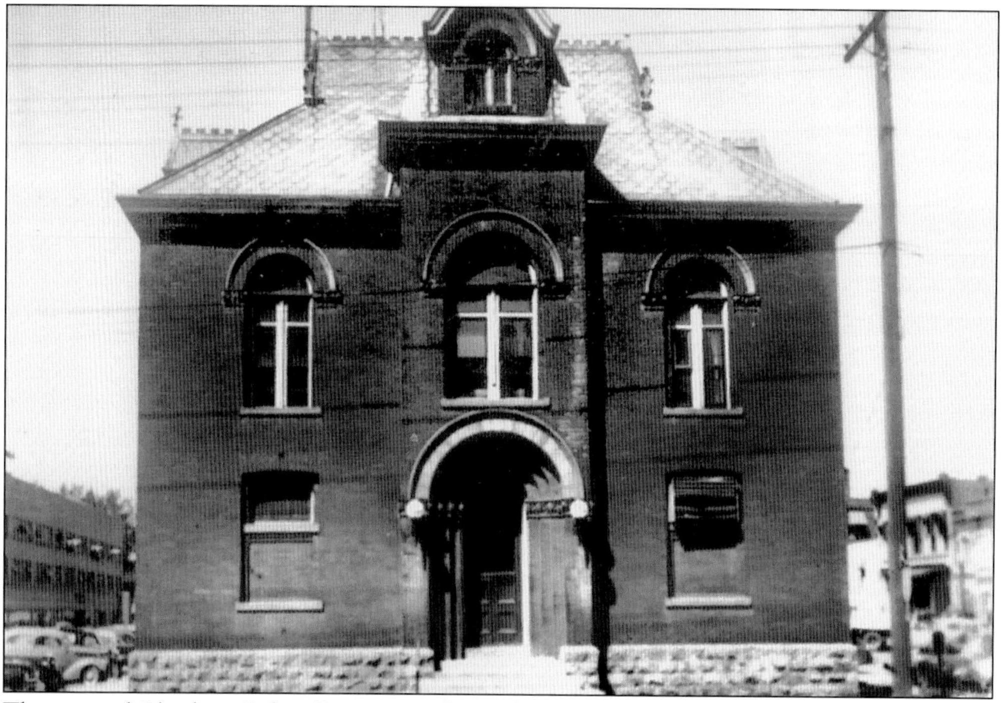

The original Chatham Police Station was located in North Chatham just over the Fifth Street Bridge, near the location of the current Lower Thames Valley Conservation Authority. In 1905, a new police station, seen here *c.* 1930, was erected at the south end of the Market Shed on Wellington Street South and at the opposite end of the original Chatham Town Hall. (Courtesy Mollie French.)

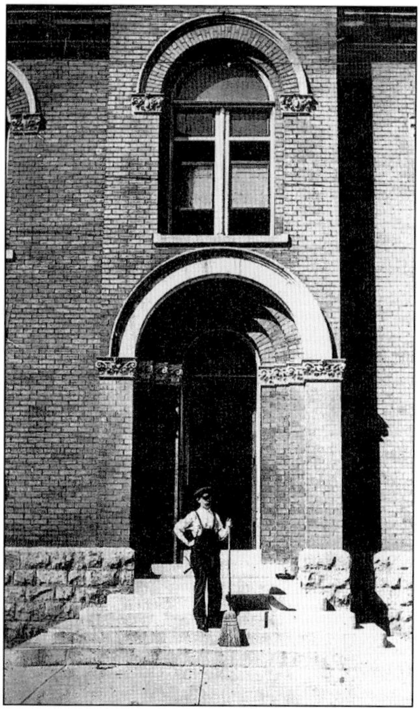

In this *c.* 1910 photograph, longtime market clerk and caretaker Walter Huson stands on the front steps of the 1905 Chatham Police Station on Wellington Street South. The police station was replaced in 1965 by the present station situated at the southeast corner of King and Third Streets. The first police chief at this 1905 structure was longtime policeman A.B. Baxter. (Courtesy Marg Mills.)

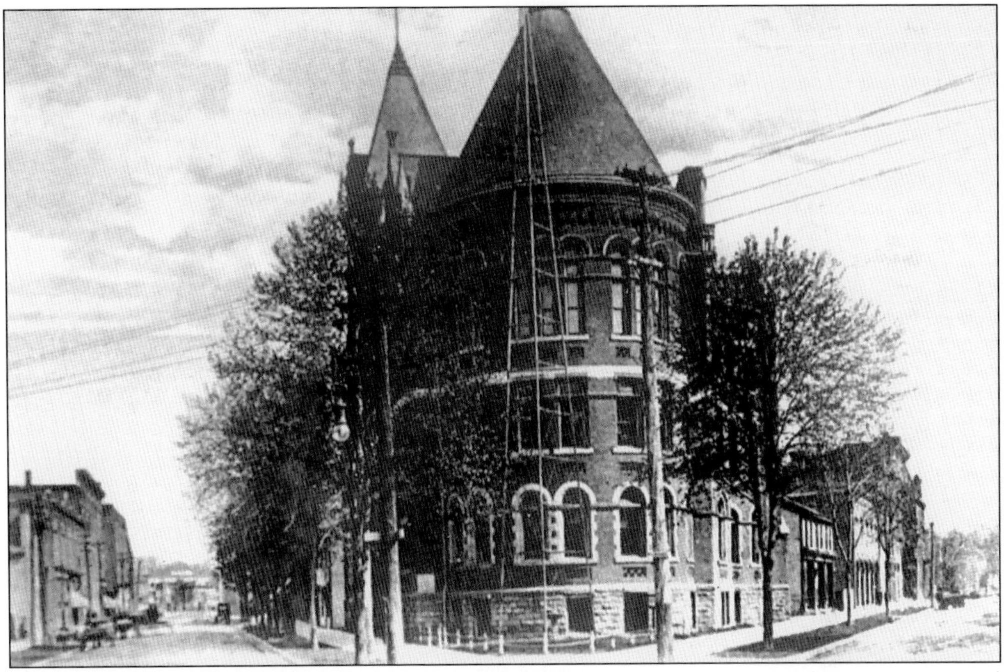

On June 16, 1889, the town and county agreed to allow the construction of a joint municipal building. This site, a gore lot between Fifth and Sixth Streets opposite Central School, seen here *c.* 1910, was determined to be as close as possible to the centre of town. (Courtesy Chatham Kent Museum.)

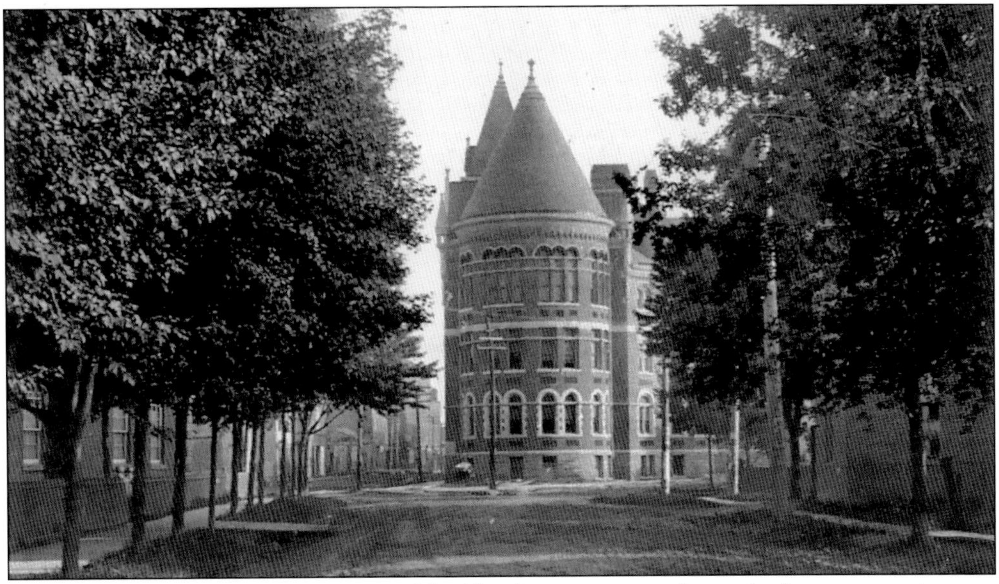

The new joint town-county municipal building's costs were split, with the town paying one third ($9,550.77) and the county paying two thirds ($28, 682.32). The building's cornerstone was laid on August 27, 1889; the construction was finished in 1890, and the building officially opened on July 1, 1891. It was named Harrison Hall in honour of Hon. Robert Alexander Harrison, chief justice of the Queen's Bench. This *c.* 1912 J.S. Butler postcard shows Harrison Hall in a most picturesque manner. (Courtesy Dr. Dick Charteris.)

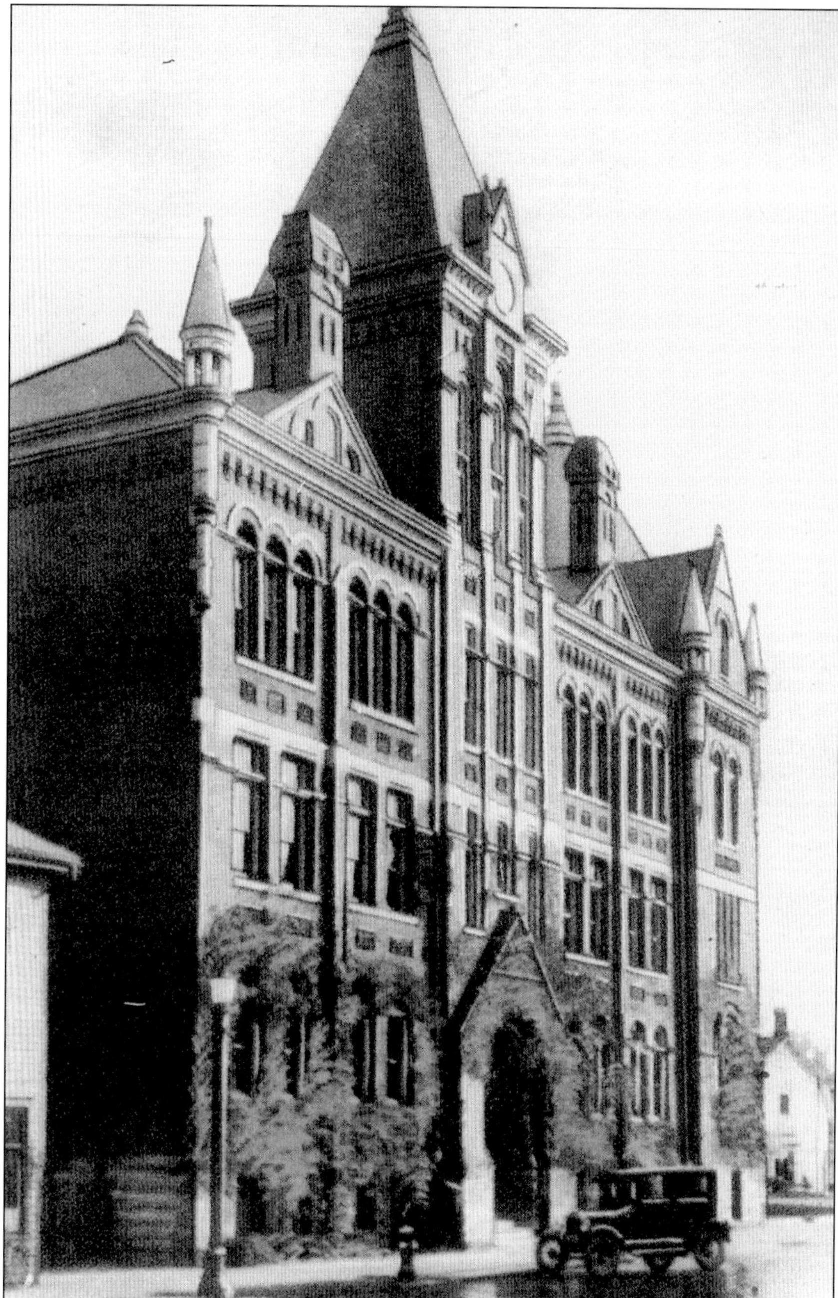

This *c.* 1920s view of Harrison Hall, taken from Fifth Street, represents an interesting variation from the normal photographs of the hall. Key features of the modified Byzantine architecture (Richardsonian Romanesque) are seen more clearly, as well as local architect T.J Rutley's variations (arched windows used on top of mullions and high corbelled chimneys). Built in 1889–1890 at a cost of $38,000, this structure complemented Central School and the First Presbyterian Church, built on the two other corners facing Harrison Hall. For Canada, this style of architecture was somewhat exotic but very practical, functional, and attractive. (Authors' collection.)

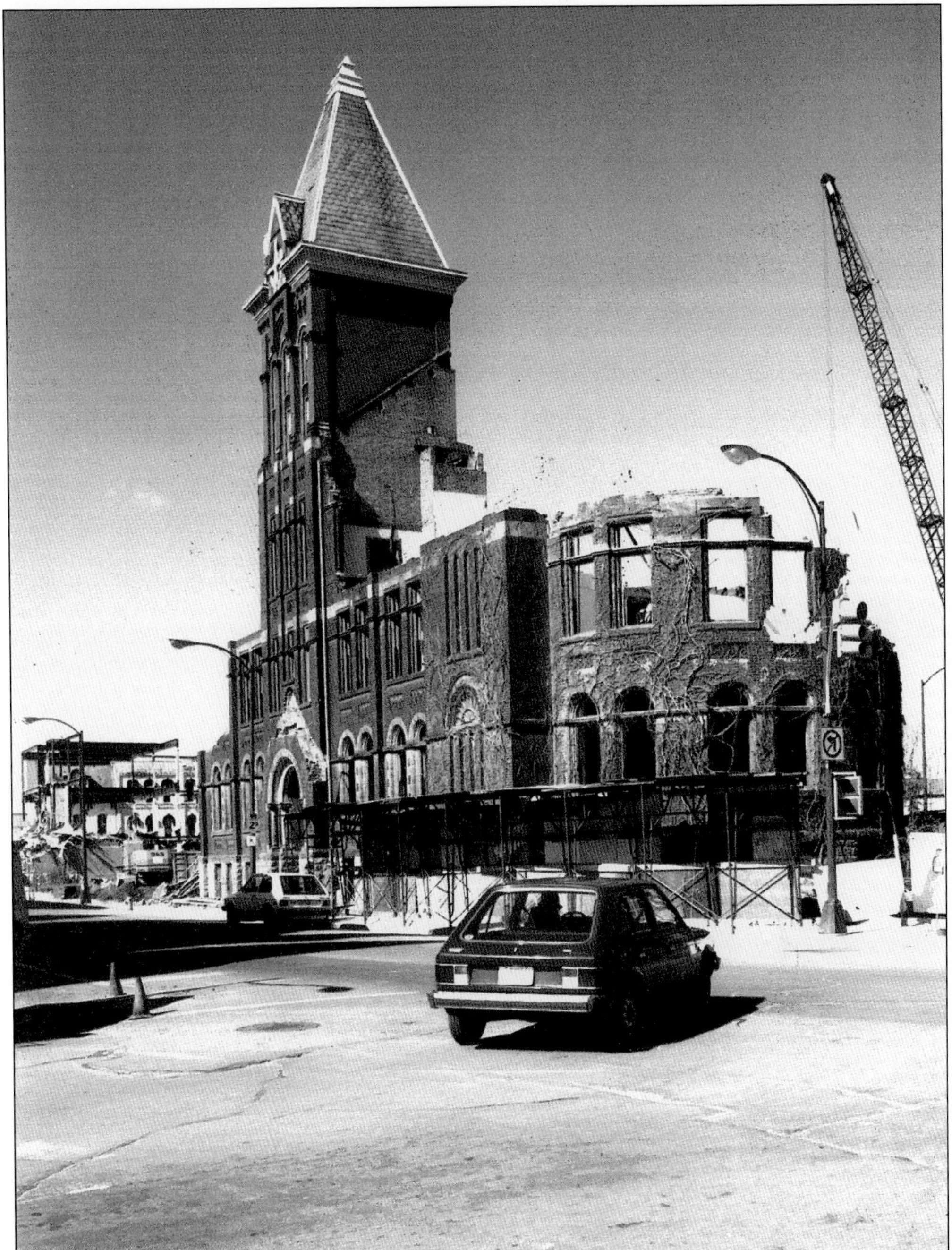

Amid much controversy, Chatham's second city hall, Harrison Hall, was torn down in 1981, along with a good portion of the old downtown area, in order to make way for the new Downtown Chatham Centre. Supporters of the project felt that a brick, graceless monolith of a modern shopping centre would transform Chatham's downtown area into an exciting, dynamic, and prosperous place. This photograph was taken in 1981. (Courtesy Doug and Dienne Howard.)

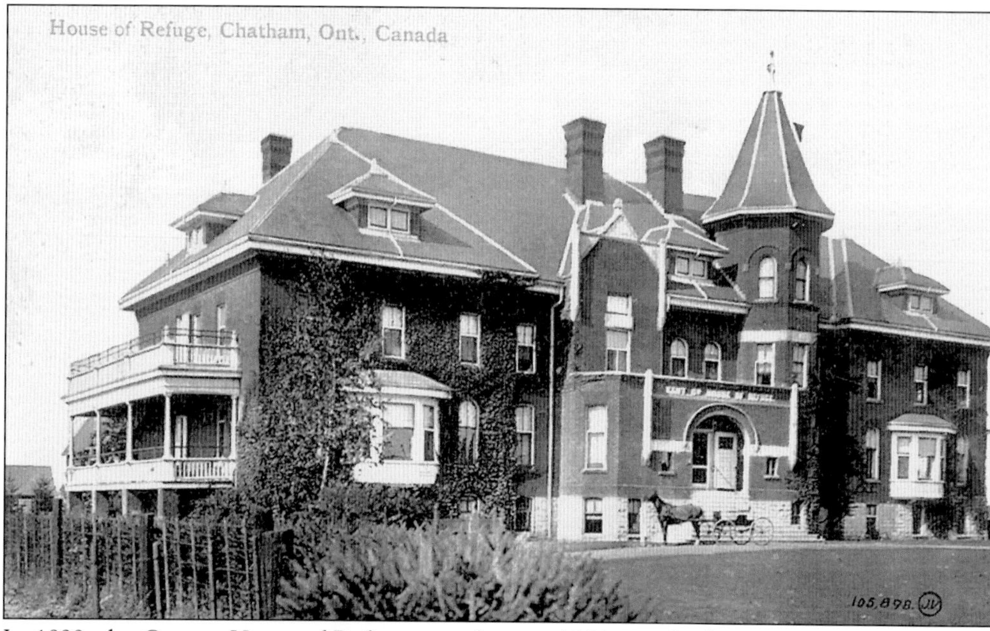

In 1899, the County House of Refuge, seen here *c.* 1904, was built in Dover Township, just west of the Chatham city limits, after being considered at 34 other sites. In honour of Queen Victoria's Diamond Jubilee, the structure was officially named the Kent County Jubilee House of Refuge; however, the more common name quickly became, and remained, simply the County Home. (Courtesy Al Mann collection.)

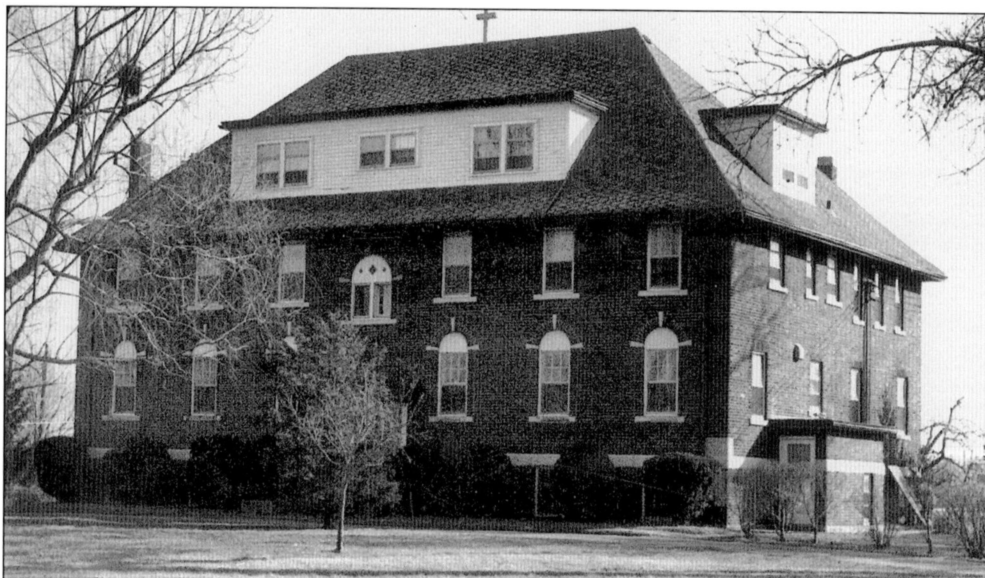

In 1911, Francis Moore died and left $12,000 to the Children's Aid Society to purchase the Atkinson Estate on Park Avenue East. In Moore's honour, the building became the Francis Moore Children's Shelter. In 1929, the old shelter was torn down and this one, pictured *c.* 1930, was constructed. In later years, it was called both Mercy Shelter and Sunnydale Manor. This building was torn down as well in the 1980s and replaced by an apartment complex. (Courtesy Doug and Dienne Howard.)

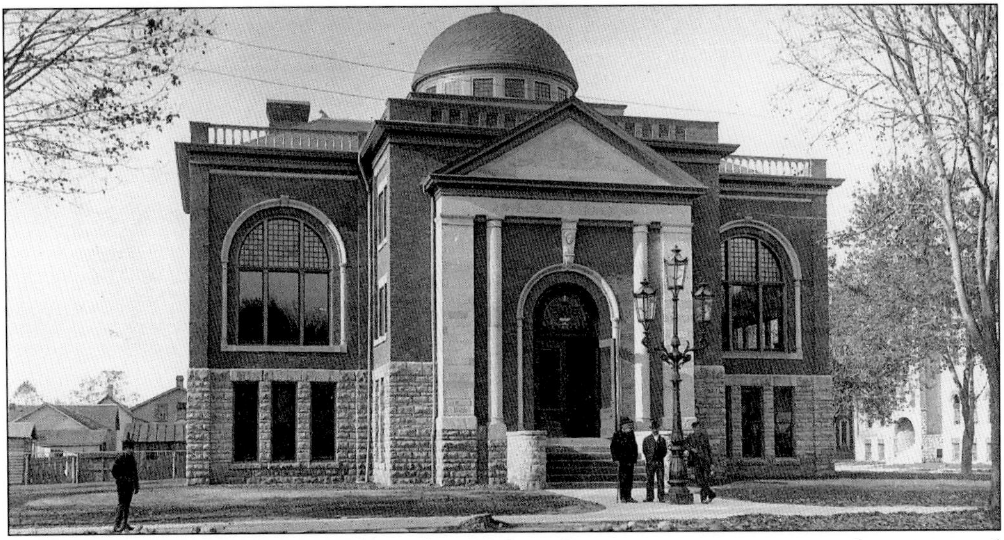

In the early 1900s, American industrialist Andrew Carnegie set out to ensure that cities and towns all over North America had a decent, architecturally attractive, functional library. Chatham successfully petitioned Carnegie for a library thanks, in part, to early Canadian author and Chatham resident A.S. Holmes. The cornerstone was laid in 1902, and the formal opening occurred on September 14, 1903. Built on the corner of Queen and Cross Streets, the structure, seen here *c.* 1904, was torn down and replaced by the current library in Canada's centennial year, 1967. (Courtesy Chatham Kent Museum.)

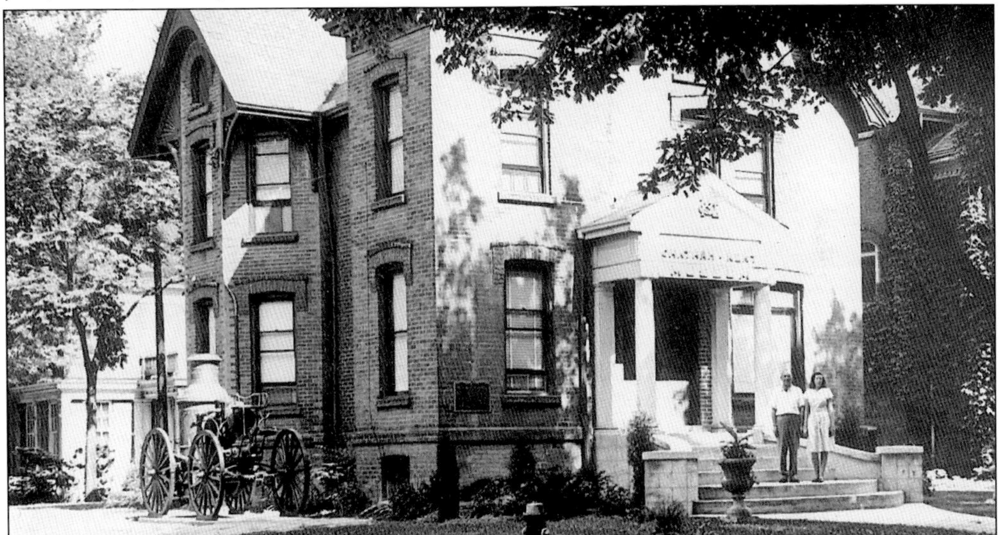

In 1944, the Chatham Kent Museum was established, due to the gift of their impressive home to the city by the family of the late Mr. and Mrs. Robert Milner. Mr. Milner, a local industrialist, was the owner of Milner Carriage Works, and Mrs. Milner was a local artist of note. Their home was ideally situated on William Street North in the heart of downtown Chatham and directly across the street from historic Tecumseh Park. In its early days, the museum centred its collection around items donated by E.B. Jones, H.A. Dean, Edwin Sandys, and G.W Sulman. Today, this building exists as a restored period home of the 1890s. This photograph was taken *c.* the 1940s. (Courtesy Chatham Kent Museum.)

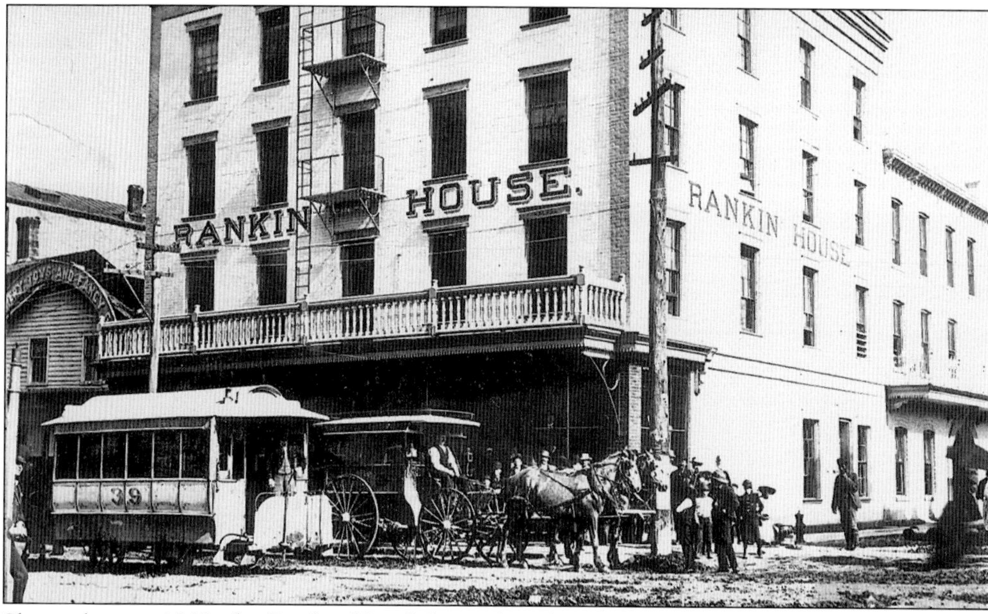

Shown here *c.* 1908, the Rankin Hotel, located at the corner of King and Fourth Streets, was built by the flamboyant Arthur Rankin in 1852; he not only gave his name to the hotel, but also to the main port of entry on the Thames River in Chatham, the Rankin Dock. Not only did this fine establishment offer alcoholic refreshments, but it also boasted "the finest fresh lobsters, oysters, pickled pigs' feet and pickled tripe." It was sold by Rankin in 1861 to the Bank of Upper Canada for the then princely sum of $10,000. (Courtesy Chatham Kent Museum.)

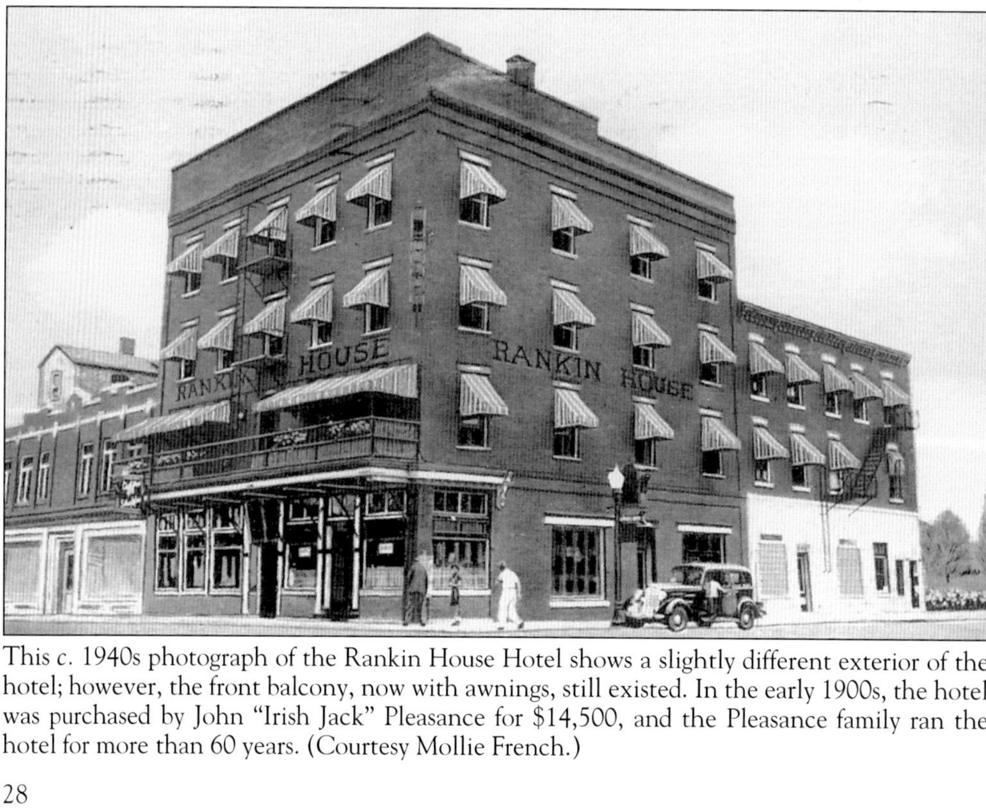

This *c.* 1940s photograph of the Rankin House Hotel shows a slightly different exterior of the hotel; however, the front balcony, now with awnings, still existed. In the early 1900s, the hotel was purchased by John "Irish Jack" Pleasance for $14,500, and the Pleasance family ran the hotel for more than 60 years. (Courtesy Mollie French.)

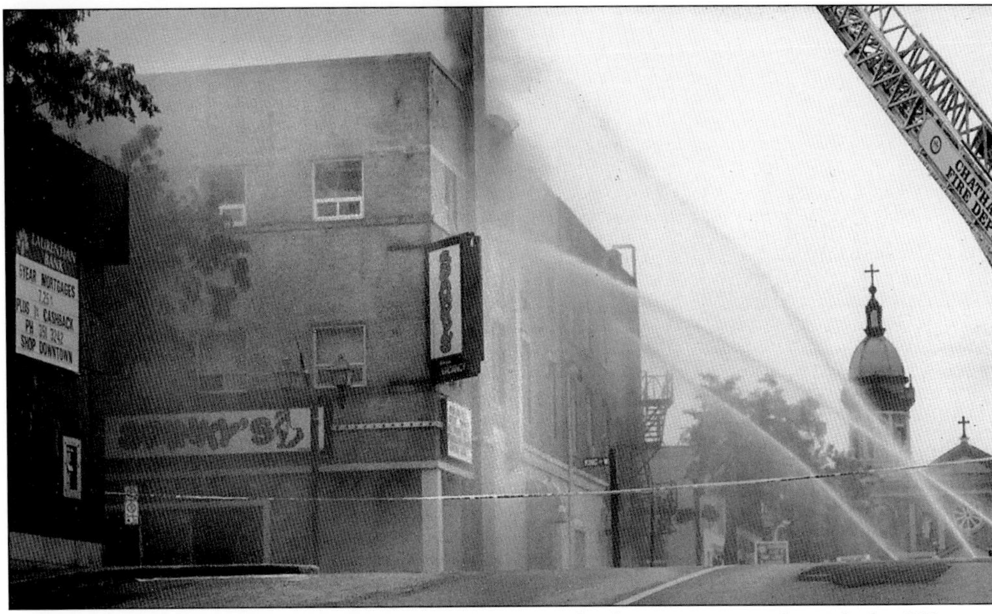

In August 1999, an early-morning fire, later determined to be arson, swept through the 150-year-old structure formerly known as the Rankin Hotel and currently known as Spanky's. In a short period of time, flames shot through the roof. In this picture, taken from the slope leading down to the site of the old Rankin Dock, the fire is seen at its peak, with several fire hoses playing, in vain, on the raging fire. In the right centre of the photograph is St. Joseph's Church at the south end of Fourth Street. (Authors' collection.)

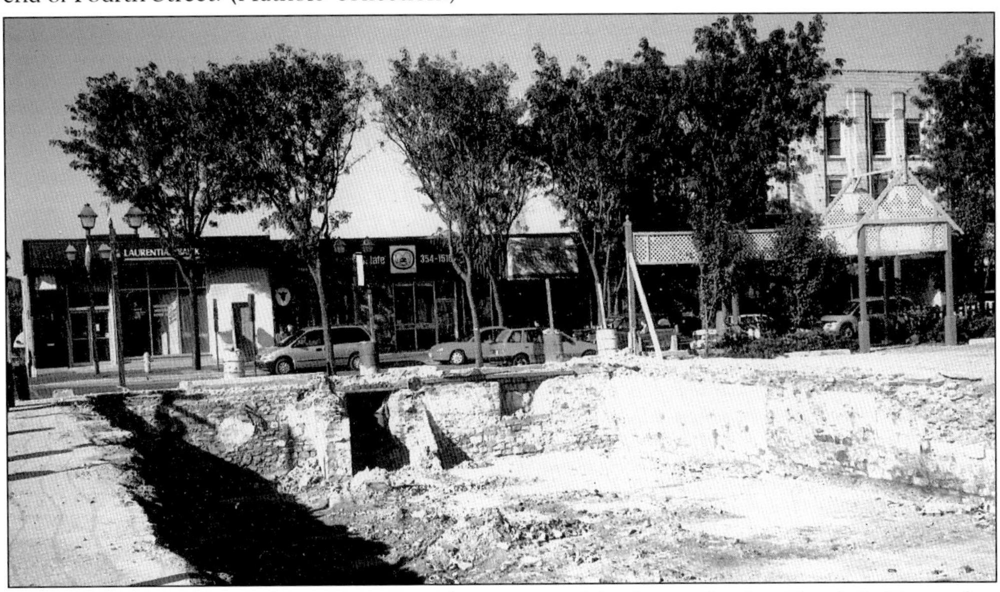

This photograph depicts the final stages of destruction of the former Rankin Hotel. By November 1999, a hole in the ground was all that was left of King Street's oldest (*c.* 1852) commercial structure. Rumours of a mysterious tunnel in the basement of the original Rankin Hotel leading to the Thames River were further fueled by "the cave," which became visible in the excavation of the burned-out site. No doubt it was merely a storage area, but it does add a certain amount of personality and charm to a lost structure. (Authors' collection.)

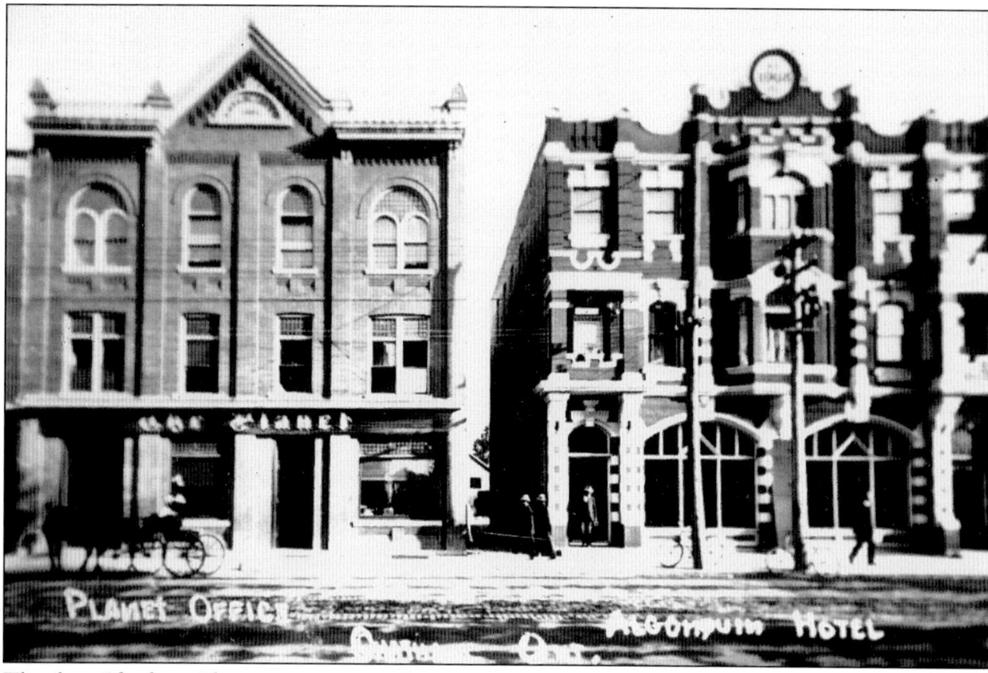

The first *Chatham Planet* newspaper office, pictured on the left *c.* 1900, was built in 1891 and burned down in 1913, with the loss of two lives. It was rebuilt by owner Syd Stephenson into a brick and concrete structure that still stands today at 202 King Street West. The building on the right is the Algonquin Hotel, which later became a liquor store and now exists as Lionel's Men's Wear. (Courtesy Doug and Dienne Howard.)

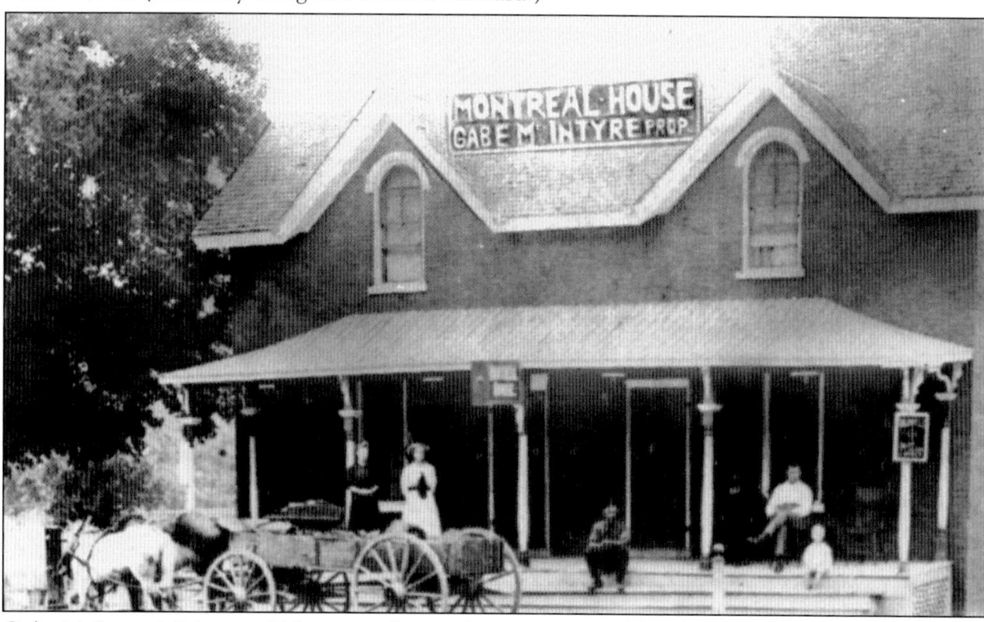

Gabe McIntyre's Montreal House, at the northwest corner of Sandys Street and Grand Avenue, has been a favourite watering hole in Chatham for many years, starting as an early stagecoach stop. This casual drinking establishment looks very similar today, except for the exterior colours, to how it appears here *c.* 1905. (Courtesy Doug and Dienne Howard.)

Two

Street Scenes and Home Scenes

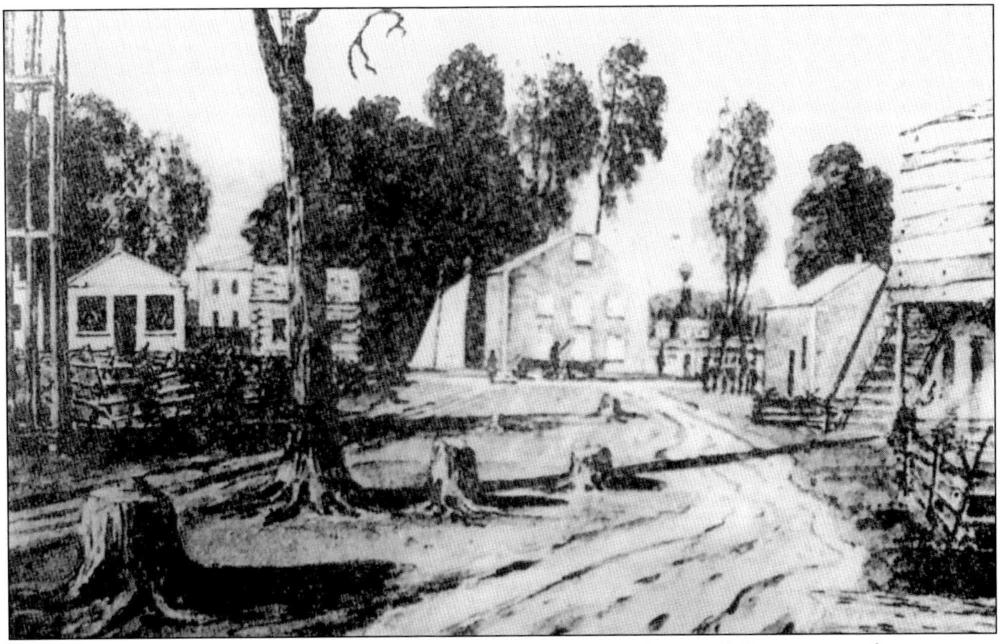

This *c.* 1843 sketch of Chatham's Sixth Street includes evidence of the stumps of trees, even in the middle of the road. The area of trees visible in the centre background is Tecumseh Park, and the sail passing by is a small sailing craft headed toward the Thames River on McGregor's Creek. (Sketch by Lt. Col. P. Brainbrigge; courtesy Chatham Kent Museum.)

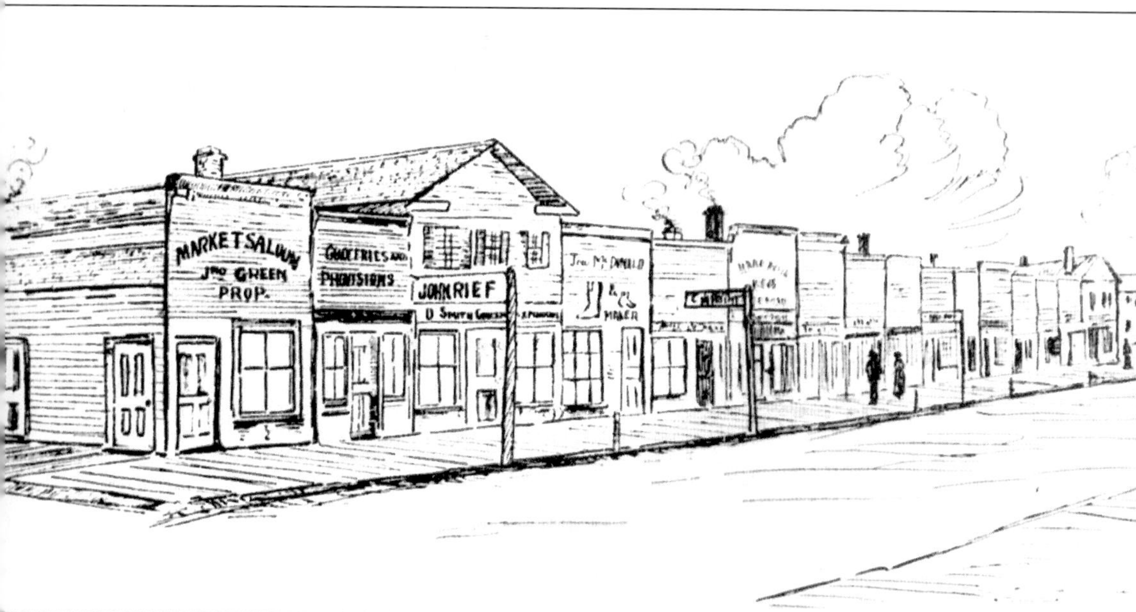

OLD PORK ROW, BURNED 1867

At the corner of King Street beyond Market Square stood John Green's Market Saloon and a line of primarily one-storey frame shops. Many of these shops were butchers or various provision stores, which coined the nickname for this area of King Street, Pork Row. In 1867, a devastating fire swept the Pork Row area, and the obvious inadequacies of fighting this fire made town officials realize that the purchase of modern firefighting equipment could wait no longer. (Courtesy Chatham Kent Museum.)

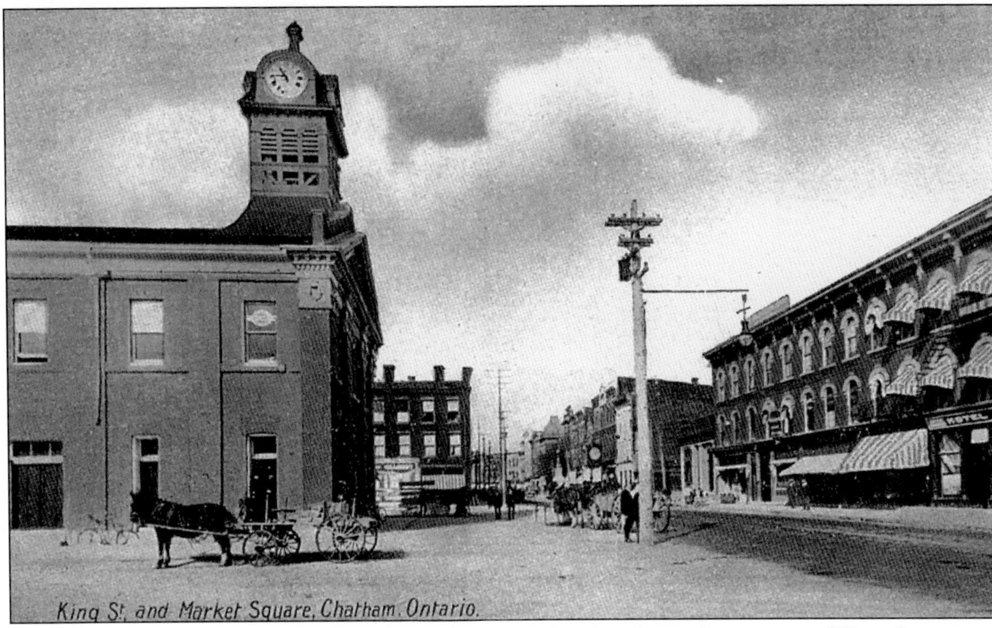

Chatham's early town hall, built *c.* the 1850s, was a landmark on the corners of King Street and East and West Market Streets. In the middle of this postcard, a tall hydro pole supports a police call light. When policeman were on foot patrol and this light was lit, they knew they were to return to the station for further orders. A number of these lights existed around Chatham in its early years. This view looks west down King Street *c.* 1908. (Authors' collection.)

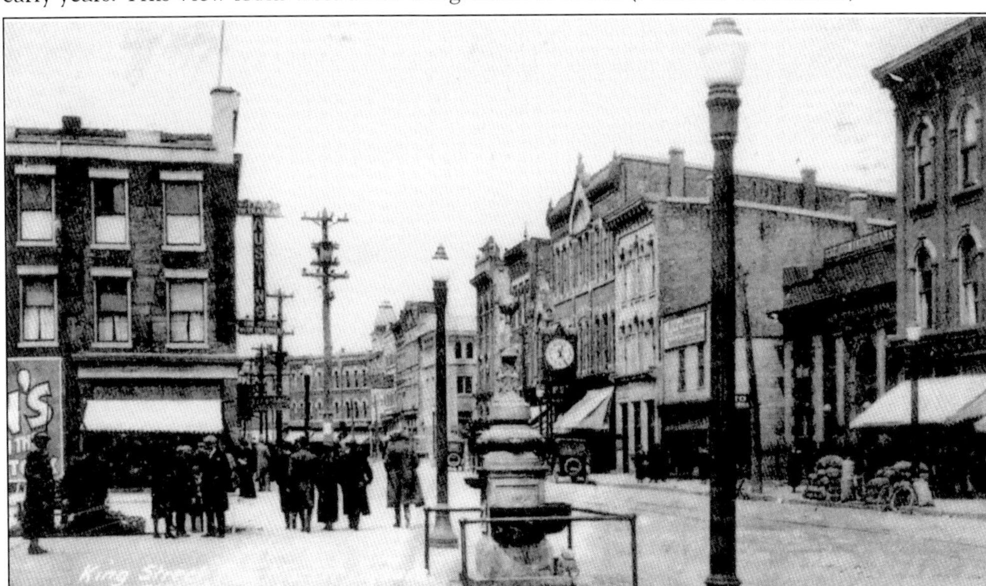

The ornate horse trough situated in front of the old Chatham Town Hall on Market Square was a King Street landmark for many years. In this *c.* 1930s photograph, the view looks toward the west, and the taller building on the right is the Chatham Department Store (formerly the Charles Austin Department Store), which, in later years, became the T. Eaton Department Store. In the 1980s, it was torn down and became part of the Downtown Chatham Centre. (Courtesy Mollie French.)

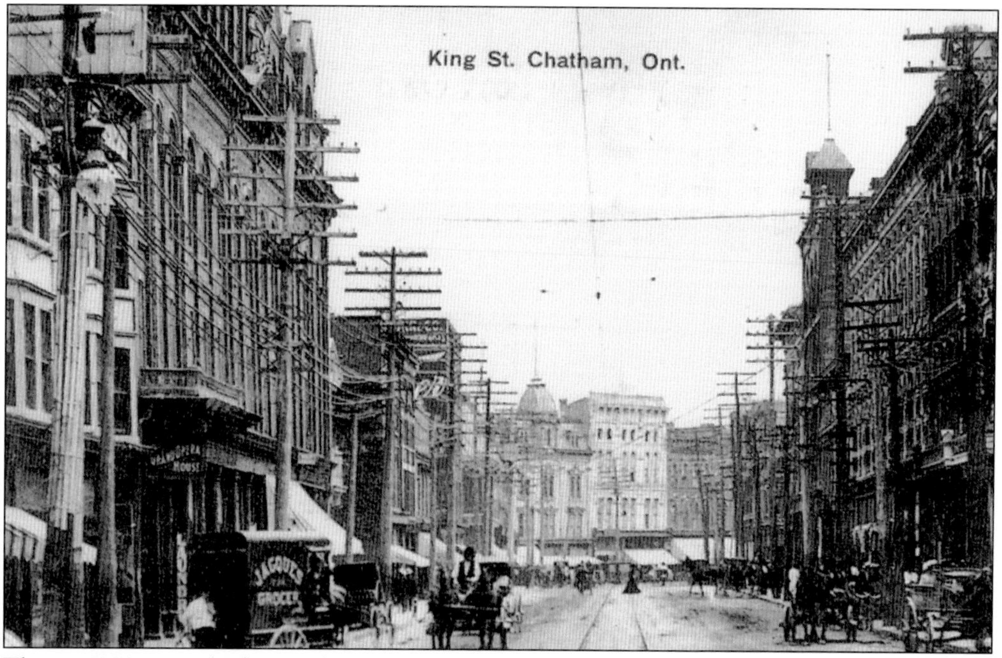

This *c.* 1880s view looks east from Fourth Street down King Street, virtually on the streetcar tracks. To the left, a grocer's wagon is parked in front of the Grand Opera House. At the far end is the bend in King Street, and Hugh Malcomson's store is the tallest structure. (Courtesy Mollie French.)

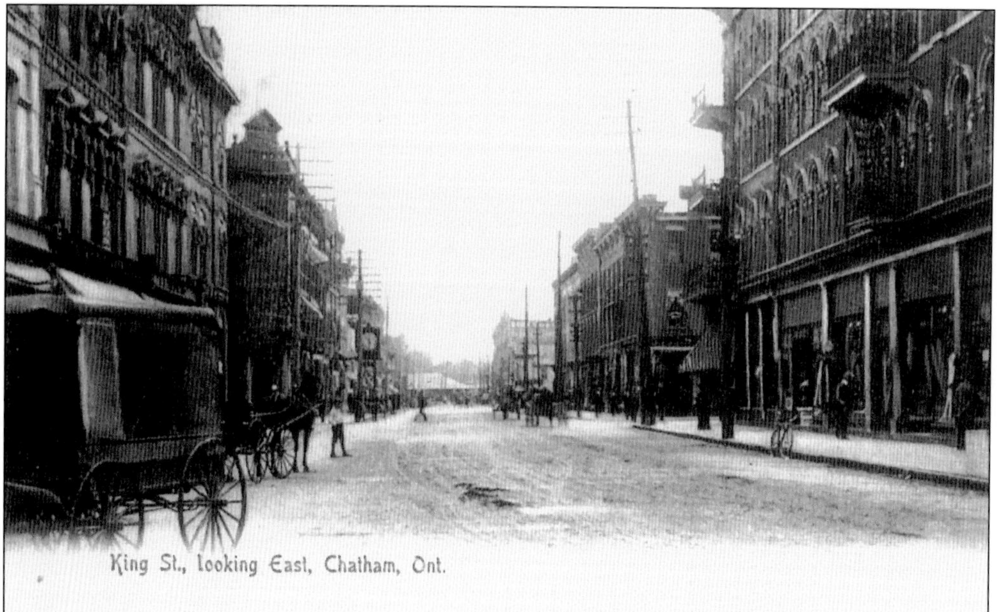

In front of Hugh Malcomson's store, just past the bend on King Street, this view looks east down King Street. To the left is the Garner Hotel, and at the end of King Street, in the distance, is the Canadian Pacific station. Note the large number of horse-drawn delivery wagons on King Street *c.* 1900.

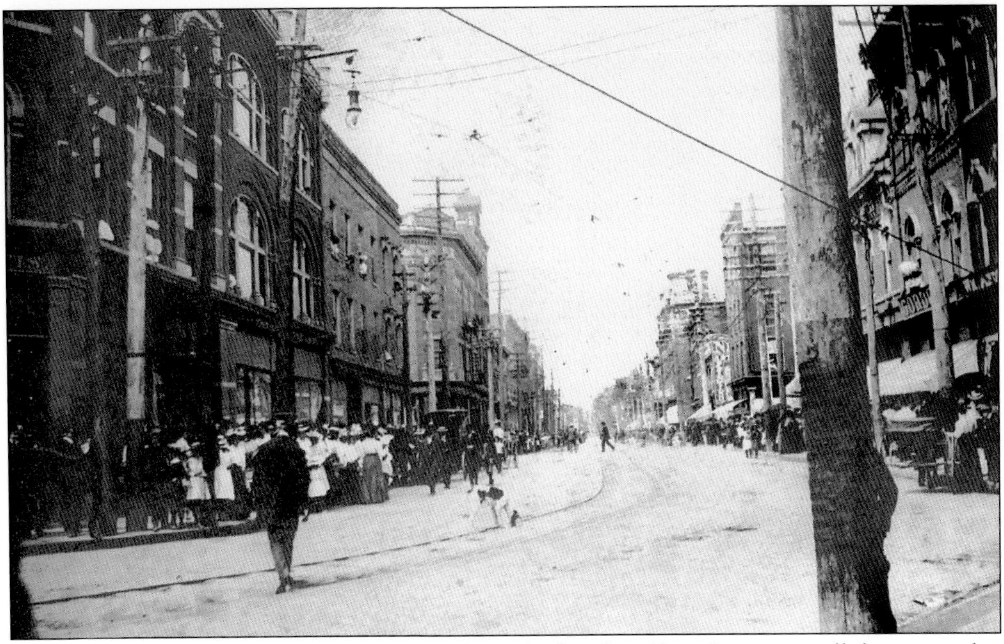

This picture reveals a view of King Street from the bend in King Street as well; however, this view looks west. A dog inspects the Chatham, Wallaceburg, and Lake Erie Railroad tracks while people crowd the sidewalks in anticipation of a possible parade. (Courtesy W.G. Glassco.)

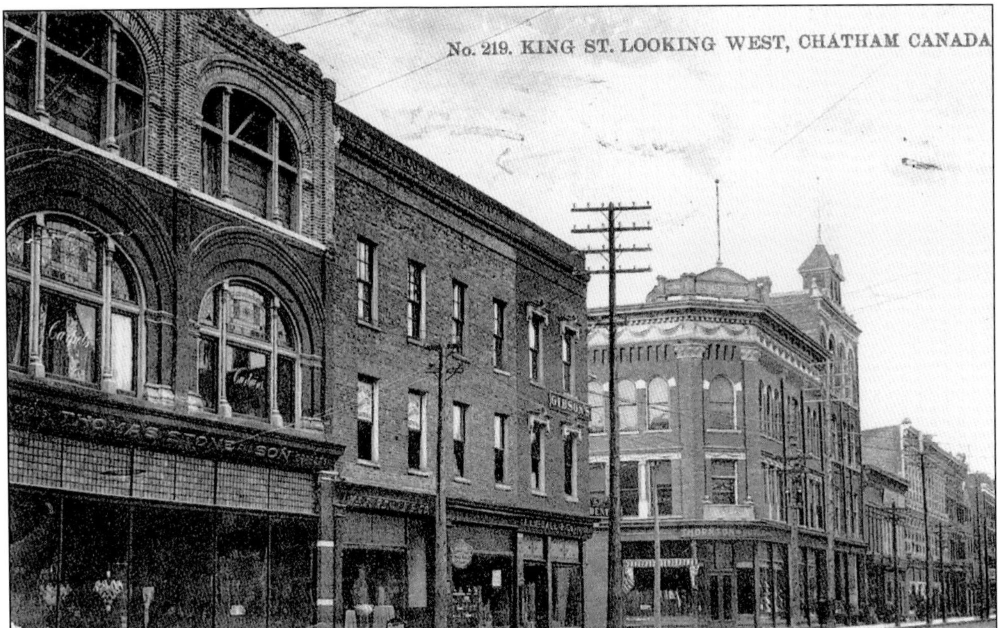

Three rather important businesses on the corner of King and Fifth Streets are pictured in this view from the early 1900s. On the far left is the Thomas Stone & Sons Store, then the Thomas Forman Store, and across Fifth Street is the Victoria Block. The latter was built after the historic Royal Exchange Hotel burned down in February 1898. (Courtesy Mollie French.)

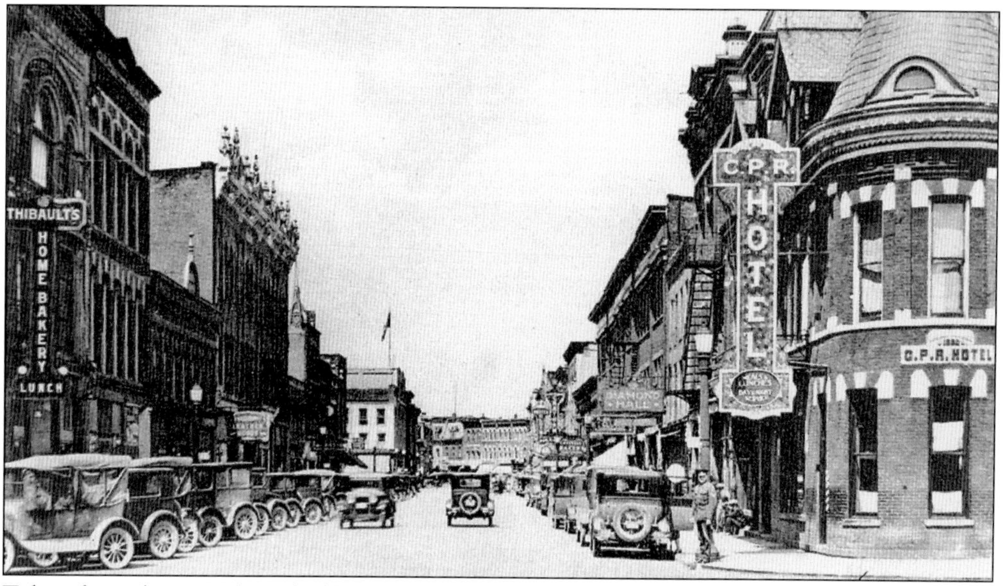

Taken from the easterly end of King Street, near William Street, this early-1920s photograph shows angle parking on the right side of King and parallel parking on the left. On the right is the CPR Hotel, and on the left is Thibault's Home Bakery. A portion of the George Stephen's Building, with its ornate ironwork on the second floor, is partially visible on the left. (Courtesy W.G. Glassco.)

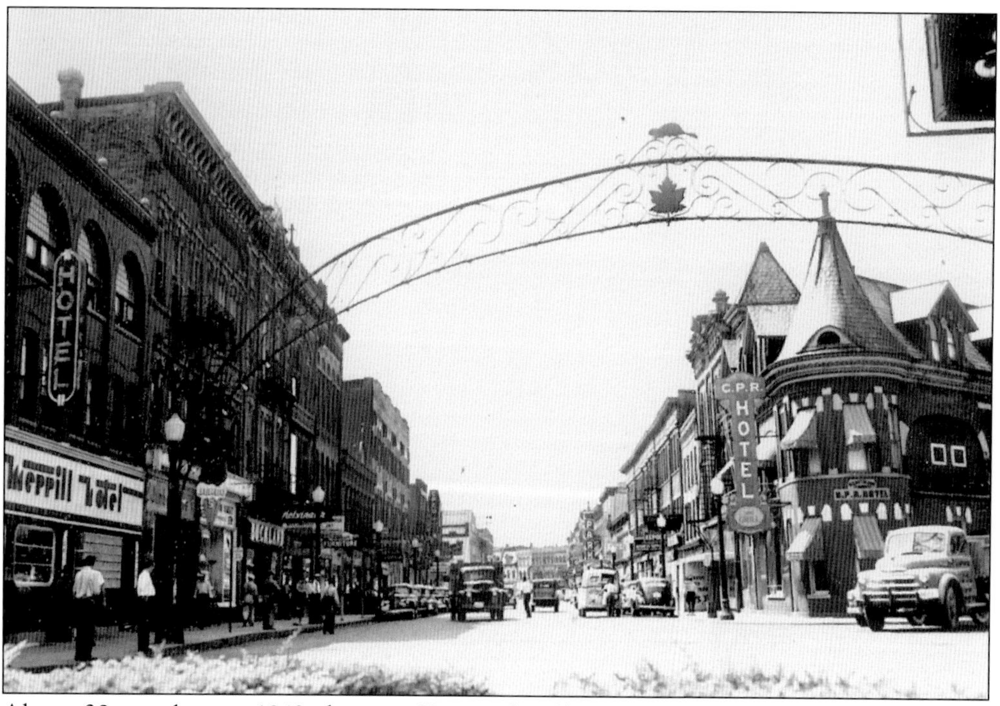

Almost 30 years later, c. 1949, this same King and William Streets corner has experienced a few changes. The CPR Hotel has added a few awnings, Thibault's Bakery seems to have disappeared, and angle parking is no longer allowed on the left side of King Street West. A beautiful arch spans the street, sporting a beaver and a maple leaf. (Courtesy Chatham Kent Museum.)

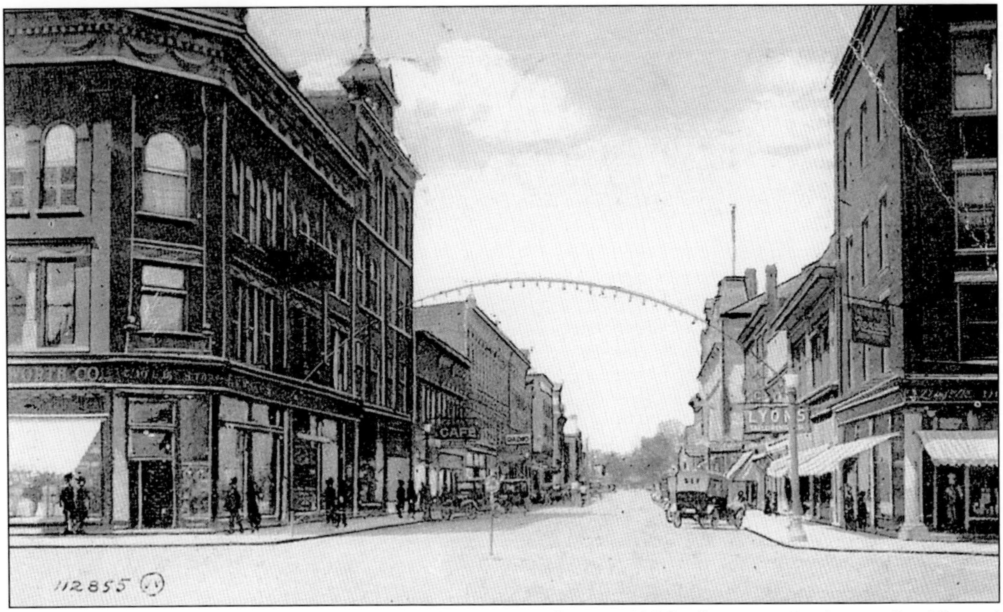

Taken from the corner of King and Fifth Streets, this *c.* 1923 photograph shows the Eberts' Block on the right and the Victoria Block on the left. On the street level of the Victoria Block was the Woolworth department store. Note the decorative iron arch that extended over King Street. It seems to be a less ornate version of the one spanning King Street near William Street. (Authors' collection.)

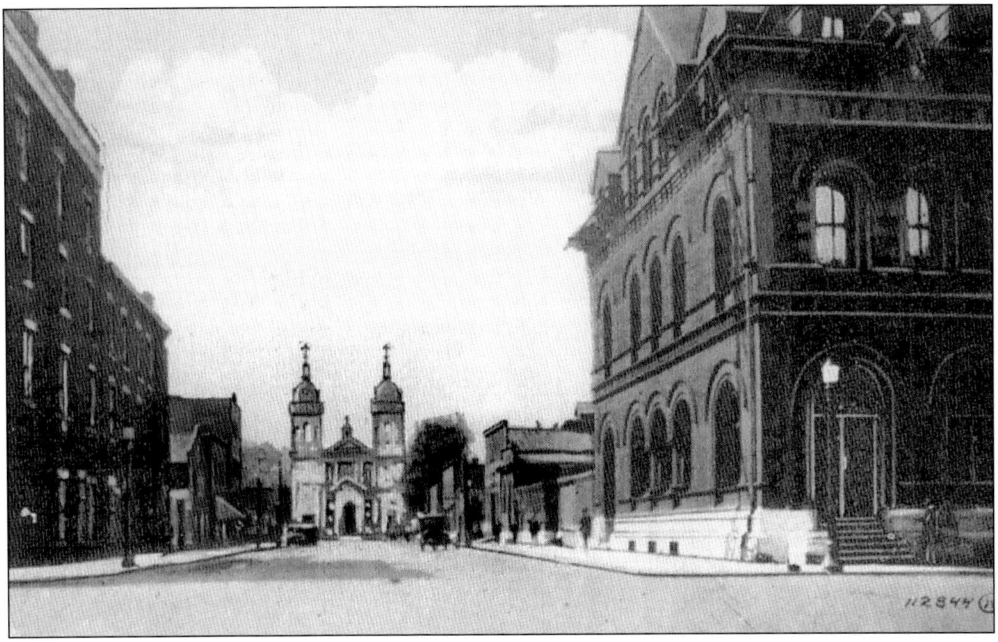

Looking south down Fourth Street from the approach to the old Rankin Dock at King Street, this view reveals a portion of the Rankin Hotel on the left, as well as the beautiful Chatham Post Office, on the right. In the middle background stands St. Joseph's Church. This rather impressive view greeted visitors to Chatham when they stepped off an excursion steamer at the Rankin Dock. (Courtesy Mollie French.)

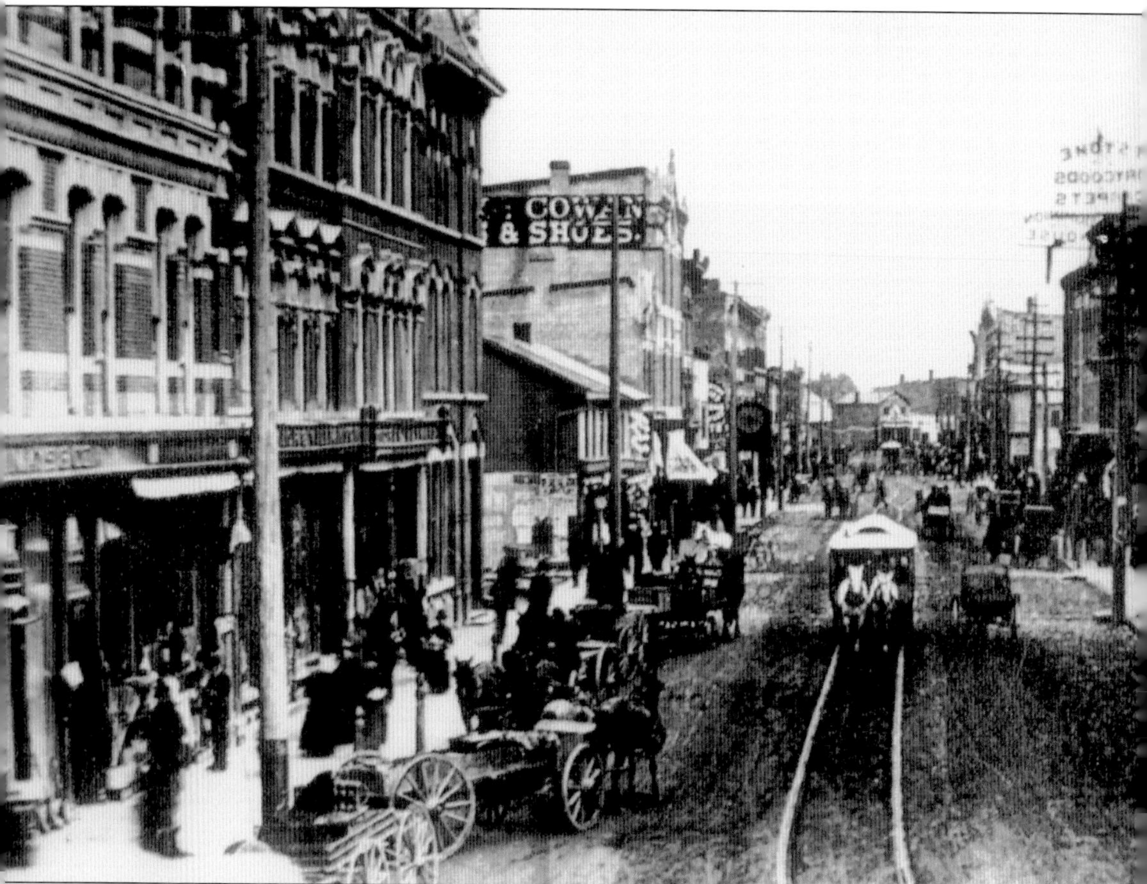

Chatham's horse-drawn streetcars were a very unique feature in the city and were well used from their inception. In this *c.* 1880s picture of King Street, looking east toward Sixth Street, a streetcar moves toward the camera, and beyond that, near the old Chatham Town Hall, sits the crossover track, where streetcars met and passed by one another. At this time, King Street was not paved. Note the many horse-drawn buggies parked on either side of the street. (Courtesy W.G. Glassco.)

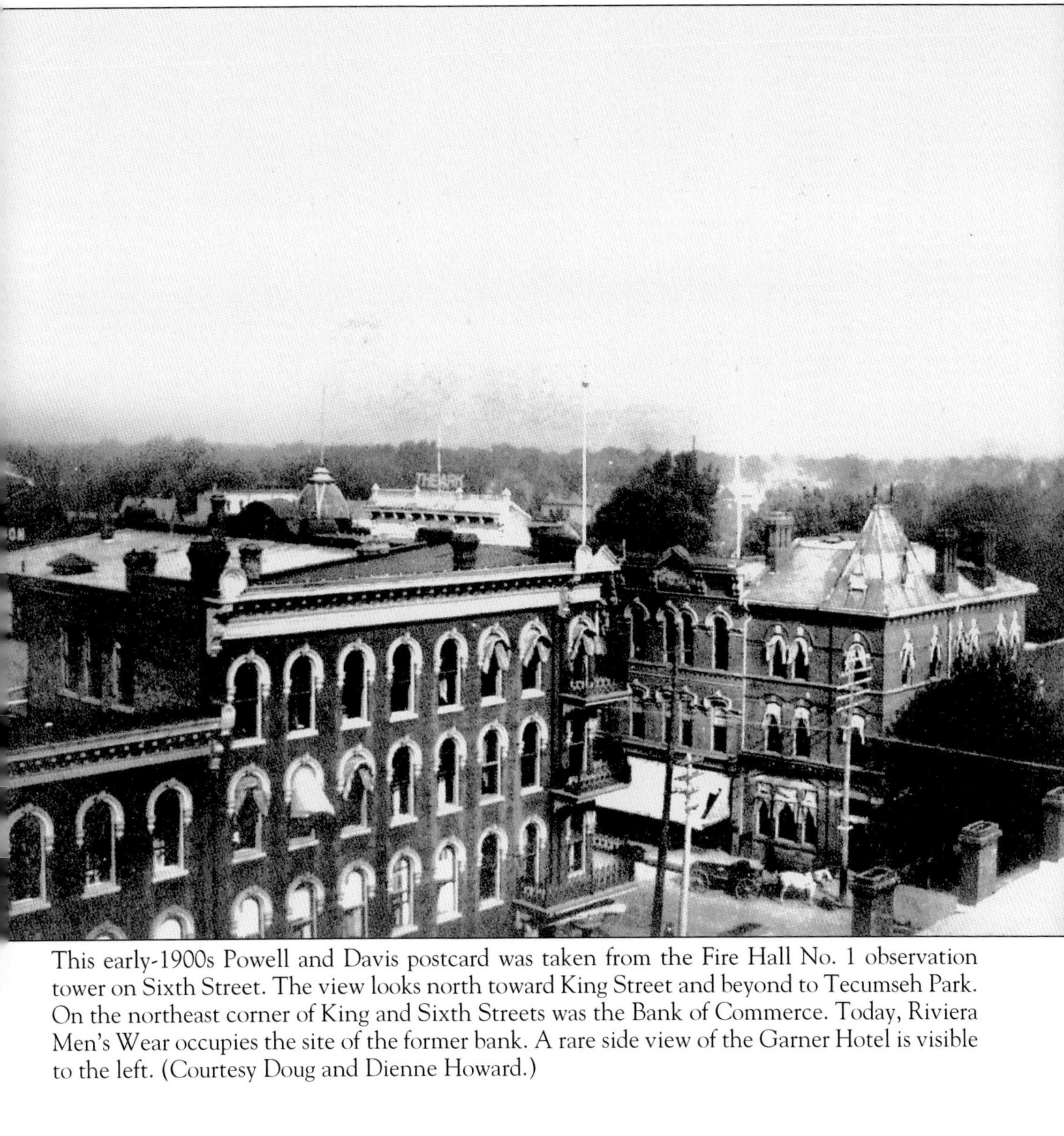

This early-1900s Powell and Davis postcard was taken from the Fire Hall No. 1 observation tower on Sixth Street. The view looks north toward King Street and beyond to Tecumseh Park. On the northeast corner of King and Sixth Streets was the Bank of Commerce. Today, Riviera Men's Wear occupies the site of the former bank. A rare side view of the Garner Hotel is visible to the left. (Courtesy Doug and Dienne Howard.)

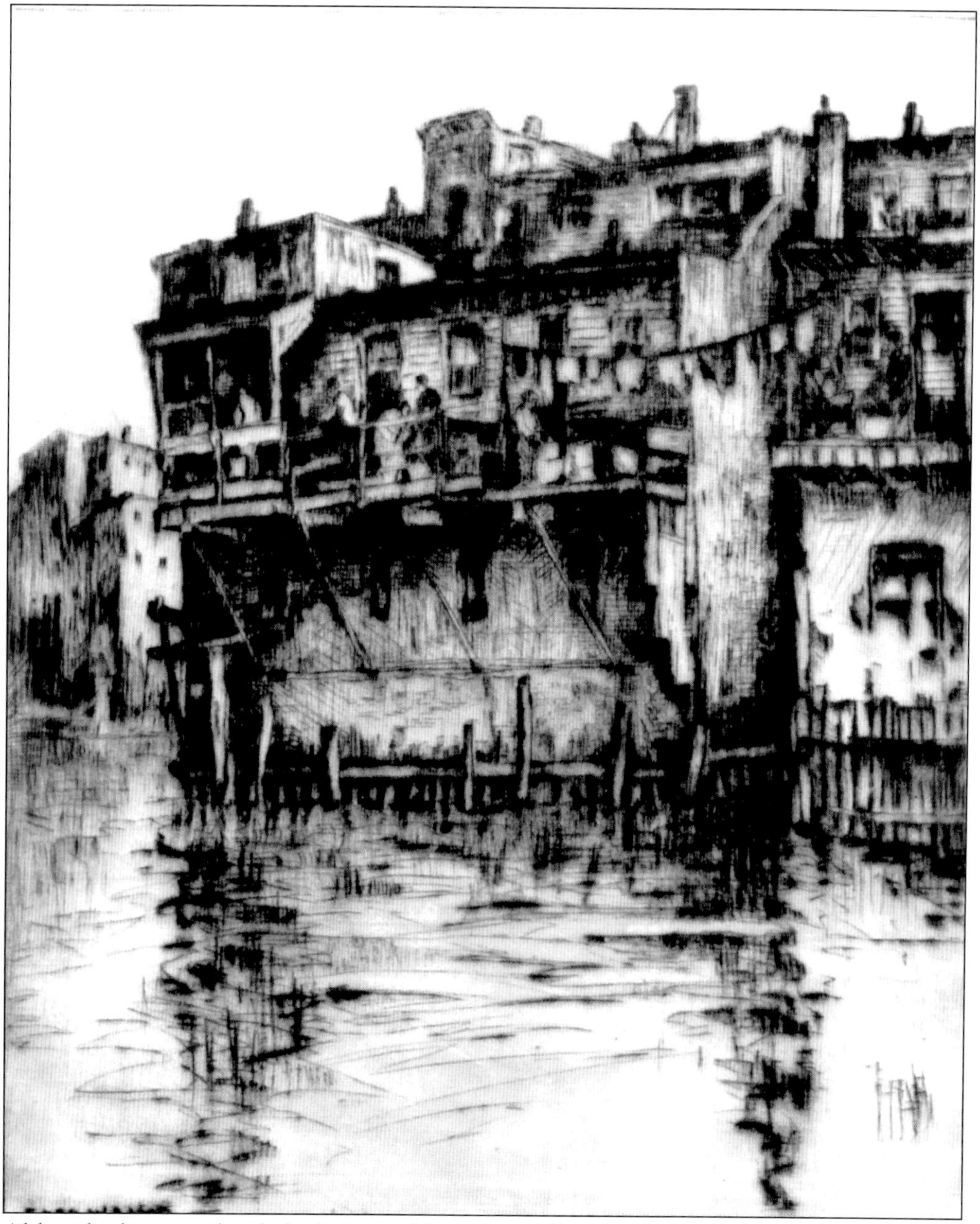

Although this rare sketch looks more like a scene from Dickens's Victorian London than Chatham, it is, nevertheless, a drawing of the apartments overlooking McGregor's Creek. In 1932, a visiting artist from New York, Fred Wright, completed it from a vantage point behind the armouries in Tecumseh Park. It shows the rear view of the apartments located between Chatham's former Park Theatre and the former CPR Hotel. (Courtesy Mary Ellen Hunter.)

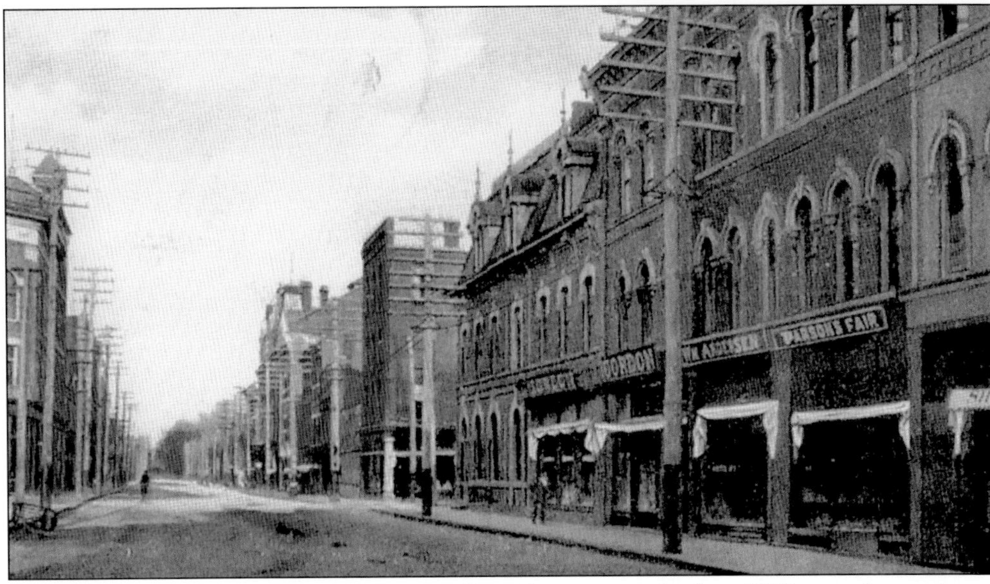

One of the most attractive streetscapes on King Street since the late 1880s was the section of buildings on the north side near Fifth Street. Impressive awnings stretched over the sidewalk, ornate windows, and unique architectural features made this area a very desirable home for such shops as Gordon's, Parson's Fair, William Anderson, and Merchant's Bank. In 1925, this plant became the home of Canadian Leaf Tobacco, and it was torn down in 1965. (Courtesy Darren French.)

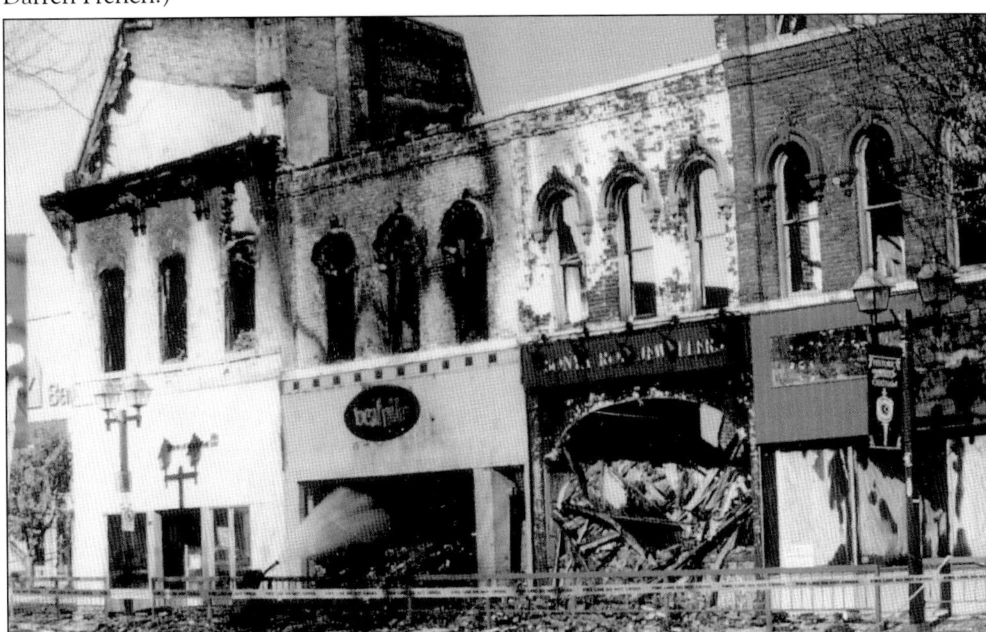

In the fall of 2000, an early-morning fire swept through this section of buildings on the north side of King Street near Fifth Street and devastated most of the buildings. This fire, coupled with the 1999 fire that destroyed the former Rankin Hotel on King Street, obliterated some of the street's oldest and most historically significant structures. (Courtesy Doug and Dienne Howard.)

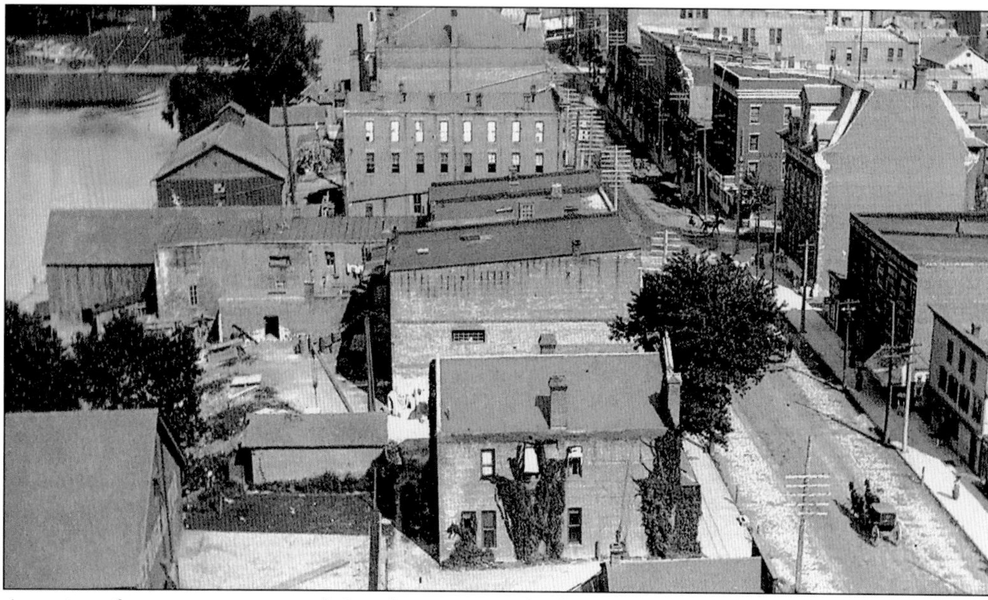

A series of unique pictures of the downtown Chatham area was taken in the early 1900s from the Chatham, Wallaceburg, and Lake Erie Power House chimney on King Street by an enterprising and rather fearless reporter. The first of the three pictures selected for this publication shows a view of King Street, looking east. The large building in the upper right corner is a section of Harrison Hall, while the large buildings on the south side of King Street are the old Chatham Post Office and just beyond that, the Rankin Hotel. (Courtesy W.G. Glassco.)

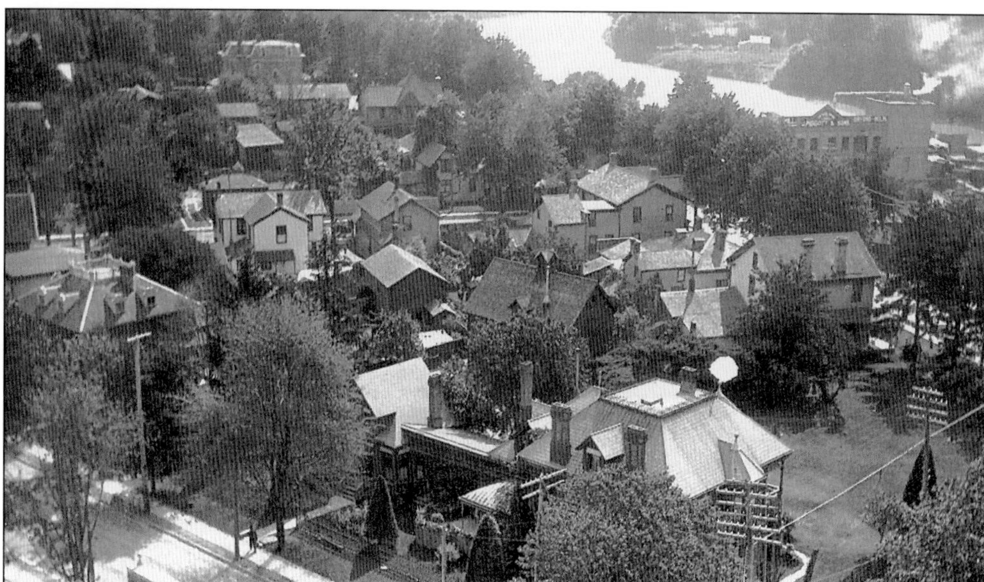

The second picture in the trio taken from the powerhouse chimney on the corner of King and Third Streets looks east down the Thames River. This corner, populated by a number of residential homes in the early 1900s, is now largely taken up by the Chatham Kent Police Services headquarters. Note the Piggot Lumber Company site on the river, which is now the approximate site of the Chatham YMCA. (Courtesy W.G. Glassco.)

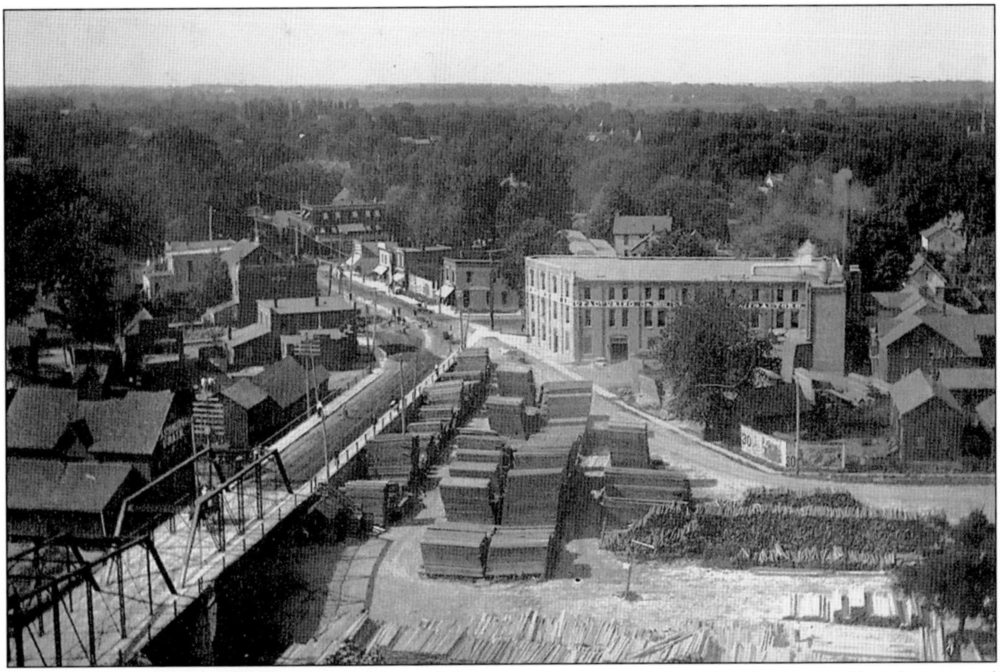

The third of three pictures shown from the vantage point of the Chatham, Wallaceburg, and Lake Erie Power House chimney on King Street West looks north across the old Third Street Bridge toward North Chatham and the Blondie Brothers plant. (Courtesy W.G. Glassco.)

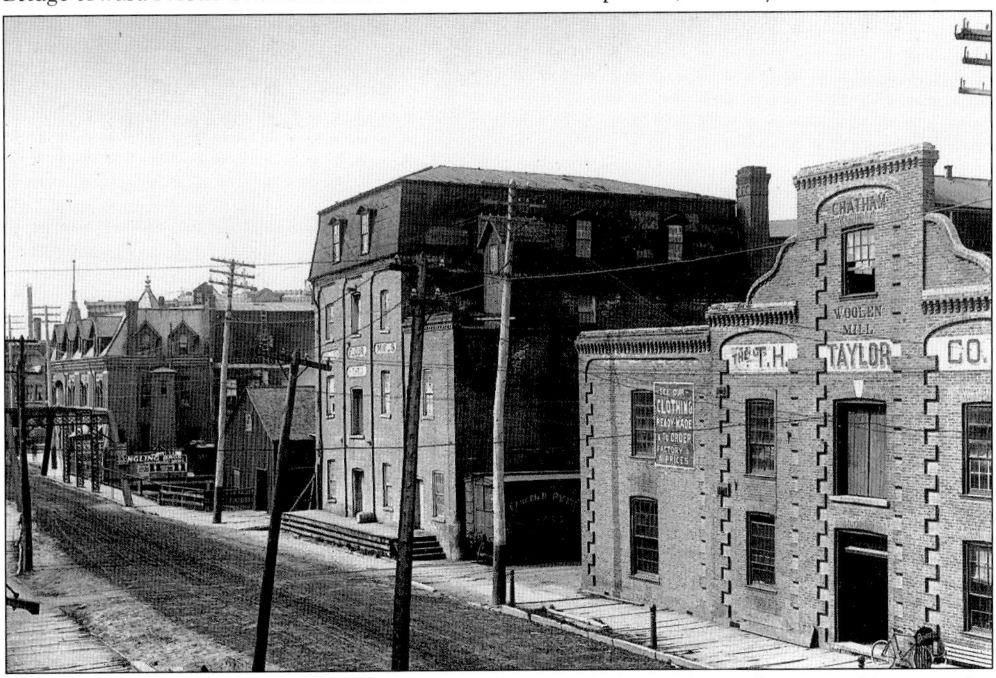

T.H. Taylor, one of Chatham's great industrialists, built the woolen mill, pictured here on the right, on the west side of William Street near McGregor's Creek in 1866. In 1872, the four-storey Beaver Flour Mill, on the left, was built by Taylor. After he died in 1891, his two sons, W.H. and W.J. Taylor, operated the Taylor empire. (Courtesy Chatham Kent Museum.)

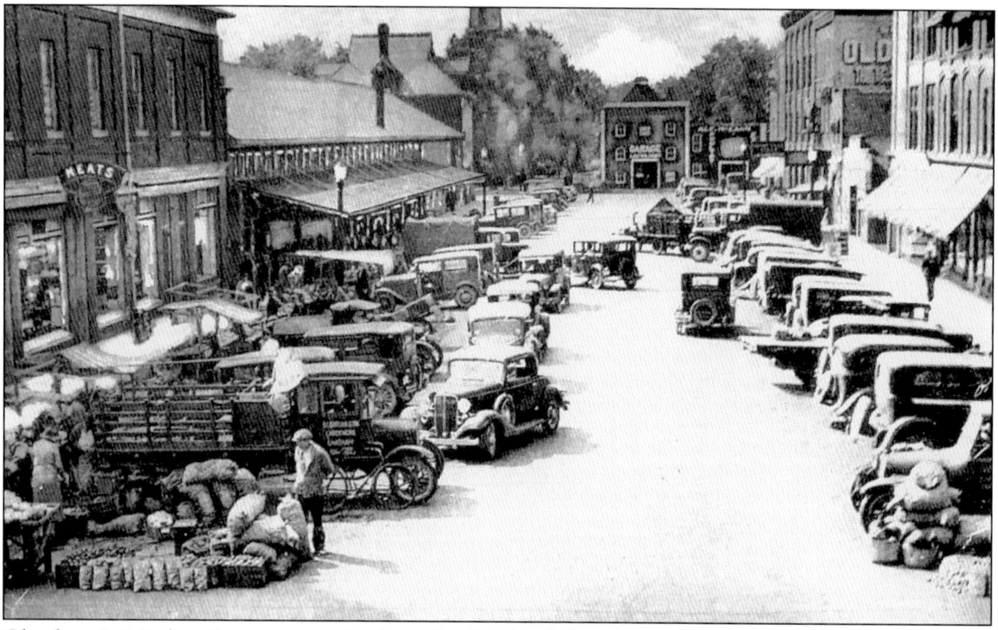

Chatham's Market Square, attached to the back of the original Chatham Town Hall, was a bustling place for much of the town's early history. In this *c.* 1930s photograph, the Market Shed stretches between the town hall in the right foreground, which fronted onto King Street, and the old Chatham Police Station in the background, which fronted onto Wellington Street East. (Authors' collection.)

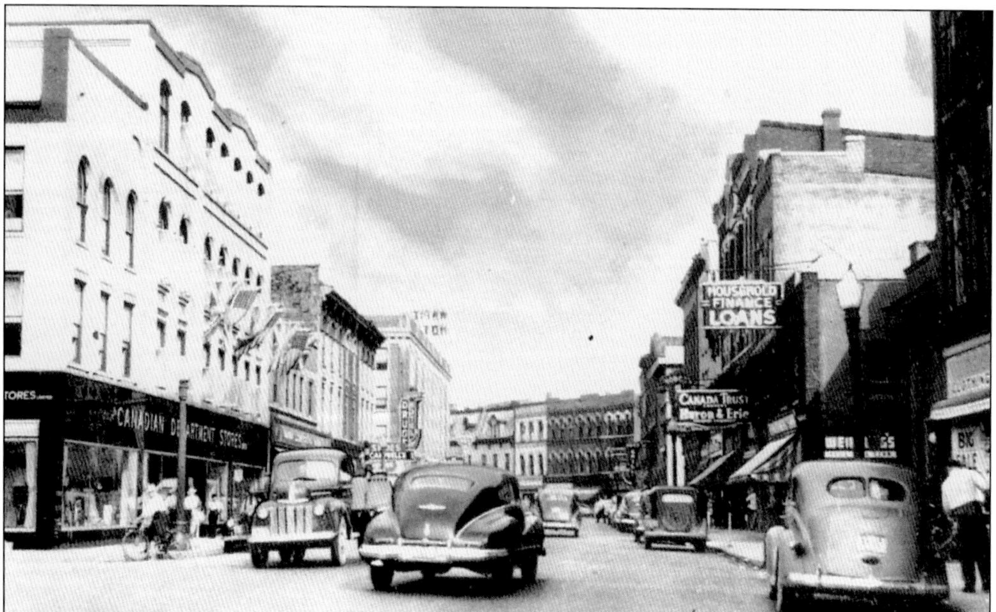

Three different department stores occupied the southwest corner of King and West Market Streets since Charles Austin opened his store in 1896. After Austin departed the corner, the Canadian Department Store, pictured here, occupied the site in the 1930s, and still later, the Eaton's Store took over. The Eaton's Store was torn down in the 1980s to make way for the new Downtown Chatham Centre. (Courtesy Jewiss family.)

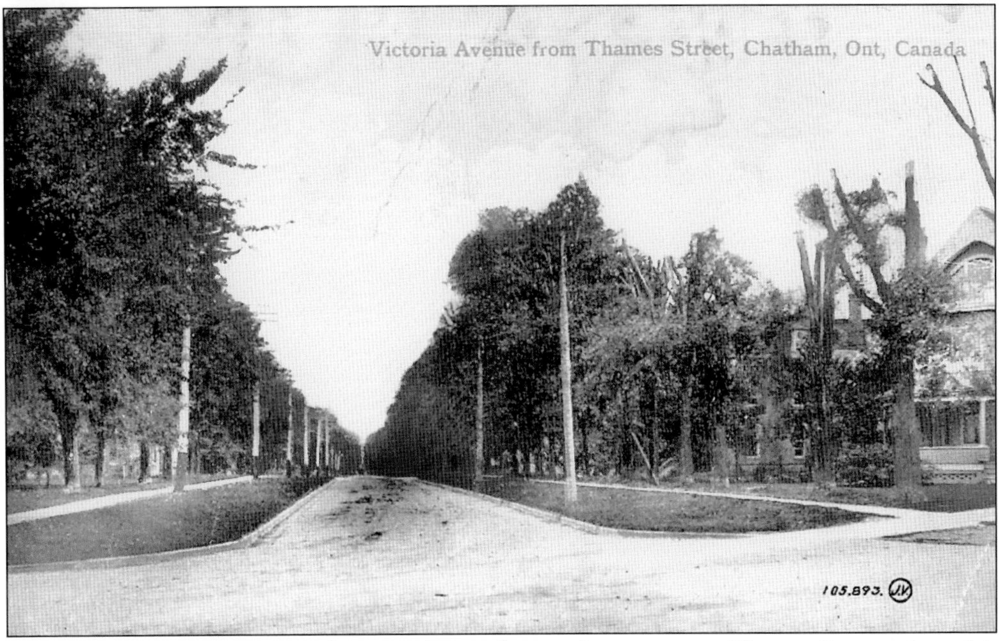

Victoria Avenue was not much more than a dirt road intersecting Thames Street when this picture was taken in the early 1900s. The house on the right still stands today and looks much the same. For many years, the lawn of this home featured the "Rebel Pup," which was a small naval cannon now housed within the Chatham Kent Museum. (Authors' collection.)

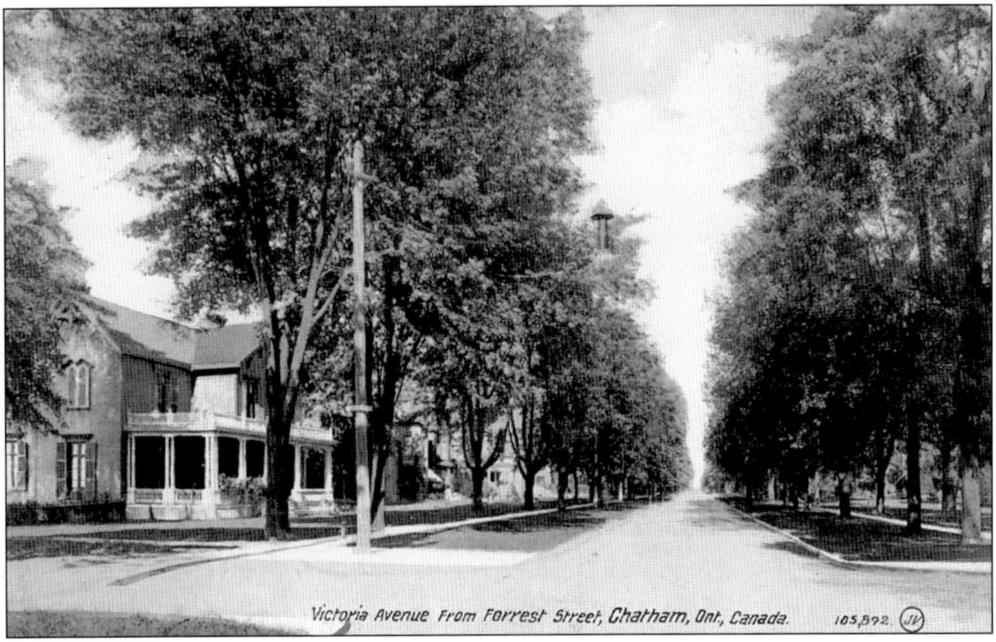

The Robert O'Hara home situated on O'Hara's Victoria Avenue estate, known as Llydican, is pictured on the left c. 1912. Robert O'Hara was a lawyer, a gifted linguist, a crack shot, and an expert on roses, which grew in great abundance at Llydican. Robert O'Hara was also the father of the famous Tin Pan Alley composer Geoffrey O'Hara, who composed, among many others, the well-known song "K-K-Katy." (Authors' collection.)

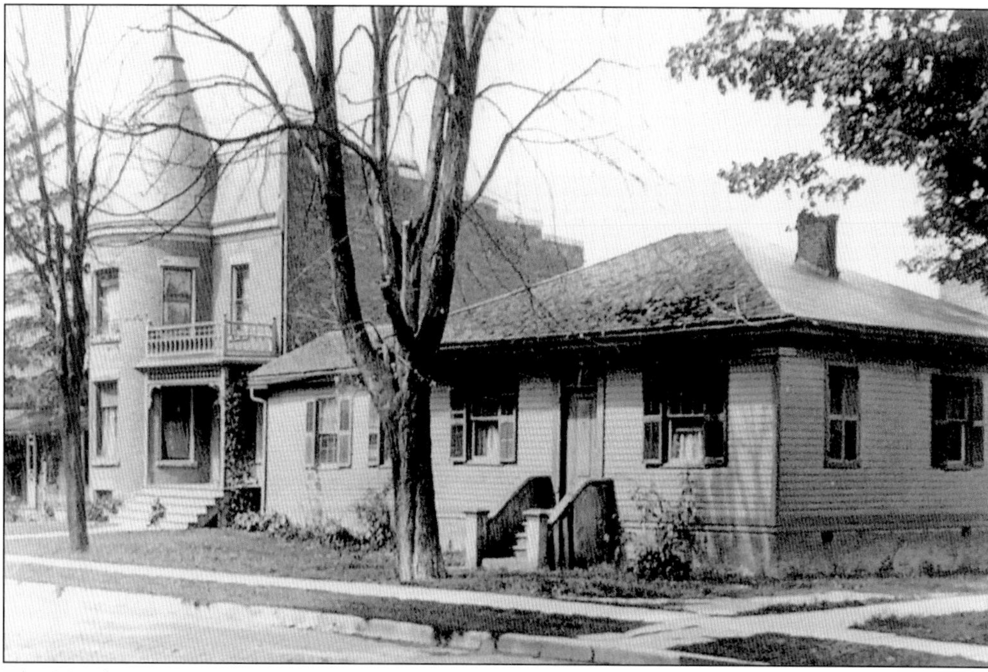

The Ursuline Sisters arrived in Chatham in May 1860 and took up residence at the home of J.B. Williams on Murray Street. They then moved to this home, pictured in the early 1900s, at the southwest corner of Wellington and Third Streets. They remained here until 1870, when they took up permanent residence at the Pines on Grand Avenue West. (Courtesy Doug and Dienne Howard.)

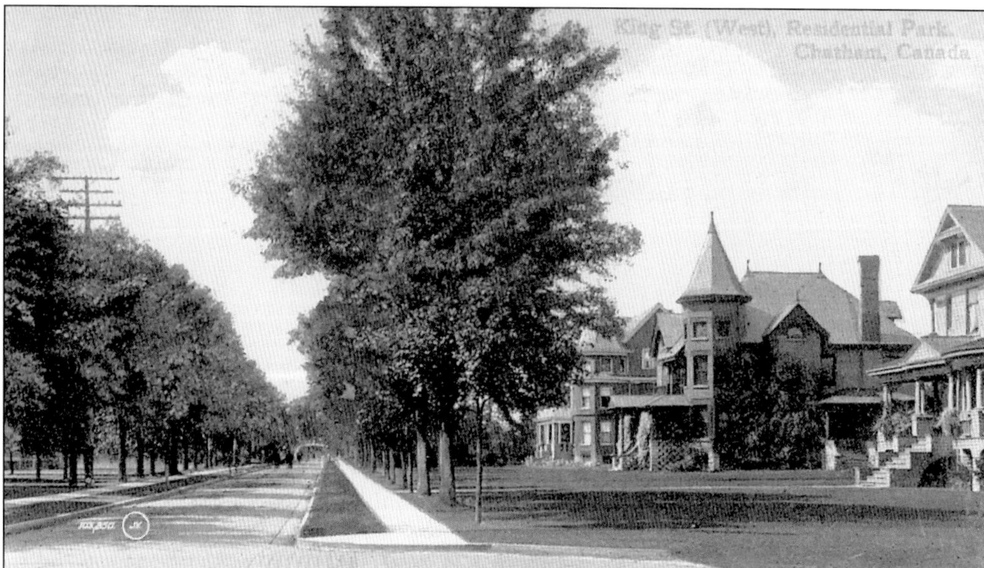

In the late 1890s, King Street West grew into a street of spacious homes and large, landscaped yards. Notable residents of the area included the Charles Austin family, the McKeough family, the Orr family, and the Patteson family. This image depicts King Street West, looking west from the corner of King and Lacroix Streets. The three homes pictured here on the right c. 1910 still exist today. (Authors' collection.)

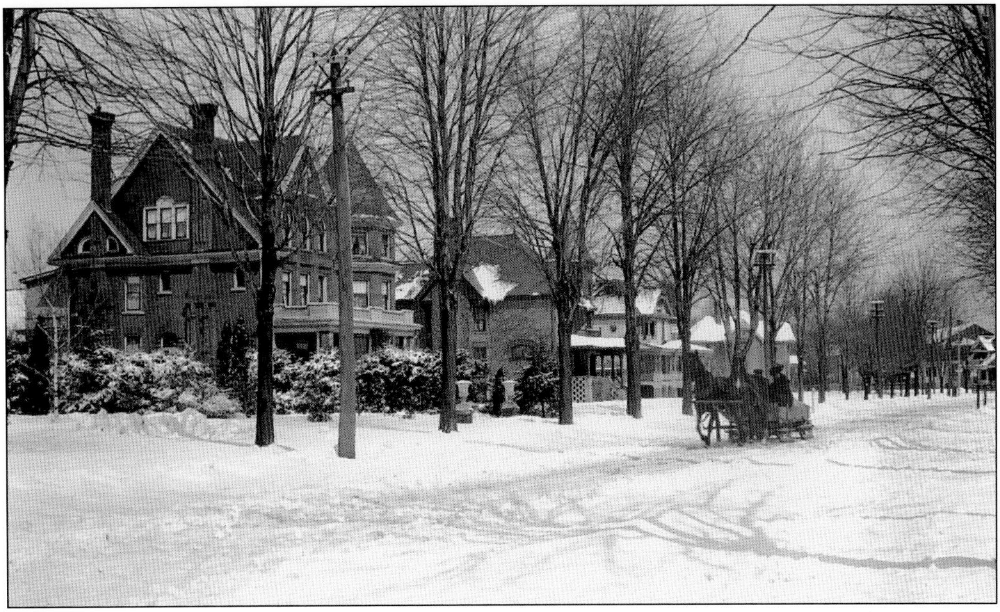

This picture, taken on a crisp winter day *c.* 1913, looks like a posed photograph for a stylish Christmas card; however, it is in reality a relatively common winter picture of the time, taken by Mrs. Charles Austin of her impressive home on King Street West. The view looks east from the corner of King Street and Inshes Avenue. Remarkably, the homes pictured here have changed very little since they were built in the early 1900s. (Courtesy Austin Wright.)

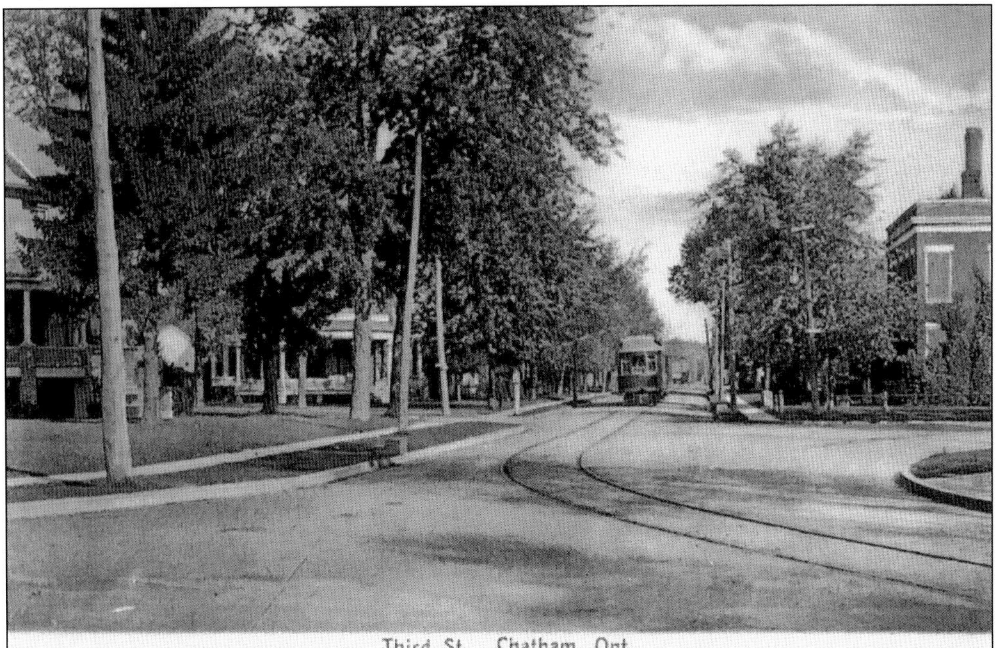

A Chatham, Wallaceburg, and Lake Erie Railroad car approaches Wellington Street from the north on Third Street. The building to the right is approximately where the Tim Horton's coffee shop stands today. The homes on the left still remain in one form or another. (Courtesy Mollie French.)

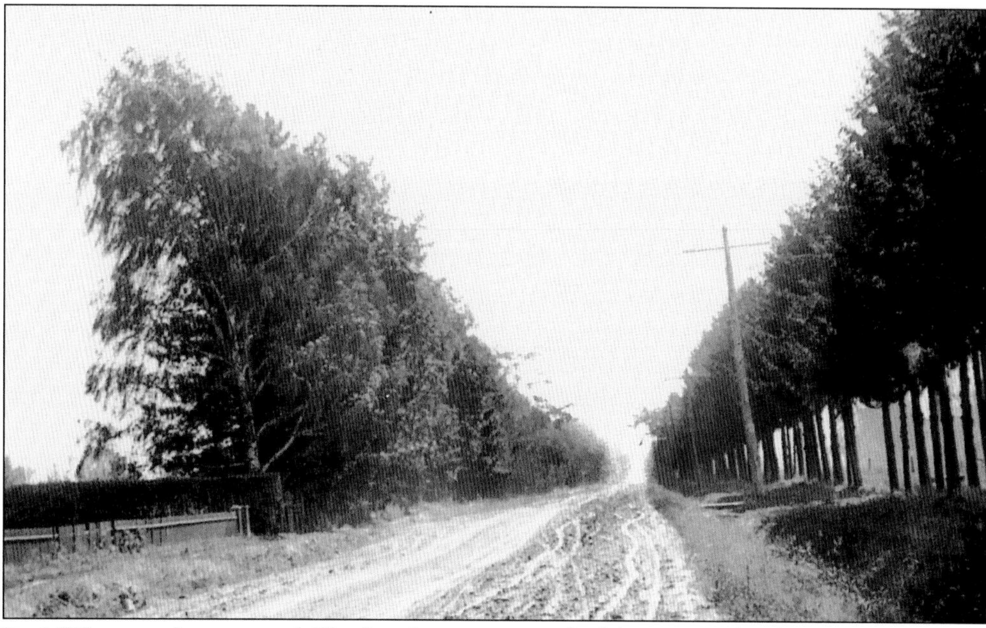

By 1905, a good portion of Chatham's core streets had been paved. The last of the main thoroughfares leading into Chatham to be paved was Queen Street (mid-1900s). This photograph shows a portion of unpaved Queen Street in the early 1900s. (Courtesy Doug and Dienne Howard.)

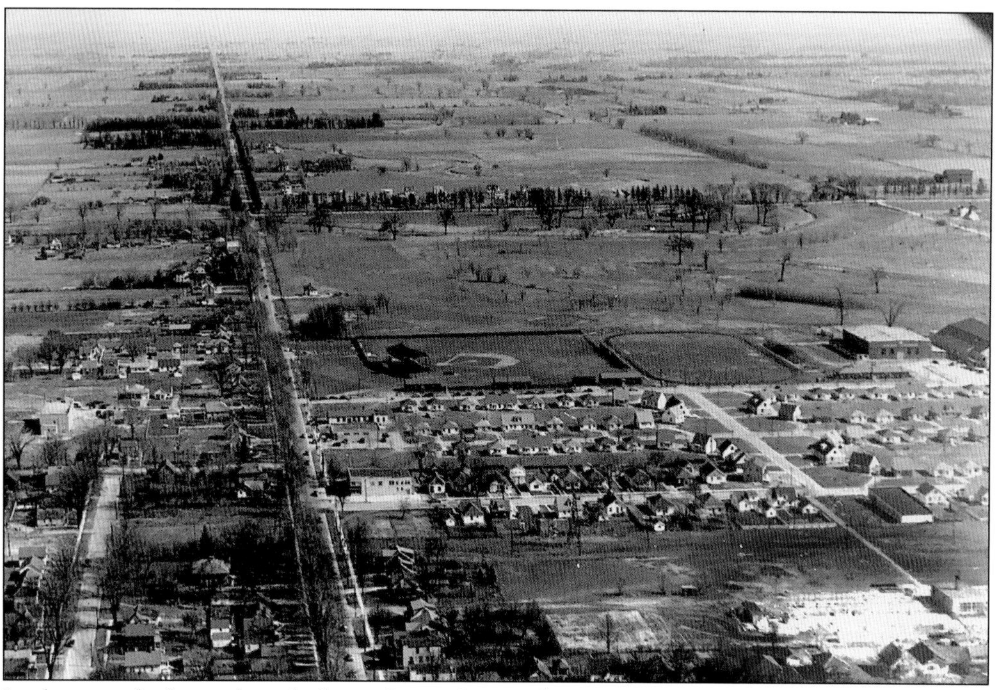

Looking south almost directly down Queen Street, this *c.* 1940s view depicts Rotary Park, with its baseball diamond and military training huts, in the lower middle. Beyond this point, to the right of Queen Street, a large open space represents Chatham's first golf course. To the middle far right, the Kinsmen Auditorium and Memorial Arena appear. (Courtesy W.G. Glassco.)

Three

Bad Times and Sad Times

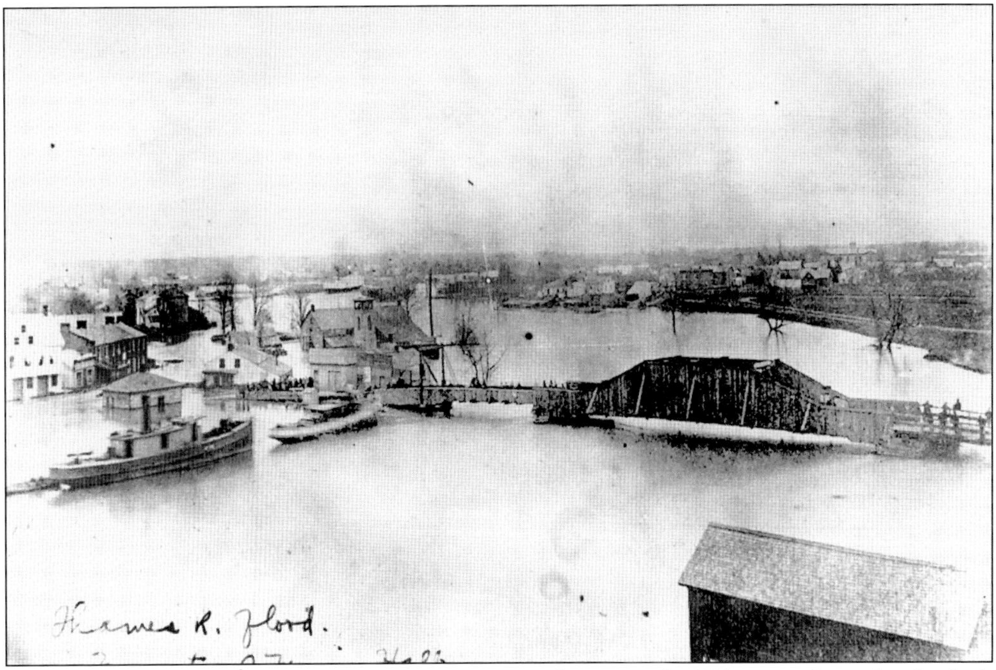

Floods have plagued Chatham since its inception. The original 1856 covered wooden bridge's superstructure was swept away by floods twice before an iron bridge was built in 1895. This picture was taken from the roof of the Chatham Opera House during the 1868 flood. (Courtesy Chatham Kent Museum.)

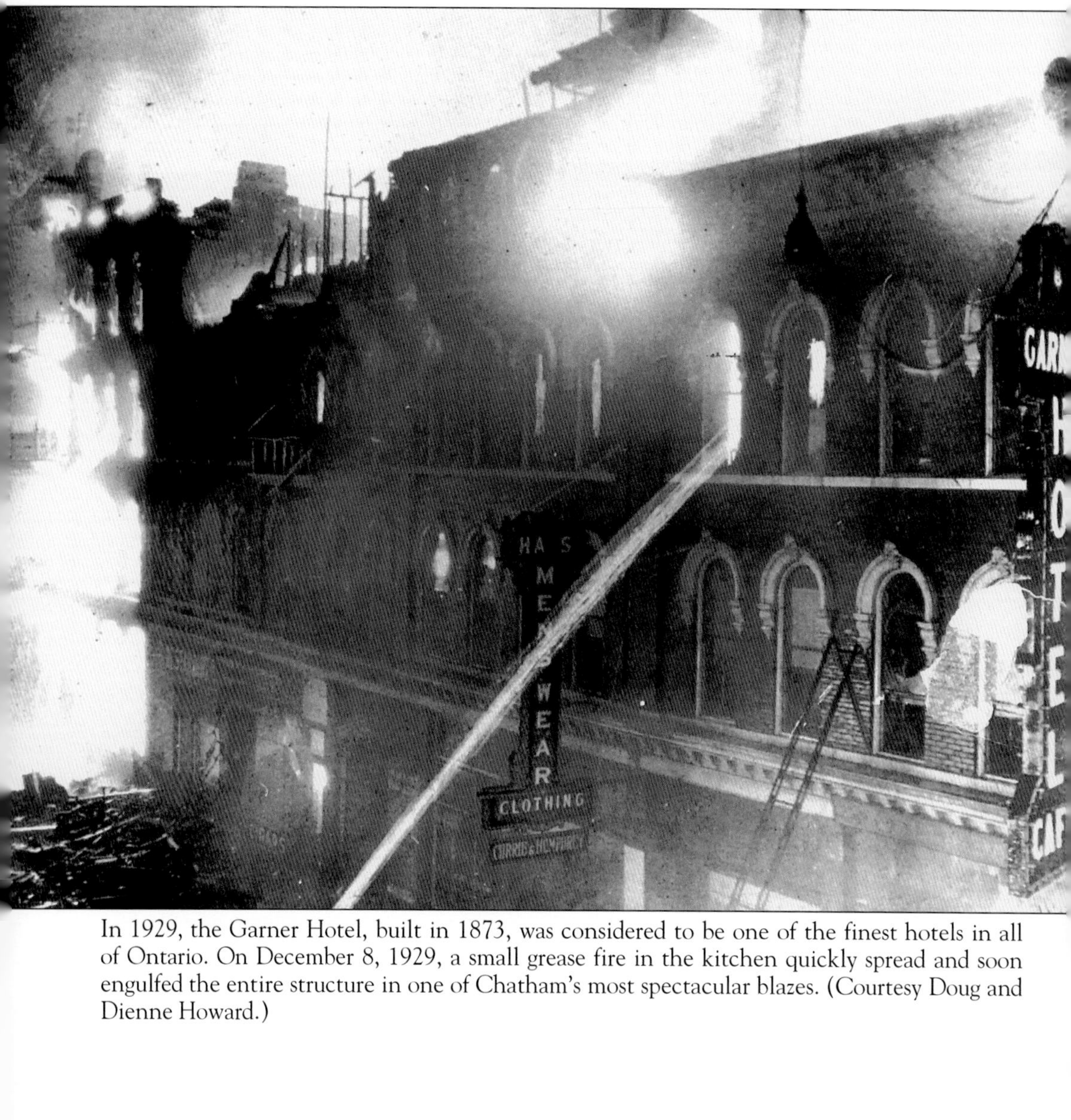

In 1929, the Garner Hotel, built in 1873, was considered to be one of the finest hotels in all of Ontario. On December 8, 1929, a small grease fire in the kitchen quickly spread and soon engulfed the entire structure in one of Chatham's most spectacular blazes. (Courtesy Doug and Dienne Howard.)

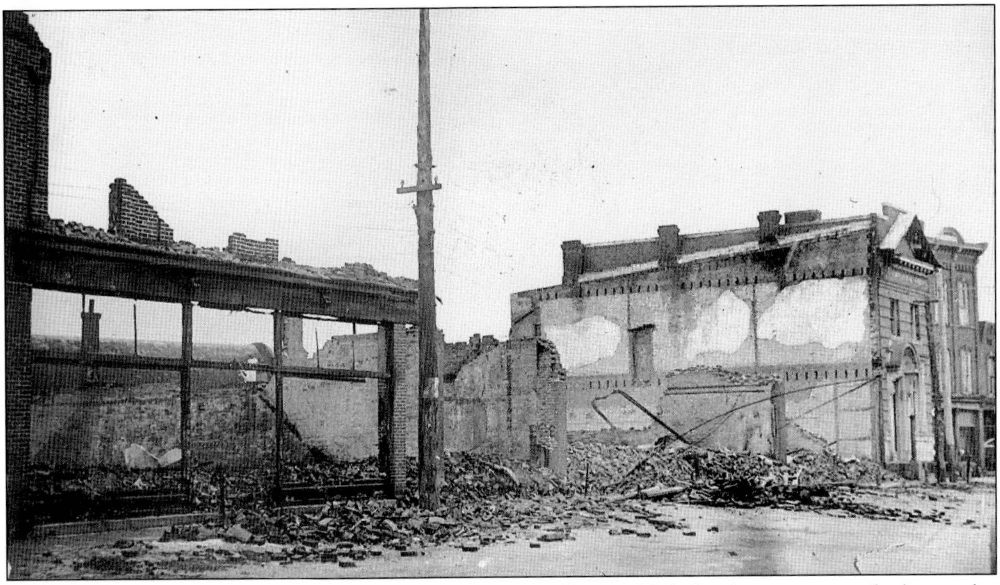

The spectacular fire that destroyed the Garner Hotel in 1929 left a huge, gaping hole on the southwest corner of King and Sixth Streets. Although fire departments from as far away as Windsor responded in record times, there was little chance of saving anything. The smoking ruin was, however, soon replaced by an even more elaborate hotel, the William Pitt, in less than a year. (Courtesy Chatham Kent Museum.)

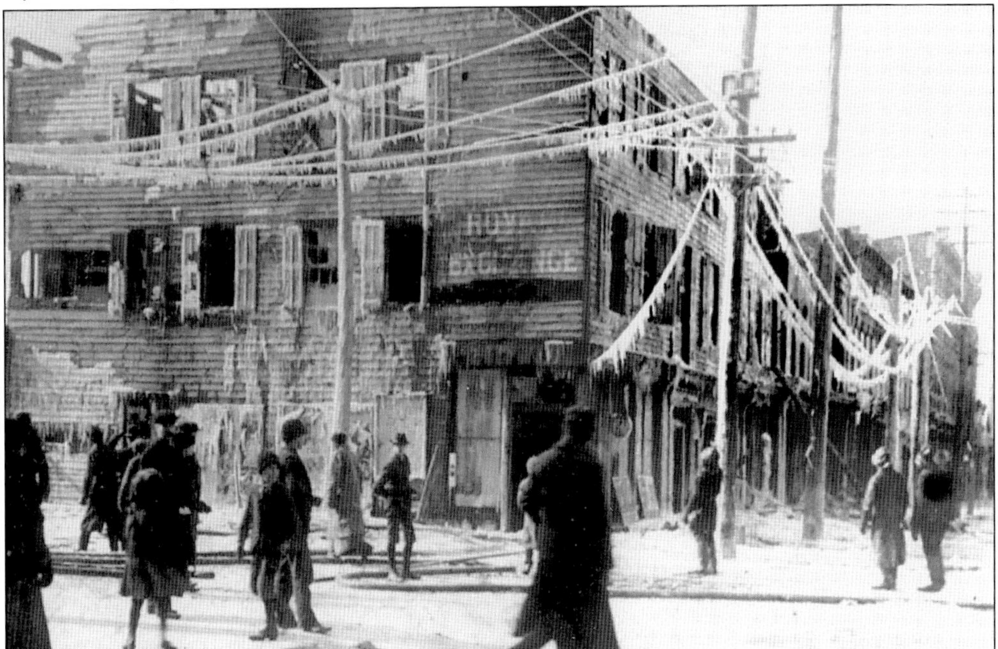

For many years, the Royal Exchange Hotel, situated on the southwest corner of King and Fifth Streets, was Chatham's premier hotel. Built in the 1830s, this frame structure was devastated by an intense fire on a cold winter's night in February 1898. Taken shortly after the fire was extinguished, this photograph shows the ice from the firefighting efforts still hanging onto wires and the burned-out Royal Exchange. (Courtesy Chatham Kent Museum.)

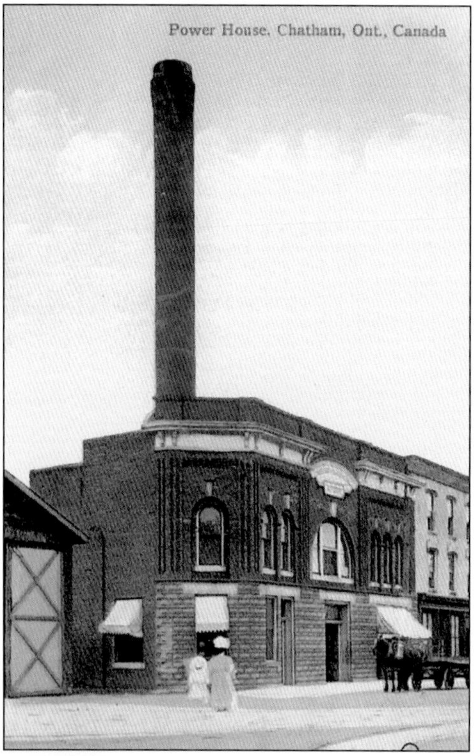

The Chatham, Wallaceburg, and Lake Erie Power House, shown here c. 1910, was located on the northeast corner of King and Third Streets. It contained two 300-kilowatt Thompson Ryan dynamos, which were driven by two McEwan tandem compound engines. The powerhouse required a great deal of energy to power the electric railroad lines on its extensive routes. (Courtesy Doug and Dienne Howard.)

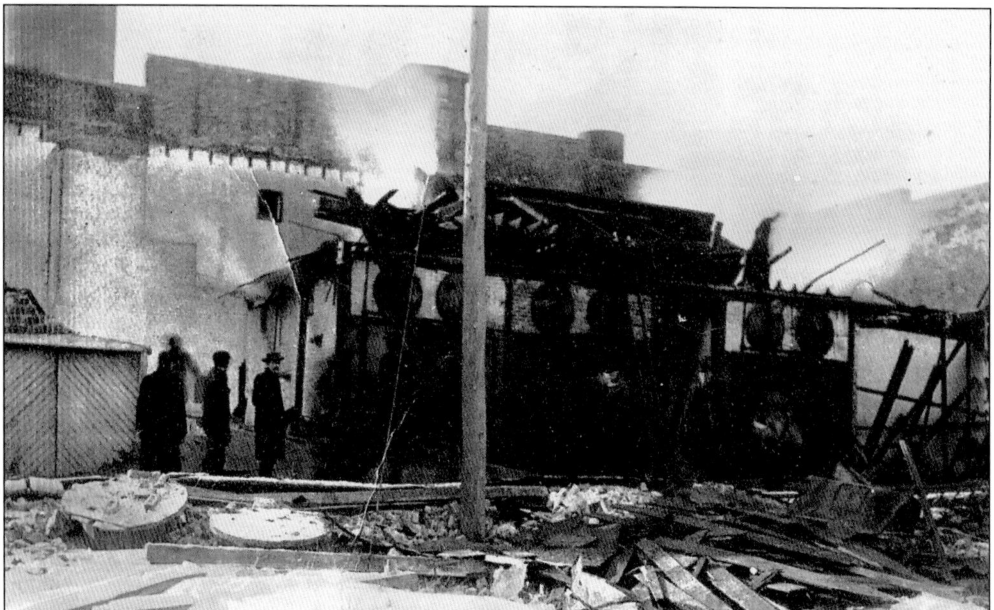

Around 8:00 a.m. on February 24, 1914, a terrific explosion rocked King Street West. The Chatham, Wallaceburg, and Lake Erie Power House had a gas leak that was ignited by the flames heating the large boilers. One man, engineer Charles Davies, was killed and two others were injured in the sudden and devastating explosion that resulted. (Courtesy Doug and Dienne Howard.)

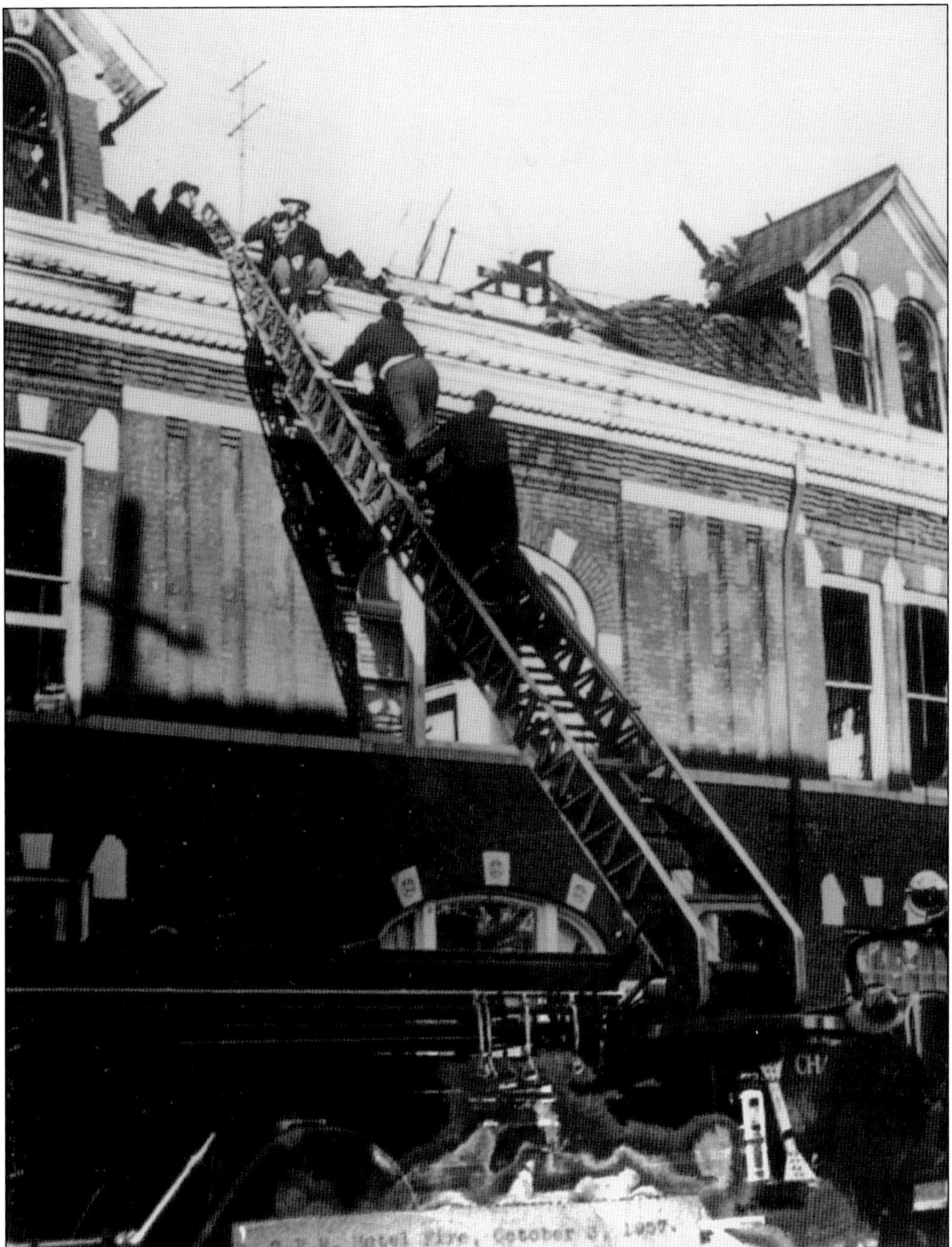

The CPR Hotel, situated on the northwest corner of King and William Streets, was built in 1890 by William Baby and burned down, as seen here, in October 1957, with the loss of four lives. In the beginning, the Canadian Pacific Railroad objected to the hotel using the CPR name since the two had no official connection. According to some reports, Baby avoided legal action by stating that the name of his hotel was really the Chatham Pool and Recreation Hotel. In this picture, firefighters ensure that all fires are extinguished. (Courtesy Chatham Kent Museum.)

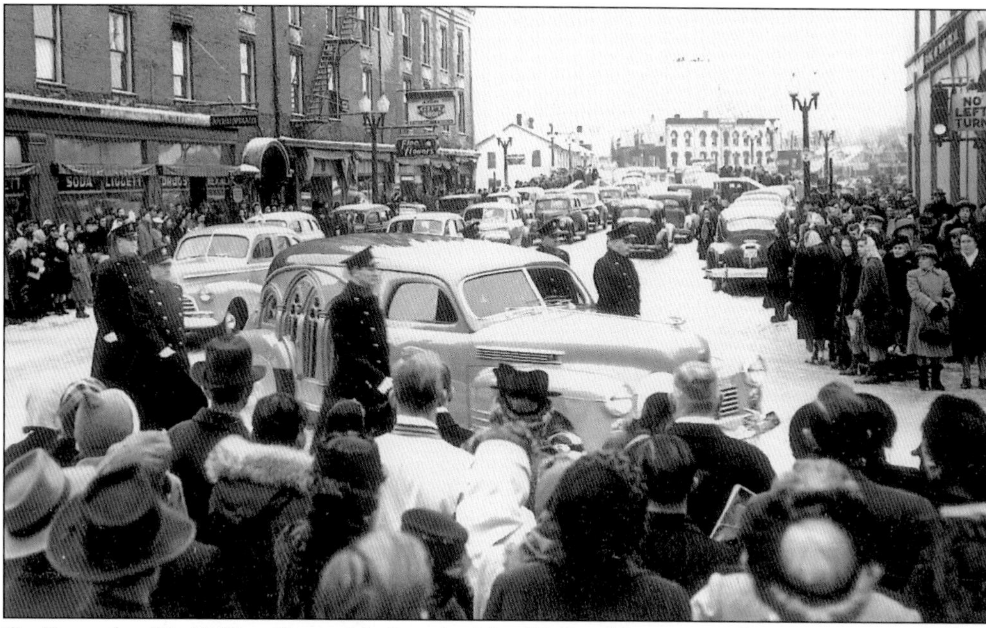

On December 28, 1947, as Constable Douglas Lloyd Reynolds attempted to arrest James Whaley, a scuffle broke out and Constable Reynolds was struck down. He died in the hospital two days later on December 30. His funeral was one of the largest Chatham had ever seen. In this 1948 picture, the unique Needham Funeral Home hearse makes the turn onto King Street from Fifth Street, carrying Reynolds's coffin. (Courtesy Stan Uher.)

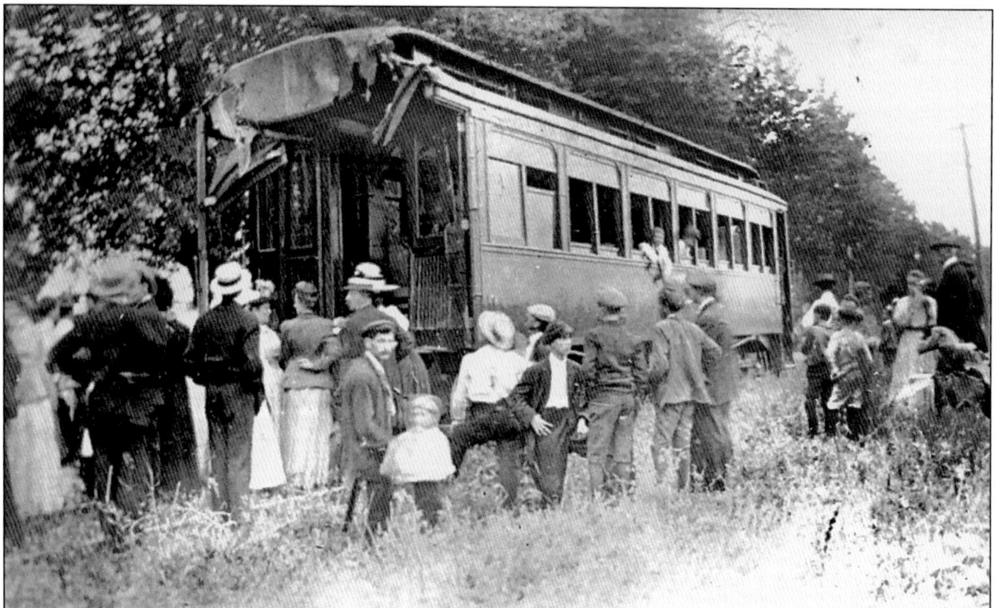

On August 10, 1908, a Chatham, Wallaceburg, and Lake Erie electric line coach was headed south on Queen Street when it stopped near Eugenie Street to drop off some passengers. The brakes of the next car coming down the line failed, and the car slammed into the back of the car pictured here. Four people were killed in the collision, shocking people throughout Chatham and Kent County. (Courtesy Chatham Kent Museum.)

Around 1:30 p.m. on June 8, 1906, a tornado hit Chatham with a great deal of destructive force. It was described as a small "cloud burst" accompanied by thunder and lightning and "a terrific wind." In some instances, entire homes, like the one pictured here on King Street East, were severely damaged. In fact, it was reported that every home in the city of Chatham had been damaged to some extent by the tornado. (Courtesy Mollie French.)

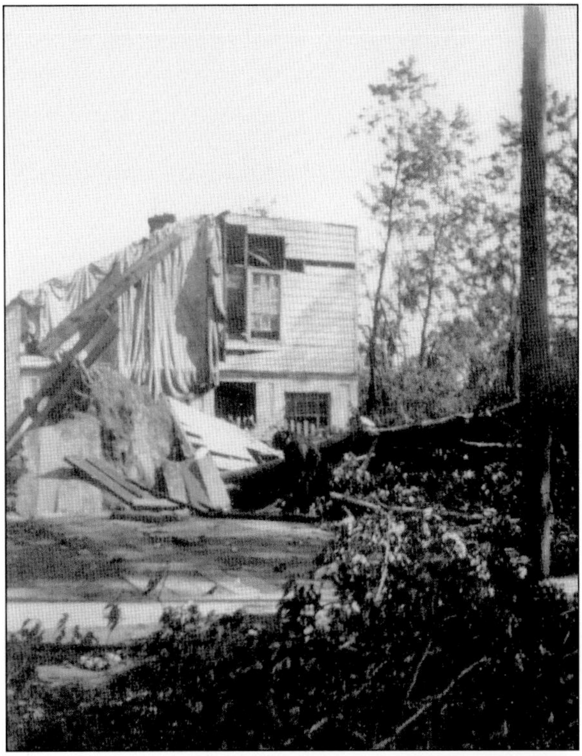

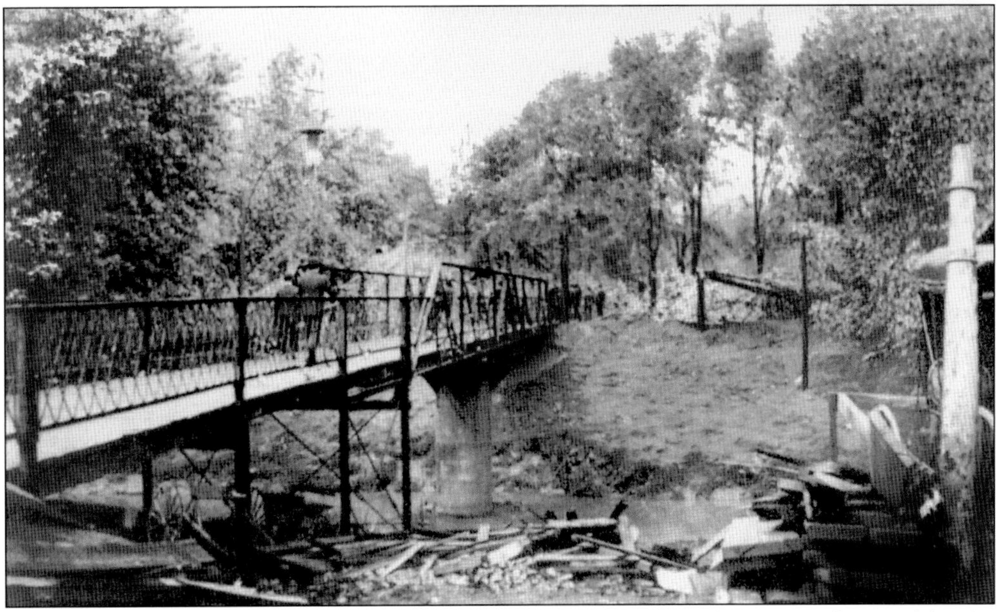

Although the footbridge over McGregor's Creek to Tecumseh Park was not damaged by the tornado of 1906, many of the trees in the park, as pictured here, were snapped off, and limbs littered the area in large numbers. In addition, the skylight and windows were blown out of the old Chatham Collegiate Institute, the trolley line between Chatham and Wallaceburg was knocked out of service, the Opera House lost all of its chimneys, and the Chatham Fire Hall was flooded. (Courtesy Doug and Dienne Howard.)

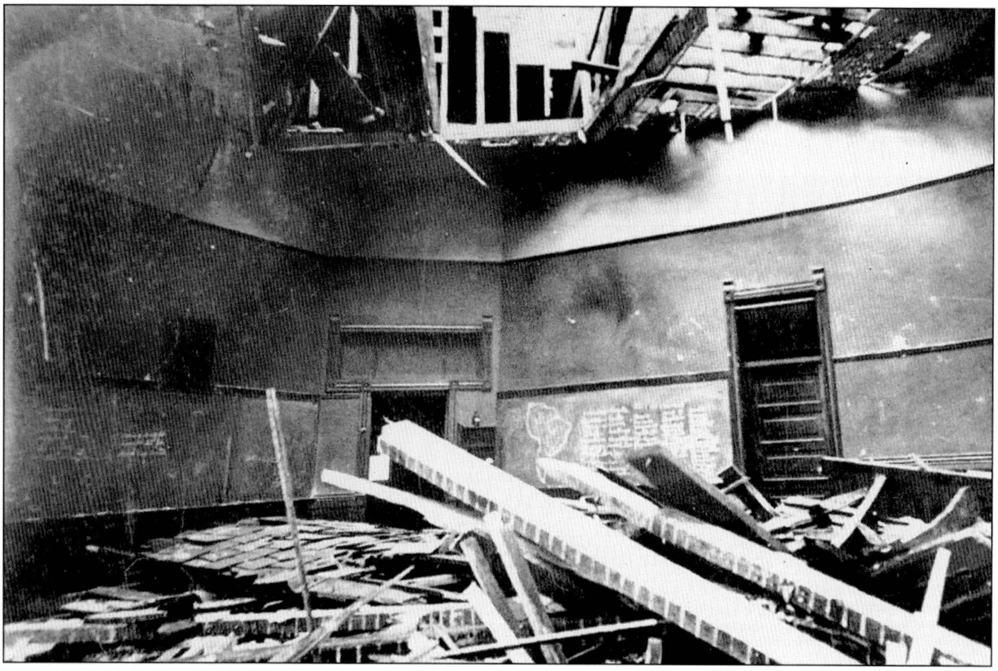

This picture purportedly shows the damage done to Chatham's Central School by the tornado of June 9, 1906. In this same storm, the steeple of the Park Street United Church toppled and was never replaced. Although many horses and cattle were killed in the storm and crop damage resulted in losses totalling thousands of dollars, not one person in Chatham was killed. (Courtesy Chatham Kent Museum.)

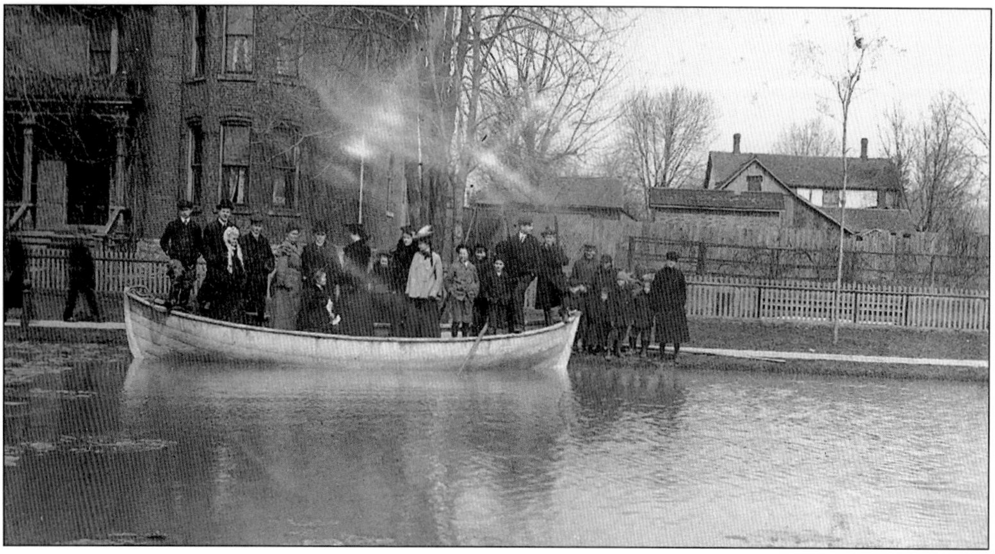

During the flood of 1904, a number of Chatham residents decided to make the best of it and go for an excursion. This picture, taken on March 28, 1904, shows a boating party on Dover Street, consisting of Mrs. N.H. Stevens, Mrs. Burk, Mrs. Strickett, Margaret Walker, Flossie Butler, Mary Rankin, Will Stevens, Douglas Stevens, Stan Stevens, Robert Tobey, George Winterstein, and a number of young lads from the neighbourhood. (Courtesy Chatham Kent Museum.)

A good portion of the downtown area of Chatham was flooded in late April 1937 long after the ice had melted and gone. Intense rainfall brought the Thames River to a record high of 594.4 feet on April 29, the day this picture was taken, near the Piggott Lumber Company on King Street West. Although Chatham had never known such water levels, the frightening event proved that the residential areas of Chatham were built on high ground and that overall the residents of Chatham fared much better than those situated in other towns and villages along the Thames River. (Courtesy Chatham Kent Museum.)

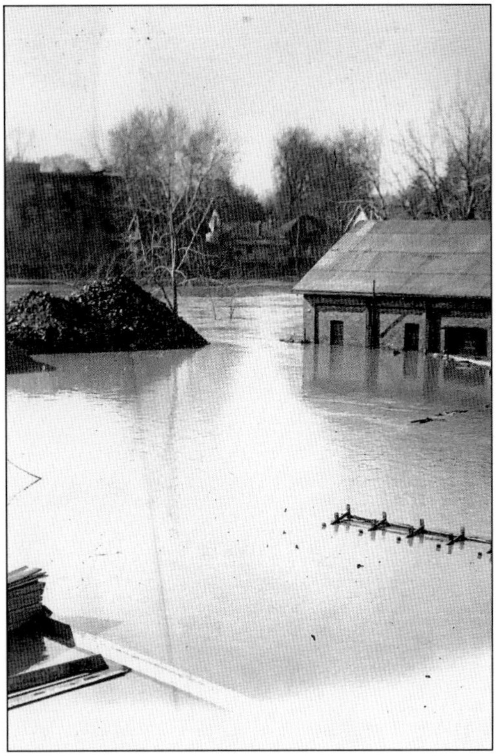

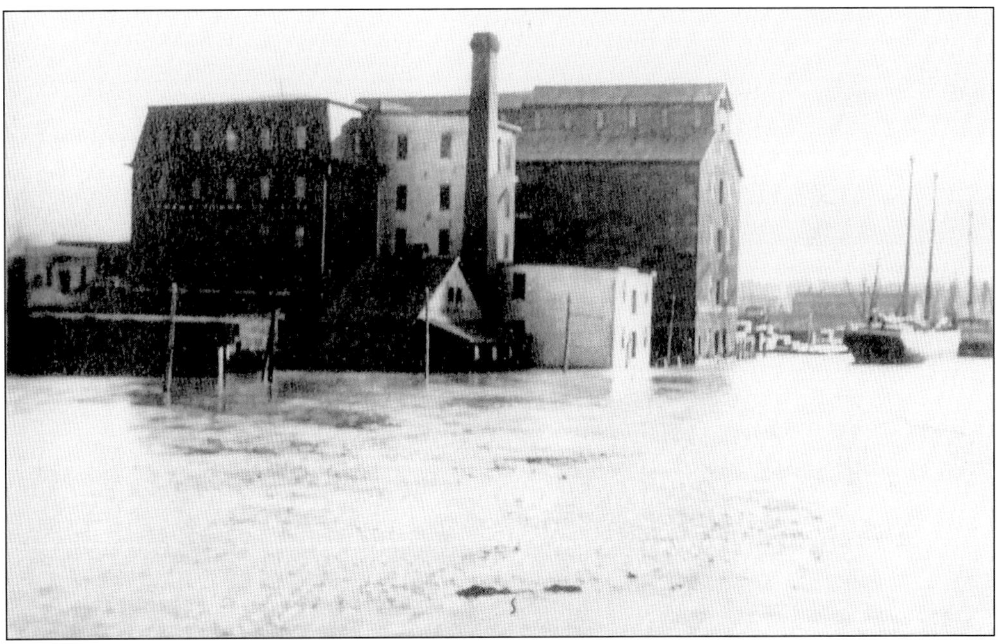

The flood of 1912 surrounded the buildings on the north side of the Thames River between the Third Street and Fifth Street Bridges. In this picture, the Kent Flour Mill is surrounded by the flooding Thames. The sailing ships pictured wintered here and in the spring began their task of bringing in barrels of salt and all types of lumber and taking out flour and other finished products produced at the Kent Flour Mill. (Courtesy Mr. and Mrs. Jamieson.)

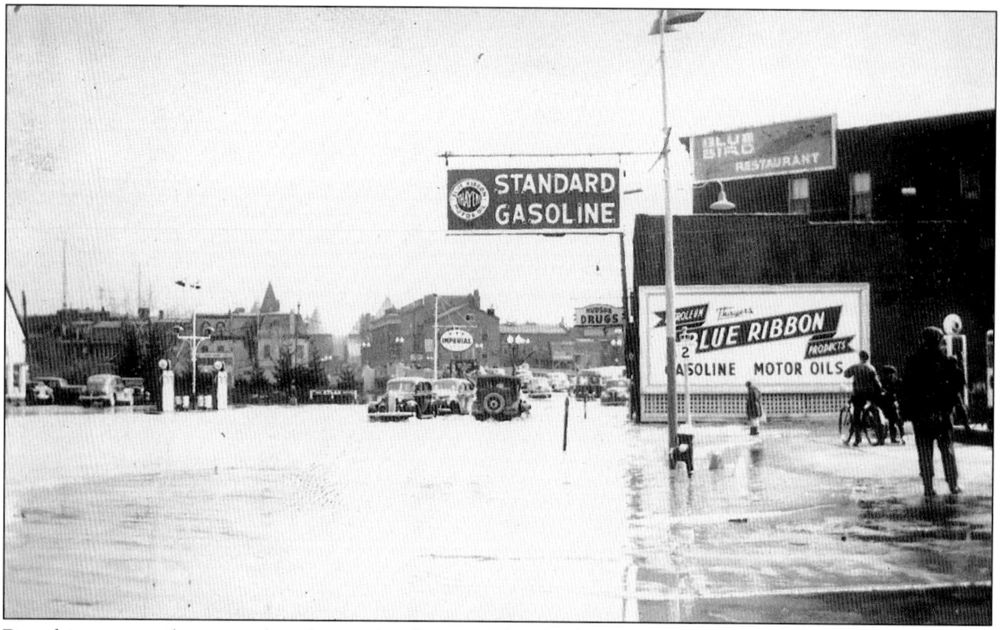

Reaching near the same height as the famous Flood of 1937, this early–April 1947 flood cost the city of Chatham thousands of dollars, nearly destroyed Public General Hospital's heating system, and forced the local Red Cross to set up an emergency centre at the Market Building. Automobiles approach the Fifth Street Bridge from Thames Street in North Chatham. (Courtesy Chatham Kent Museum.)

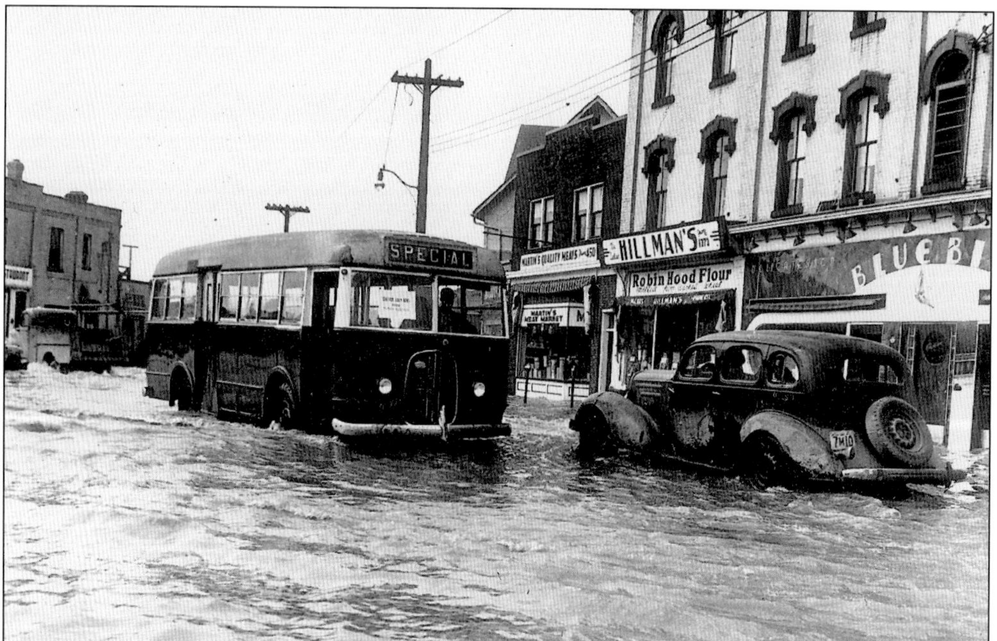

During the 1947 flood, many people were stranded in the downtown area of Chatham, forcing the fire and police departments onto 24-hour emergency duty. The Thames River covered No Parking signs in some areas, and small boats could be seen moored to parking meters. (Courtesy Chatham Kent Museum.)

The Flood of 1947 equalled the devastating flood of 10 years earlier. The area that once again received the most serious flooding was down in "the valley" on Thames and Dover Streets. In this picture, a boat is rowed toward the Thames River and the Ward Milling Company, the site of the present-day Forsyth Travel Bureau. (Courtesy Doug and Dienne Howard.)

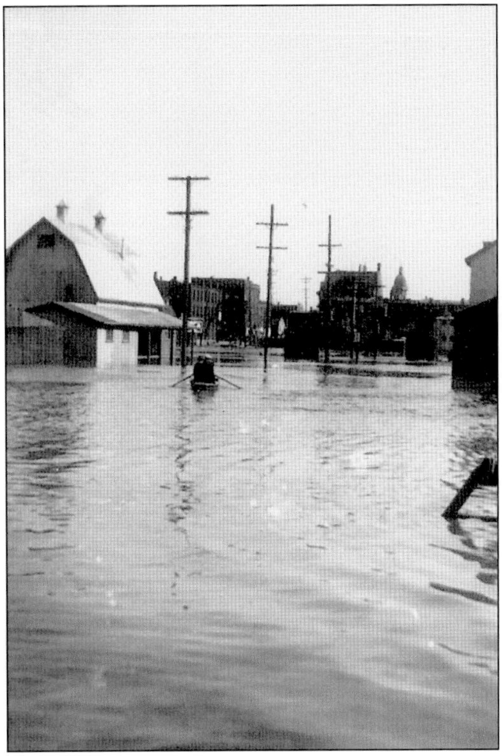

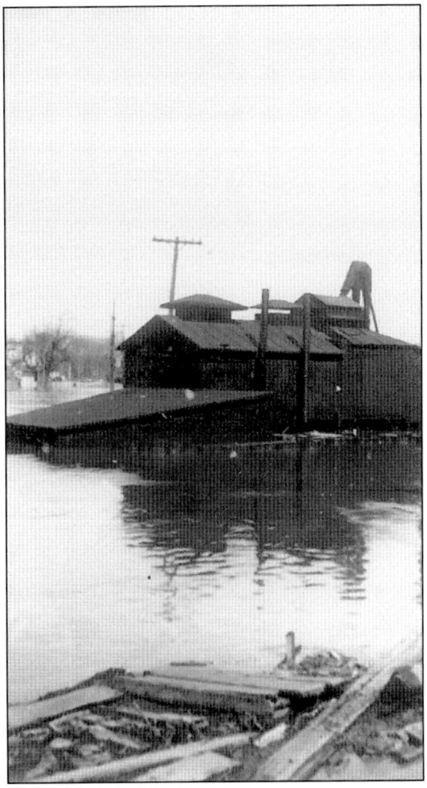

The Chatham City Works asphalt plant was situated at the west end of the valley on Thames Street, near present-day Harvey's Restaurant. In the 1947 flood, it was completely surrounded by water, as were nearly 10,000 acres of land in Chatham and Kent County. (Courtesy Mr. and Mrs. Jamieson.)

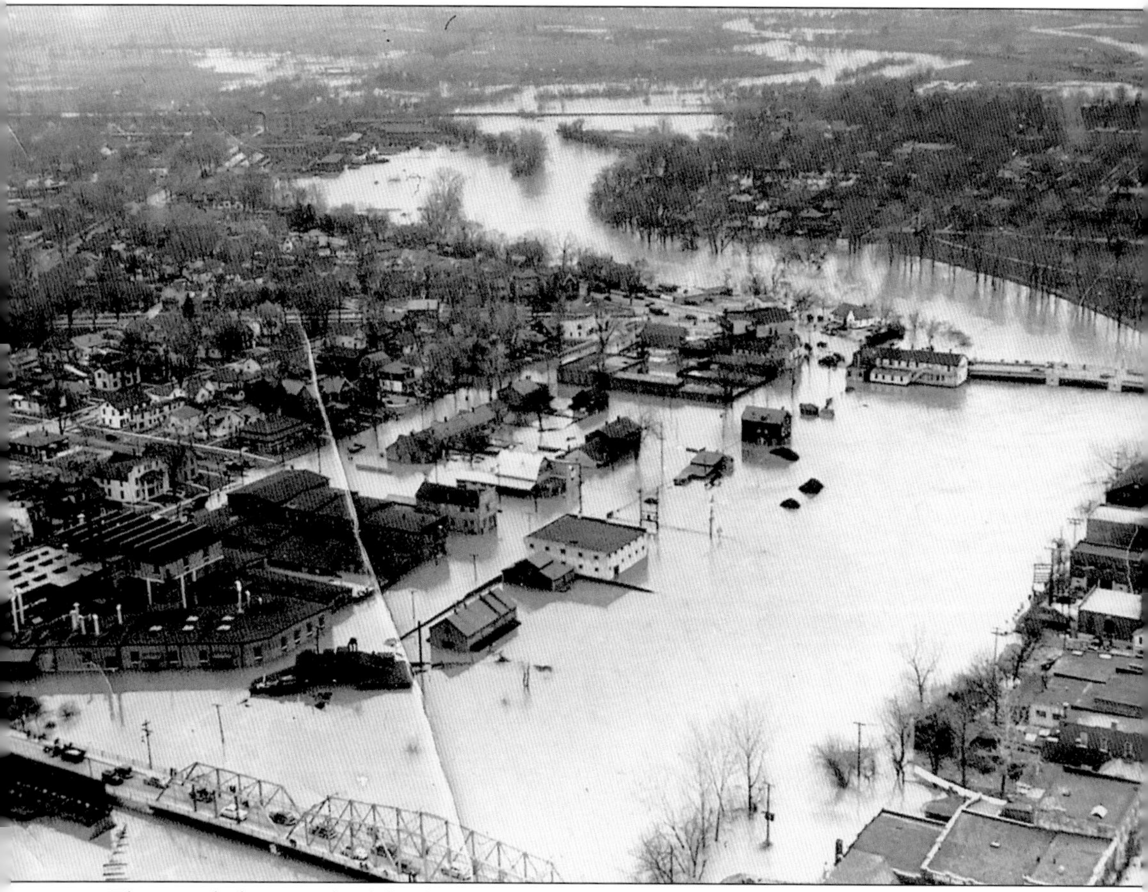

This aerial photograph of the downtown Chatham area, taken in April 1947, shows the extent of this flood. As in every flood that has hit Chatham since the earliest recorded times, the worst flooding always occurred in North Chatham (to the left of the river), and the King Street area on the south side of the river usually escaped serious flooding, as evidenced in this picture. Among the buildings on the left side of the river along Thames Street and between the Third Street and Fifth Street Bridges, the Chatham City Works' asphalt factory and the Ward Milling Company are surrounded by water. (Courtesy Doug and Dienne Howard.)

Four

Having Fun and Playing Hard

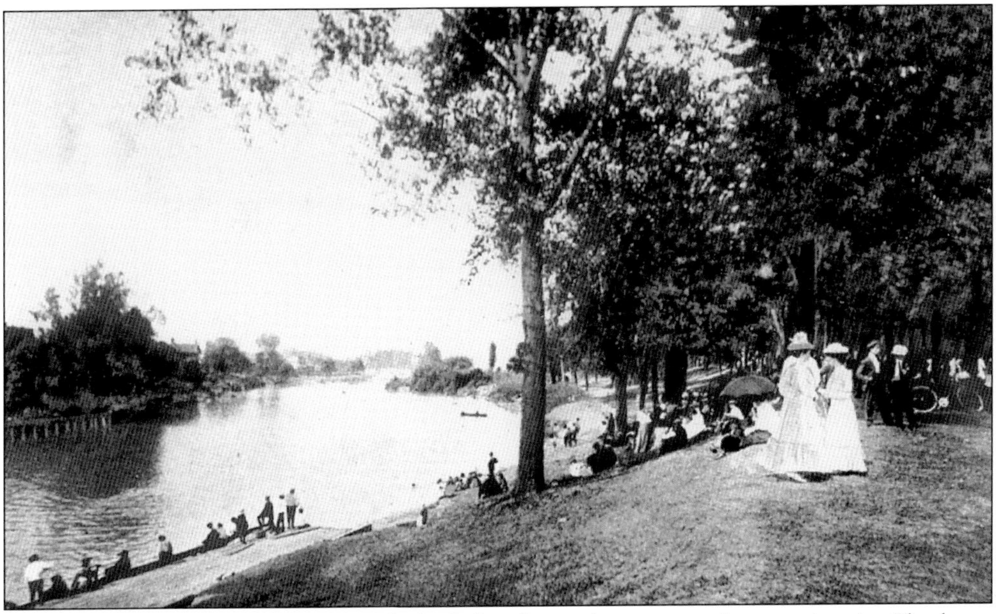

Since the spring of 1880, Tecumseh Park has been the centre of recreation in Chatham. Centrally located on the Thames River in the heart of downtown, it was originally designated as a military reserve but, beginning in the 1860s, was leased back to the former city of Chatham. When it became a park, Tecumseh was surrounded by a picket fence, with turnstiles at William Street and Gaol Street, which is now Stanley Avenue. (Authors' collection.)

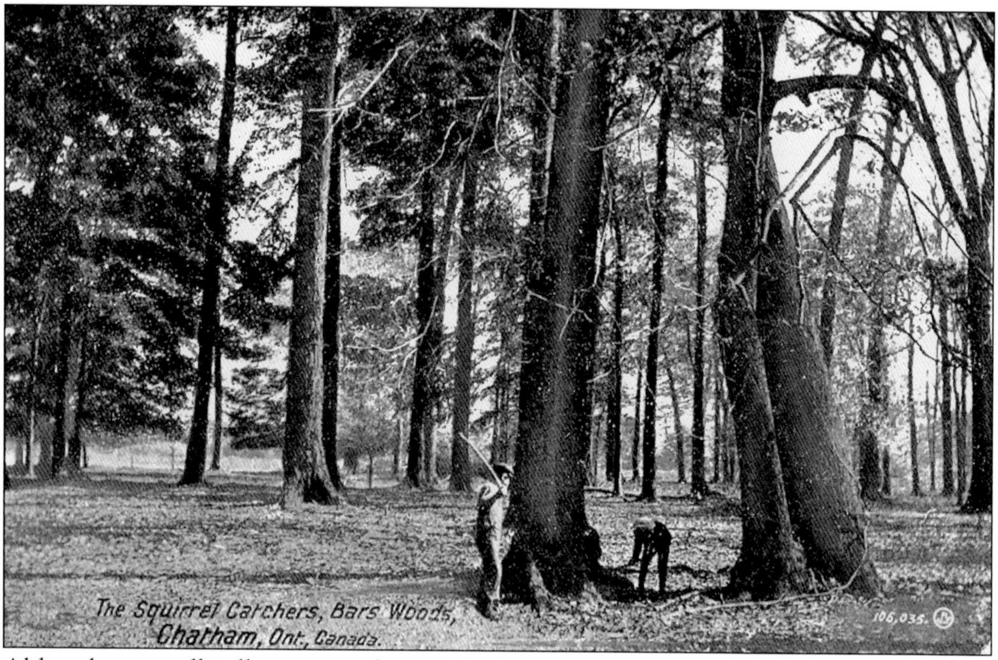

Although never officially recognized as a park, Barr's Woods, on the westerly edge of Chatham, was used by early residents for many recreational activities, including squirrel hunting, as seen in this *c.* 1911 photograph. Situated near the river, it was on a farm owned by Robert Barr. Barr's son Robert Jr. later gained fame as a newspaper editor and novelist in Canada and Great Britain. (Authors' collection.)

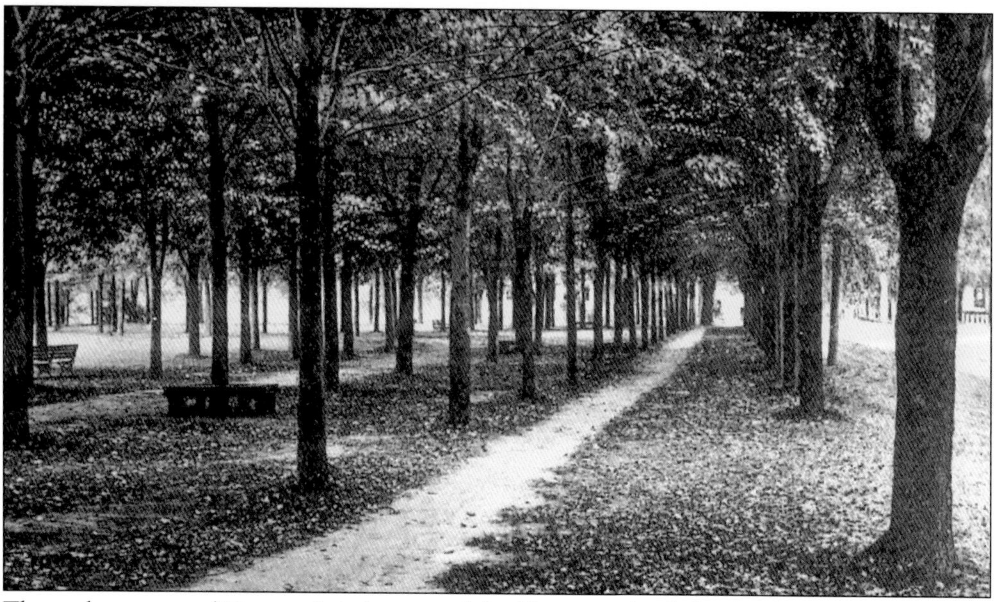
The park was named Tecumseh in honour of the Shawnee chief who fought a skirmish against American forces here on October 4, 1813, the day before he was killed a few miles upstream at the Battle of the Thames. Young couples since the mid-1800s have taken long romantic walks in this beautiful setting and along this former row of trees aptly named Lover's Walk. This photograph was taken *c.* 1900. (Authors' collection.)

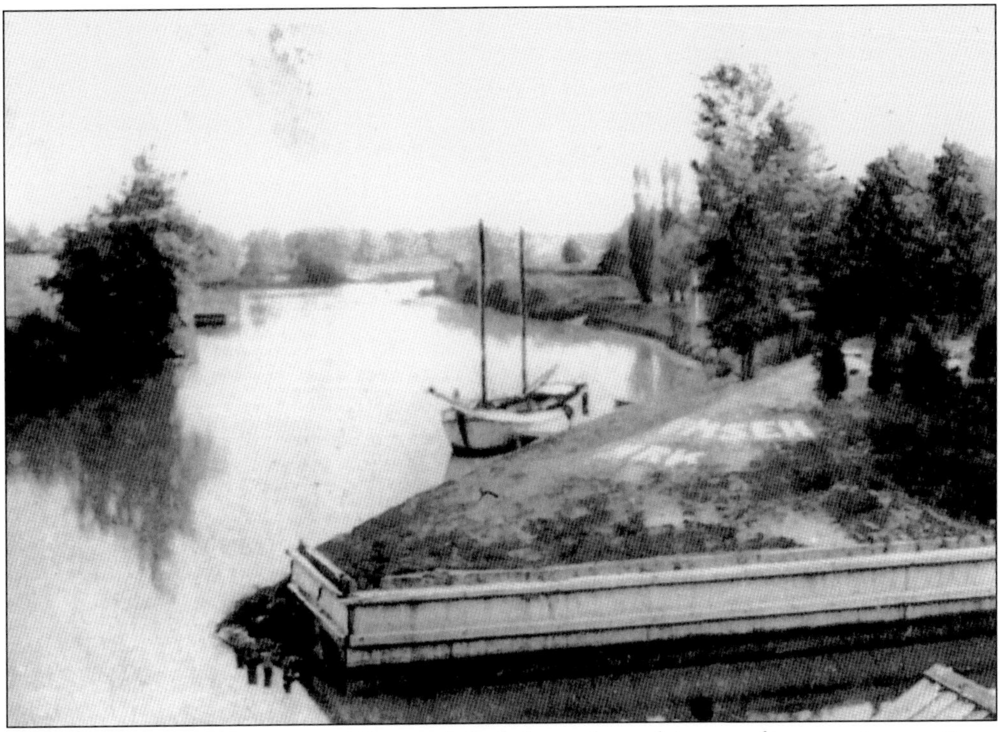

This *c.* 1890s view of the Point at Tecumseh Park shows the park in one of its many incarnations. Erosion at the spot where the Thames River meets McGregor's Creek has always been a problem. At the time this picture was taken, a wooden break wall had been installed, and Tecumseh Park had been "written" with white stones on the top of the bank. (Courtesy Doug and Dienne Howard.)

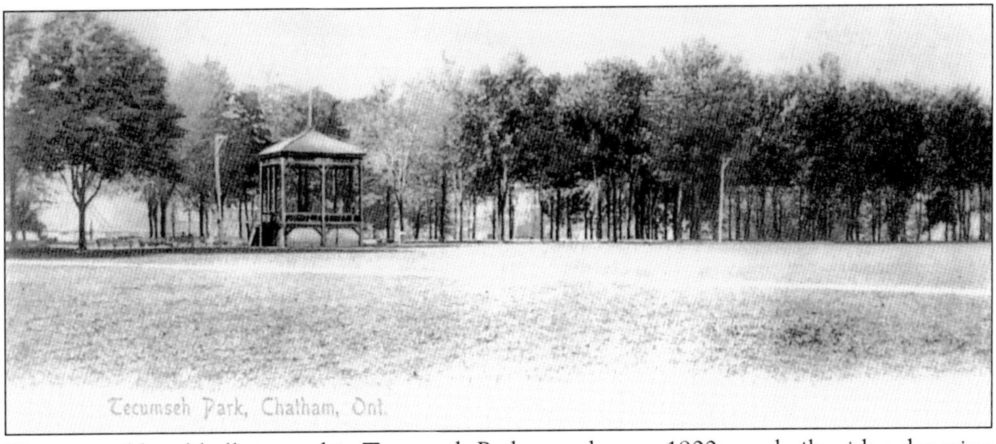

The original bandshell situated in Tecumseh Park, seen here *c.* 1900, was built with a donation from Robert Gray and underwent a number of alterations over the years before being torn down in the late 1960s. During the summer months, the bandshell was used extensively by many groups, and the tradition continues today in a newer bandshell, with the Chatham Concert Band playing every Wednesday evening in the summer months. (Courtesy Doug and Dienne Howard.)

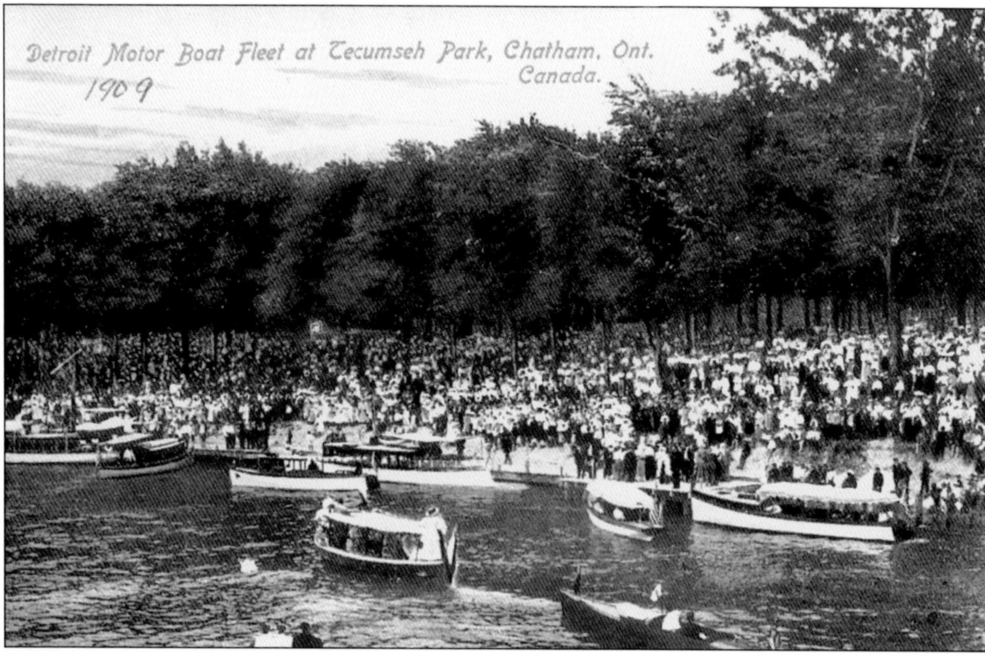

Since its earliest days in the 1890s, Tecumseh Park's waterfront has played host to a number of exciting activities. In the early 1900s, the Detroit Motor Boat Fleet navigated its way up the Thames River in order to participate in a regatta usually held on the first week in July. The impressive number of boats as well as the large crowds, pictured here *c.* 1909, attest to its popularity. (Courtesy Chatham Kent Museum.)

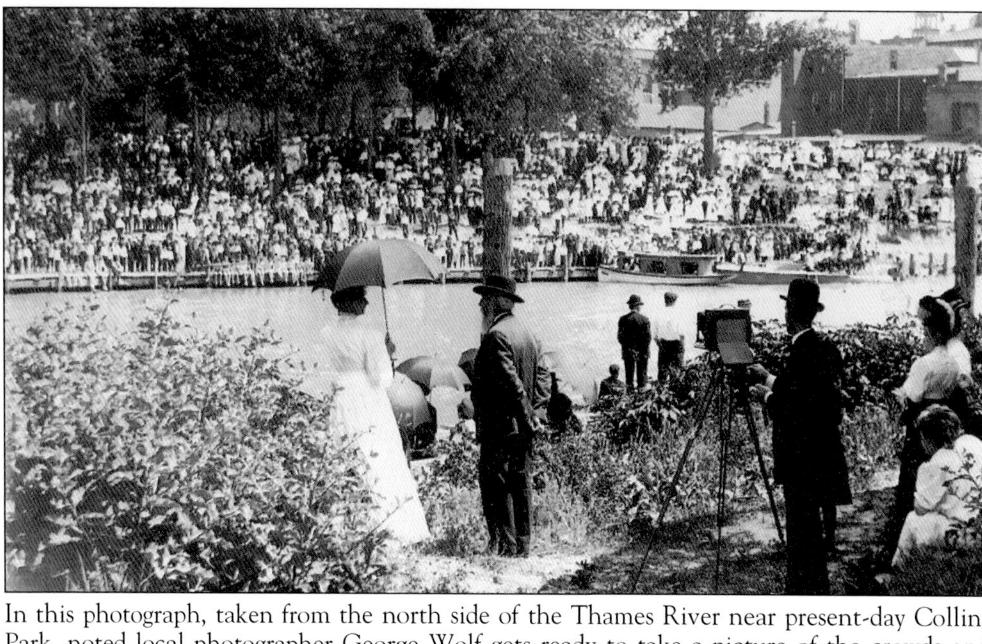

In this photograph, taken from the north side of the Thames River near present-day Collins Park, noted local photographer George Wolf gets ready to take a picture of the crowds and the boats crowding around the docks at Tecumseh Park in preparation for the summer regatta. Wolf's pictures of Tecumseh Park, as well as those of many other scenes and people in the Chatham area, were very popular in the 1900s. (Courtesy W.G. Glassco.)

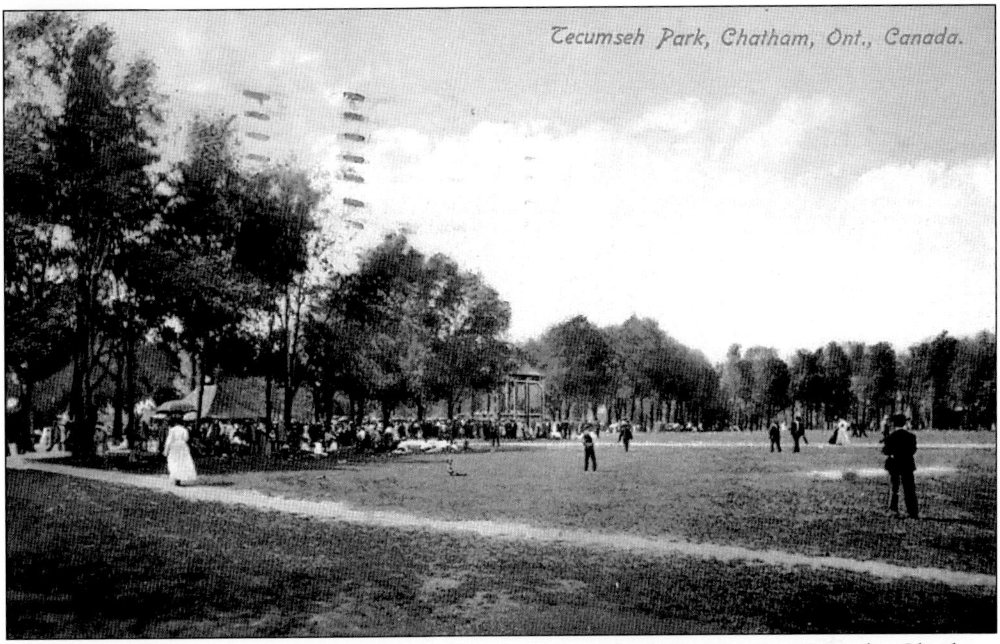

During the 1840s, cricket was a celebrated sport in the Chatham area. In 1841, the Chatham Cricket Club was organized by Thomas Dapplyn, James Reeve, and Henry Slagg. The club later took on the more formal name of the Royal Kent Cricket Club and played most of their games at Tecumseh Park, pictured here *c.* 1910. The cricket club once staged a match with Guelph for the visiting lieutenant governor. (Authors' collection.)

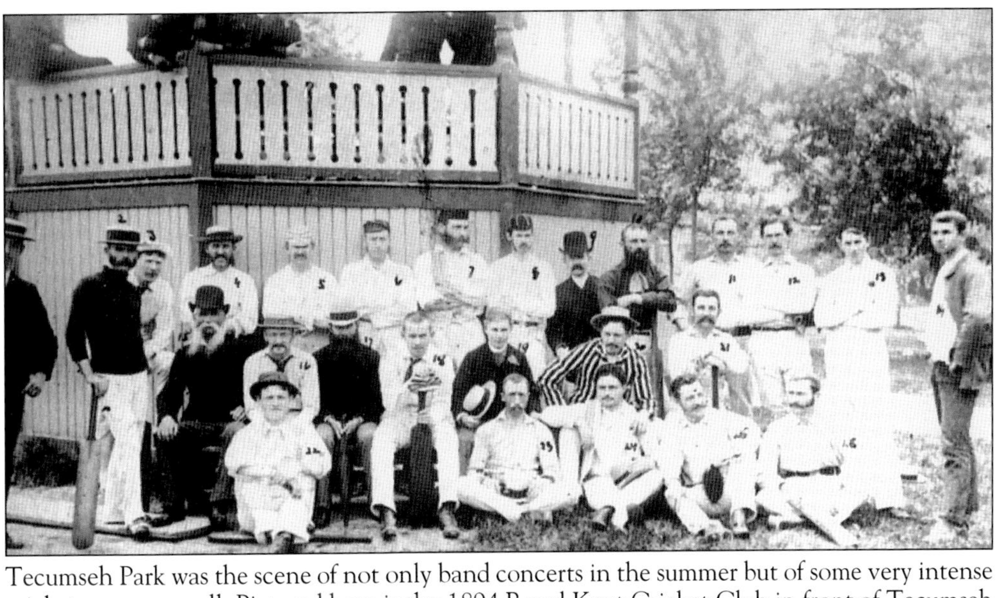

Tecumseh Park was the scene of not only band concerts in the summer but of some very intense cricket games as well. Pictured here is the 1894 Royal Kent Cricket Club in front of Tecumseh Park's bandshell. (Courtesy Chatham Kent Museum.)

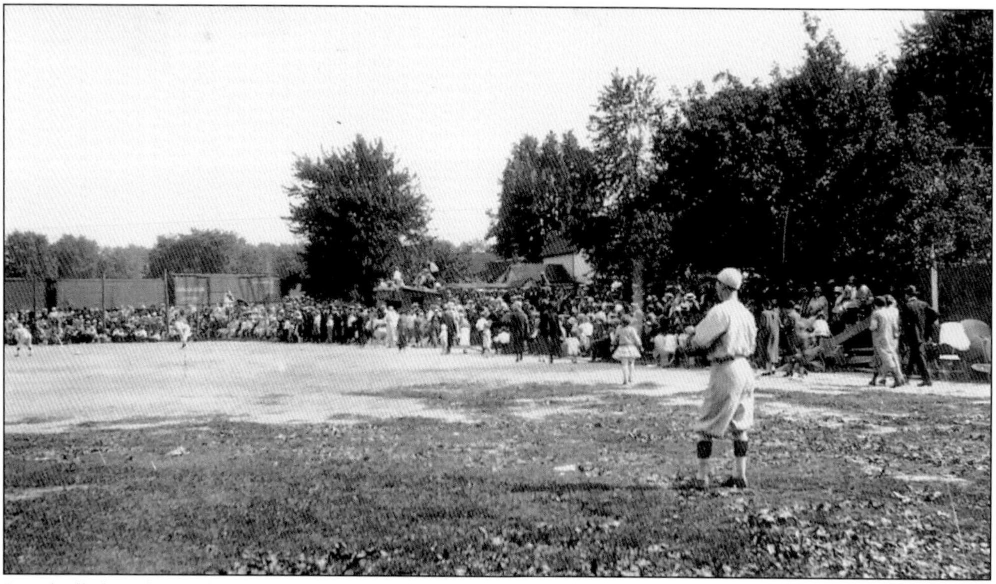

Baseball has long been a popular pastime in Chatham, dating back to the 1890s, when Chatham's team entered the semiprofessional Canadian League. This 1925 photograph shows the championship for the city league at Stirling Park. According to the note attached to this picture, the fielder closest to the camera was a man named Mason. Apparently, he caught the last ball hit in the game and, overly excited, continued to run with the ball all the way to his house! (Courtesy Chatham Kent Museum.)

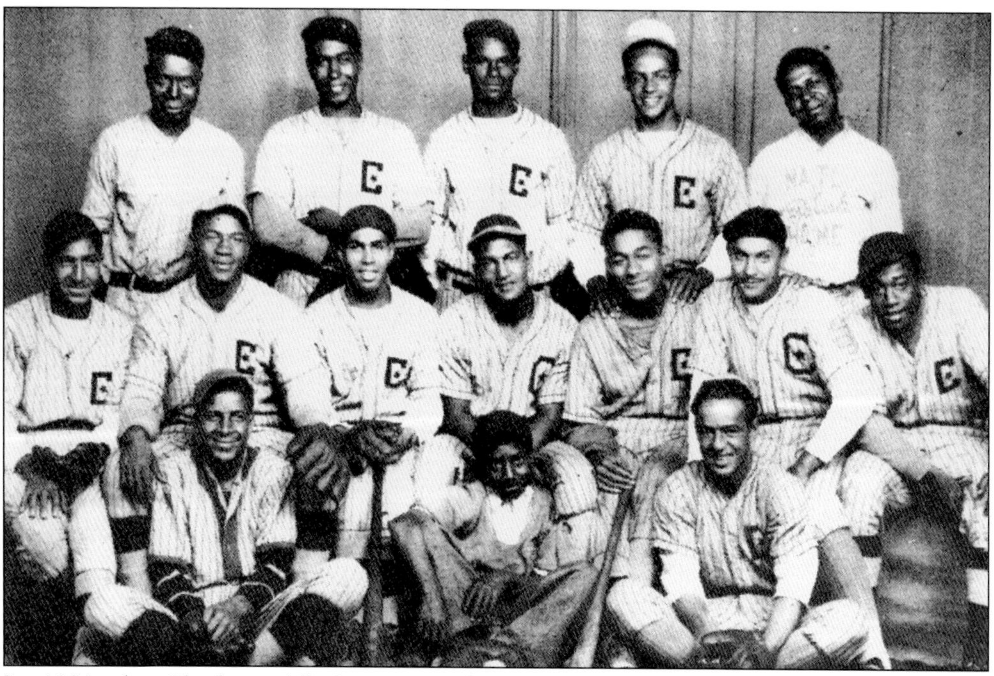

In 1934, the Chatham All Stars won the Ontario Baseball Association Intermediate Championship. The team beat stiff competition from Sarnia, Welland, Milton, and Penetang. Crowds of fans greeted the team upon its return late at night on October 23 on the Fifth Street Bridge. (Authors' collection.)

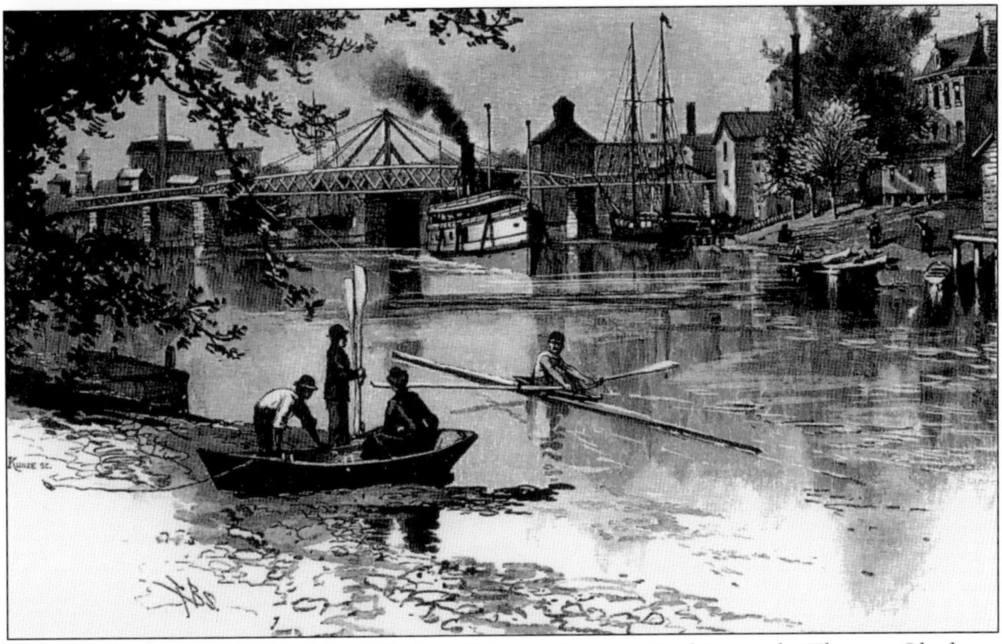

This late-19th-century sketch by F.B. Schell is simply titled *Looking up the Thames, Chatham*. The view looks from Chatham North toward the old Fifth Street Bridge. It is interesting to note the various types of recreation represented—fishing, rowing, sailing, sculling, and taking an excursion on a steamer. (Courtesy Chatham Kent Museum.)

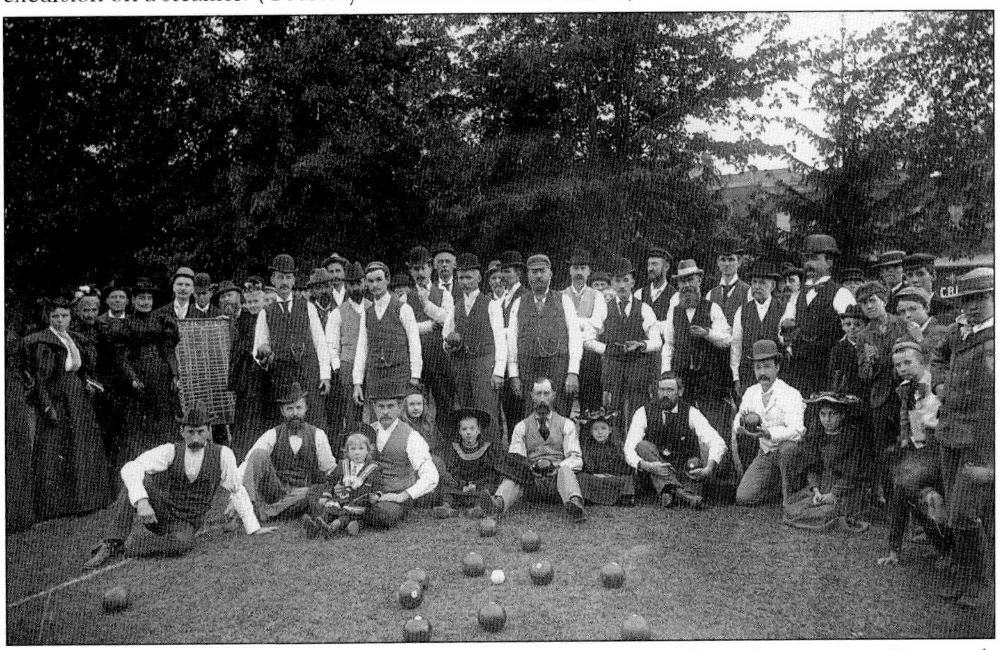

Lawn bowling has been a pastime for many years, attracting people to the greens at Tecumseh Park. The tradition continues today, as lawn bowling has retained its popularity. The Lawn Bowling Clubhouse, situated on the banks of McGregor's Creek, has long been a part of Tecumseh Park. Pictured here *c.* 1900 in Tecumseh Park is one of Chatham's early lawn bowling clubs. (Courtesy Chatham Kent Museum.)

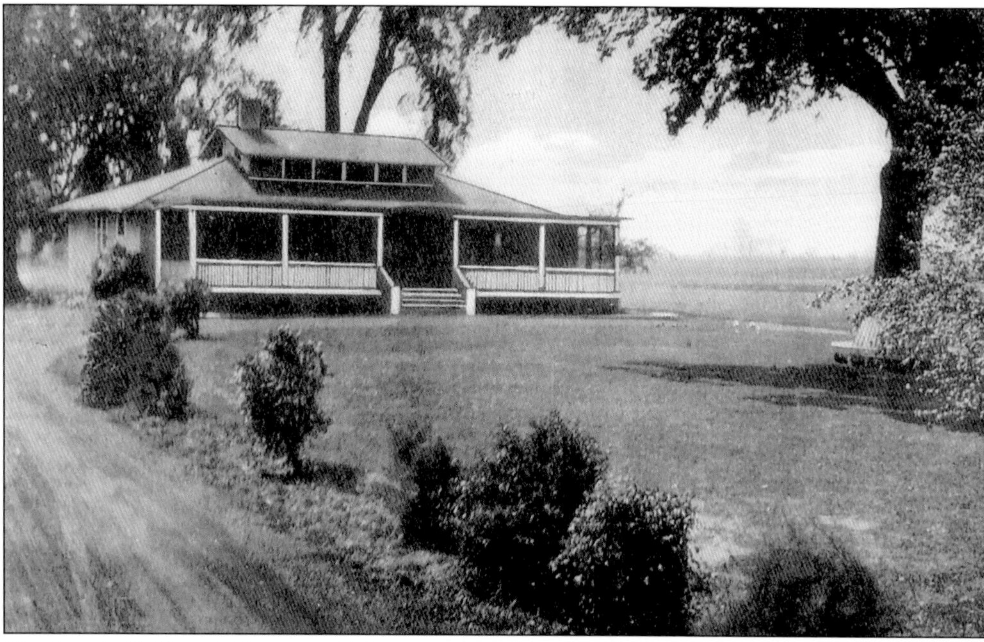

Chatham's Golf and Country Club was the earliest in the county and occupied a space of green bounded approximately by Lacroix Street, Queen Street, Tweedsmuir Avenue, and Indian Creek Road. The first clubhouse, pictured here, burned down in the 1930s. (Courtesy Mollie French.)

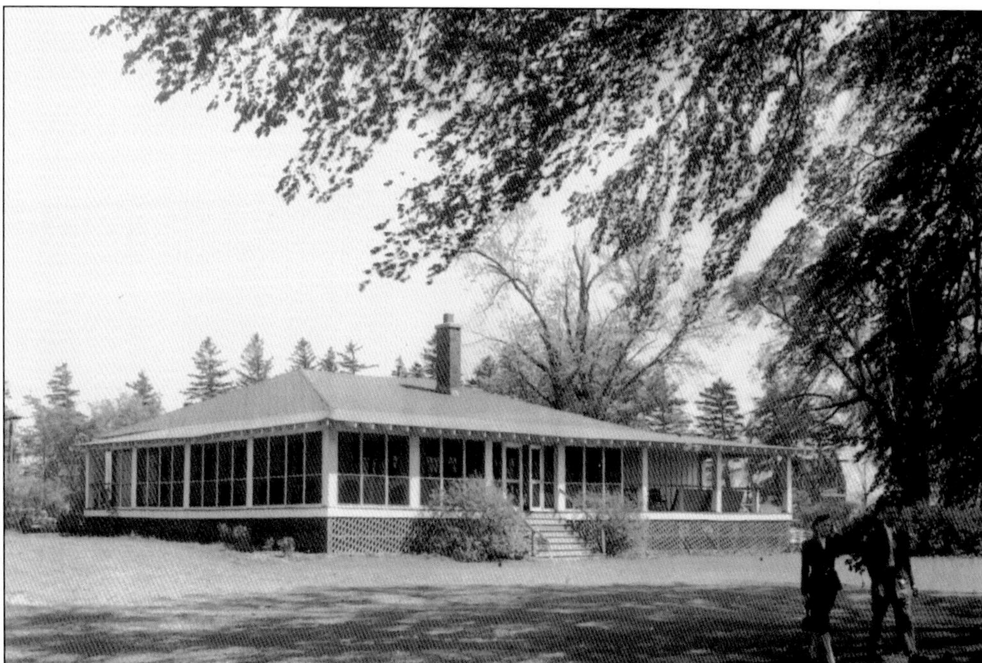

After the original clubhouse burned down, it was replaced by a slightly larger one, pictured here. The golf links continued in this area until the 1950s, when the course was turned into the Indian Crest Subdivision, a residential subdivision. (Courtesy Mollie French.)

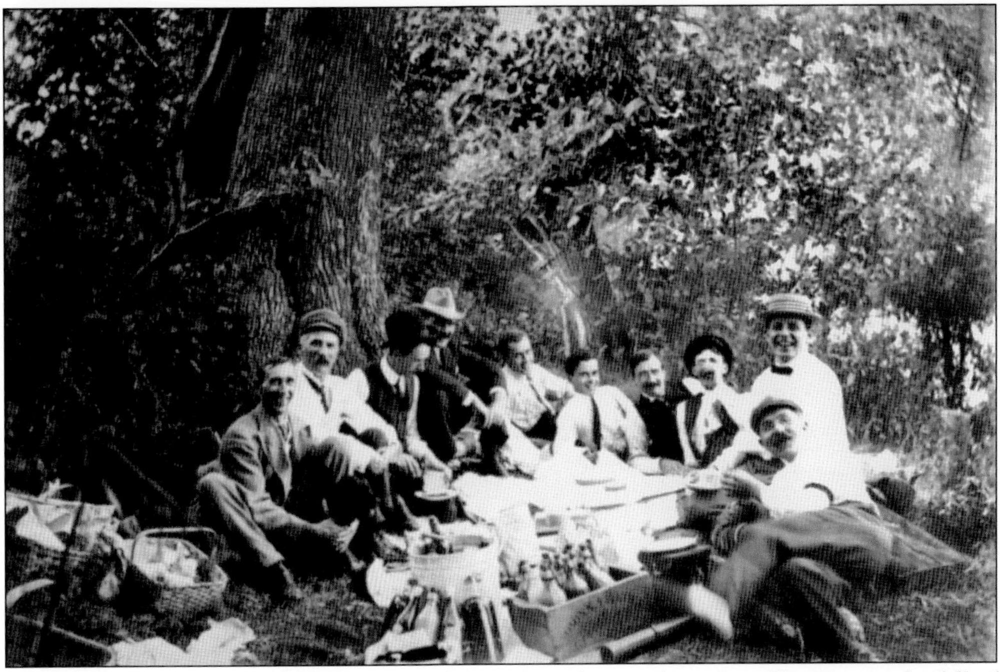

The Macaulay Club, the oldest debating club in Canada, was formed in Chatham in the fall of 1883 by four young men—R.E. Gosnell, W.K. Merrifield, Edwin Bell, and John Reeve. One of the special events held each year by the club was the annual picnic, which began with a summer canoe trip up the Thames but gradually evolved into all-day motor picnics to such "exotic sites" as Rock Glen, Kettle Point, Bright's Grove, Tyrconnell, Amherstburg, and Point Pelee. This photograph was taken *c.* 1907. (Courtesy Chatham Kent Museum.)

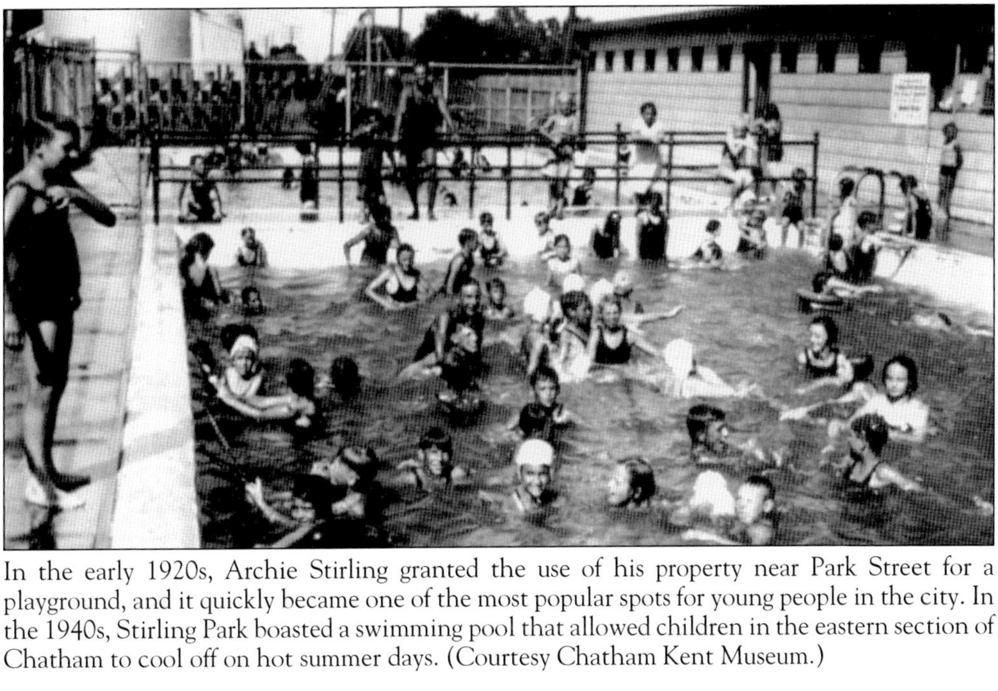

In the early 1920s, Archie Stirling granted the use of his property near Park Street for a playground, and it quickly became one of the most popular spots for young people in the city. In the 1940s, Stirling Park boasted a swimming pool that allowed children in the eastern section of Chatham to cool off on hot summer days. (Courtesy Chatham Kent Museum.)

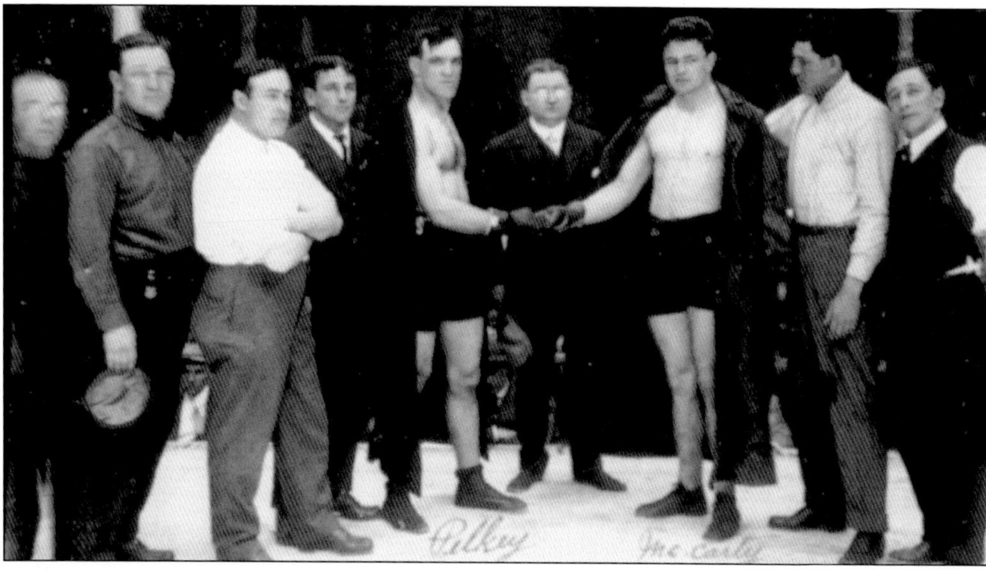

In the early 1900s, a Chatham-area gentleman became, for a brief period of time, the White Heavyweight Champion of the World. Arthur Pelkey, the East Coast White Hope Champion, faced the West Coast White Hope Champion, Luther McCarty, in Calgary. A first-round punch by Pelkey killed McCarty, and initially it was believed that Pelkey would be convicted of murder; however, further investigation revealed that McCarty had been injured in a horse-riding accident the day before, and that, rather than Pelkey's punch, was the chief cause of McCarty's death. Pelkey (left) and McCarty (right) are pictured here a few minutes before McCarty's death. (Authors' collection.)

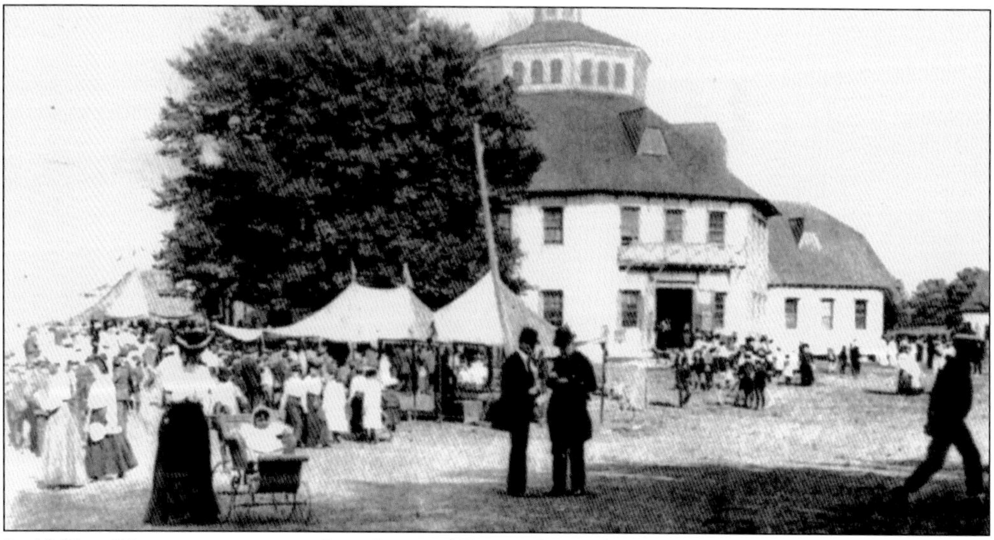

In 1881, a 20-acre site was purchased east of Queen Street between Eugenie and Mercer Streets, securing a permanent home for the West Kent Agricultural Society to hold its annual fall fair. The land cost $4,000, and the buildings housing the fair cost $8,000. The Peninsular Exhibition survived until 1925, when lack of attendance put an end to it. A variation on the fall fair continues today with the annual staging of the Faire at the Forks, a re-creation of an early-19th-century pleasure fair at Thamesgrove Conservation Area on the weekend prior to Thanksgiving. (Courtesy Mollie French.)

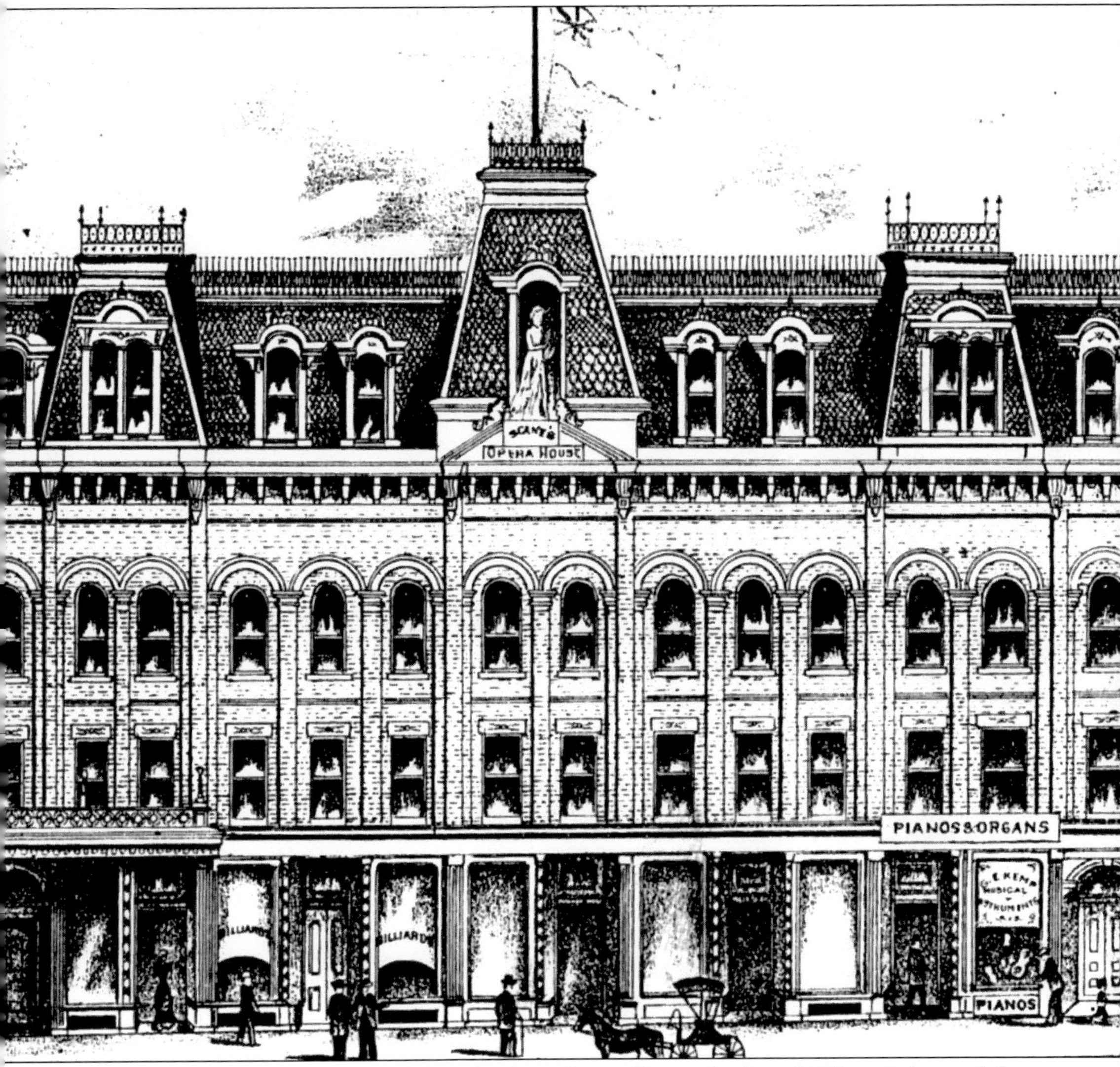

In 1875, Ebenezer Scane purchased the Chatham Opera House, built in 1872, and changed the name to Scane's Opera House. By any standards, it was a magnificent structure inside and out. Constructed at a cost of $46,000, it could seat 1,200 people in a three-storey theatrical palace that was, for many years, one of the finest theatres in Ontario. It was situated on the north side of King Street near the corner of King and Fourth Street. (Courtesy Chatham Kent Museum.)

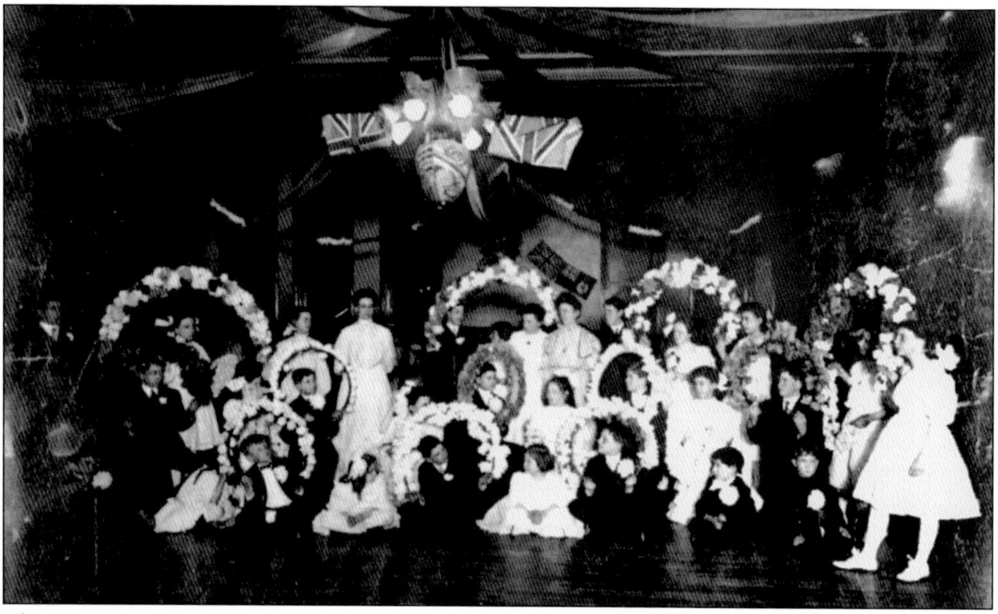

The stage was 55 feet wide, 32 feet deep, and had a height that, at its peak, extended three storeys. It was a performance area that allowed large-cast theatrical performances of the day to perform with relative ease. This *c*. 1906 photograph of a long-forgotten major production shows the immense size of the stage and the number of people it accommodated. (Courtesy Chatham Kent Museum.)

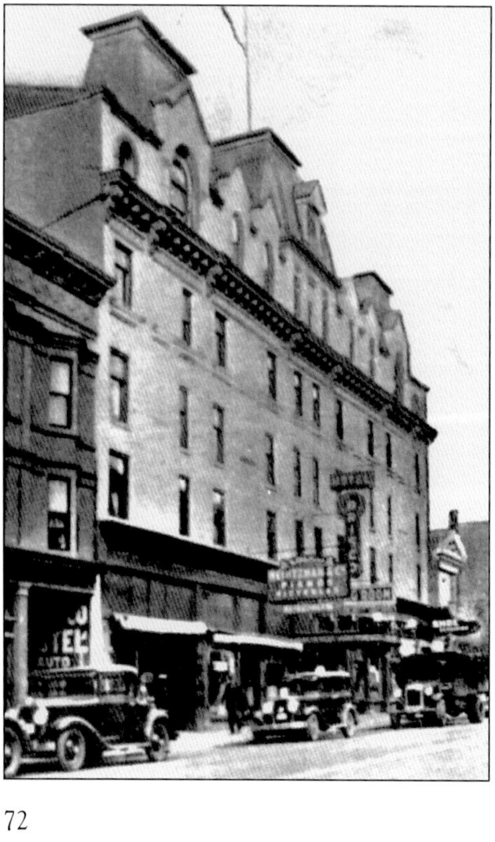

In later years, Scane's Opera House became the Chatham Opera House, the Grand Opera House, and finally the Brisco Hotel, pictured here. Eventually the upper floor was removed, covered over with a facade, and remodelled into apartments. Part of the building still exists today in a much altered state and is commonly known as the Edelstein Block. (Courtesy Mollie French.)

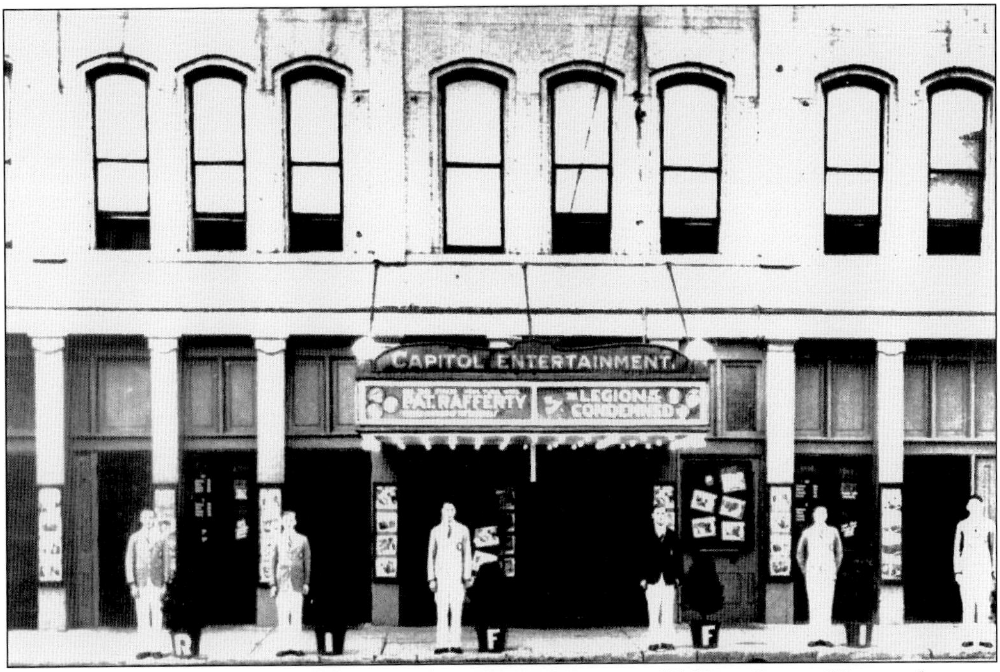

Although it started out c. 1900 as Bright's Opera House at 55 King Street West, it became known as the Wonderland Theatre c. 1910, the Family Theatre c. 1912, the Griffin Theatre c. 1914, and the Capitol Theatre in 1928. The first talking picture shown in Chatham was screened here on October 1, 1929. It later became the Park Theatre and was torn down in the 1950s. This photograph was taken c. 1928. (Courtesy Doug and Dienne Howard.)

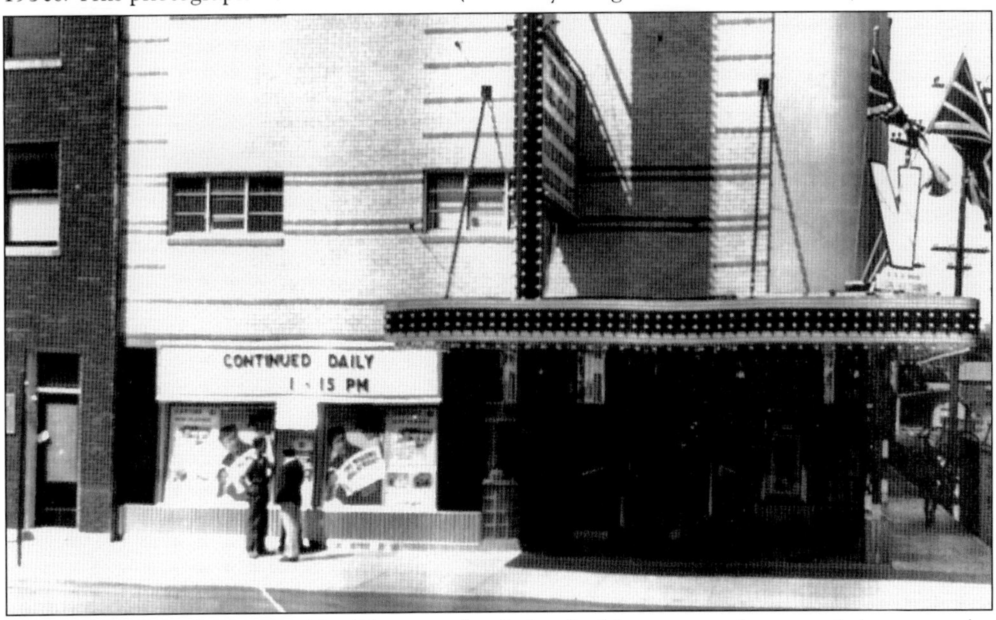

In 1940, Twentieth Century Fox Theatres decided to build a new art deco movie house on the northwest corner of King and Fourth Streets. Costing approximately $75, 000, it was called the Centre Theatre. It closed due to poor attendance in 1991 and has recently been refurbished and opened as a dance club. (Authors' collection.)

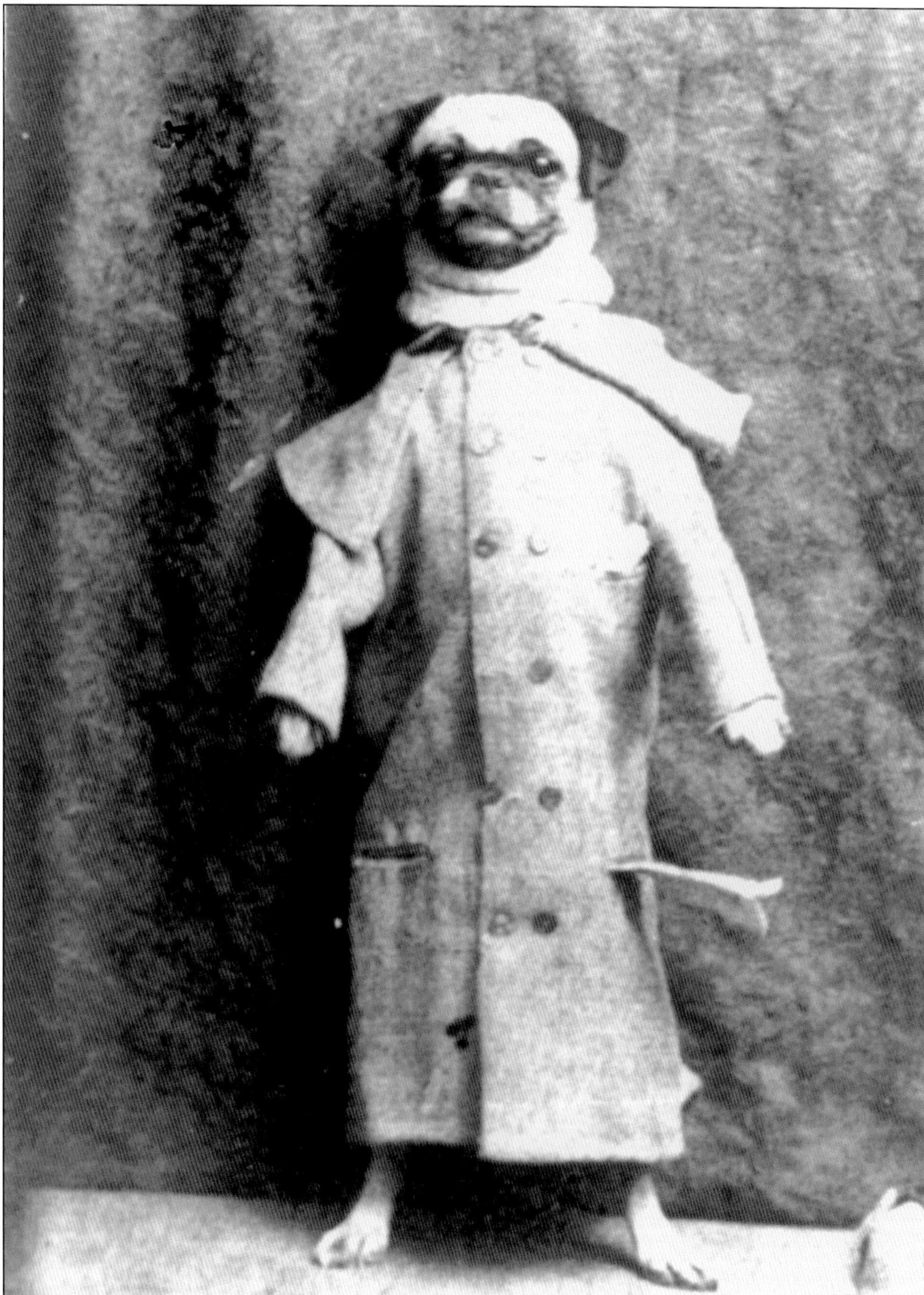

People in the early 1900s enjoyed the bizarre, the novel, and the "stupid pet tricks" as much as people do today. This picture shows Chatham's Juno the dog all dressed up but apparently with nowhere to go. Early photography everywhere was marked by such novelty photographs, which must have provided a great deal of amusement for Juno's owner. Whether Juno felt the same way is another question. (Courtesy Chatham Kent Museum.)

Five

Reading, Writing, and Praying

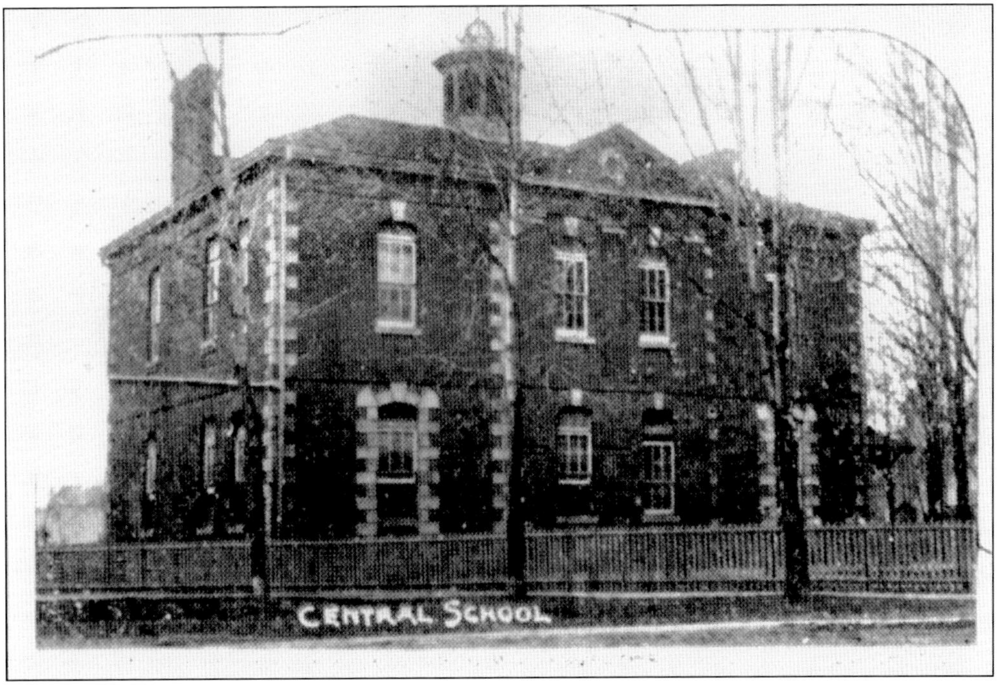

The first Central School was a frame structure constructed on the southwest corner of Wellington and Fourth Streets in 1831. It was the first official school built by the city of Chatham. An addition was completed in 1851, and a newer, much larger structure was built on the same site in 1896. This late-1850s photograph shows the first Central School after the addition was completed. The walnut paneling from the original Central School was incorporated into the woodwork of the William Edward McKeough home built in 1898 at 483 King Street West. (Courtesy Doug and Dienne Howard.)

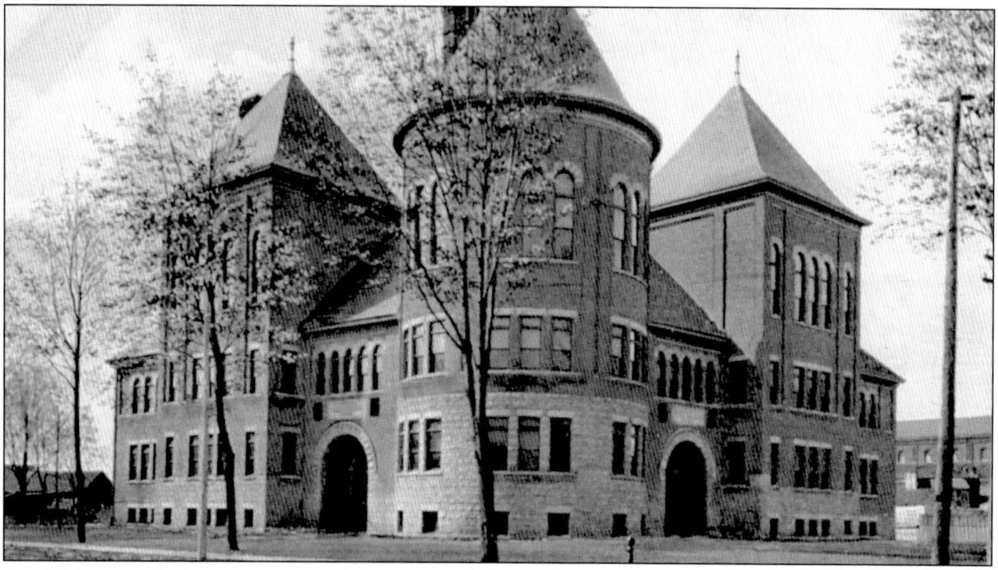

In 1896, a much larger version of the original Central School was built on the same site. It was constructed in the same Richardsonian Romanesque style of architecture that graced the First Presbyterian Church and that, a few years later, dictated the style of Harrison Hall. These three buildings, all on the same corner, made the convergence of Wellington, Fifth, and Sixth Streets a very impressive area. This photograph was taken c. 1905. (Authors' collection.)

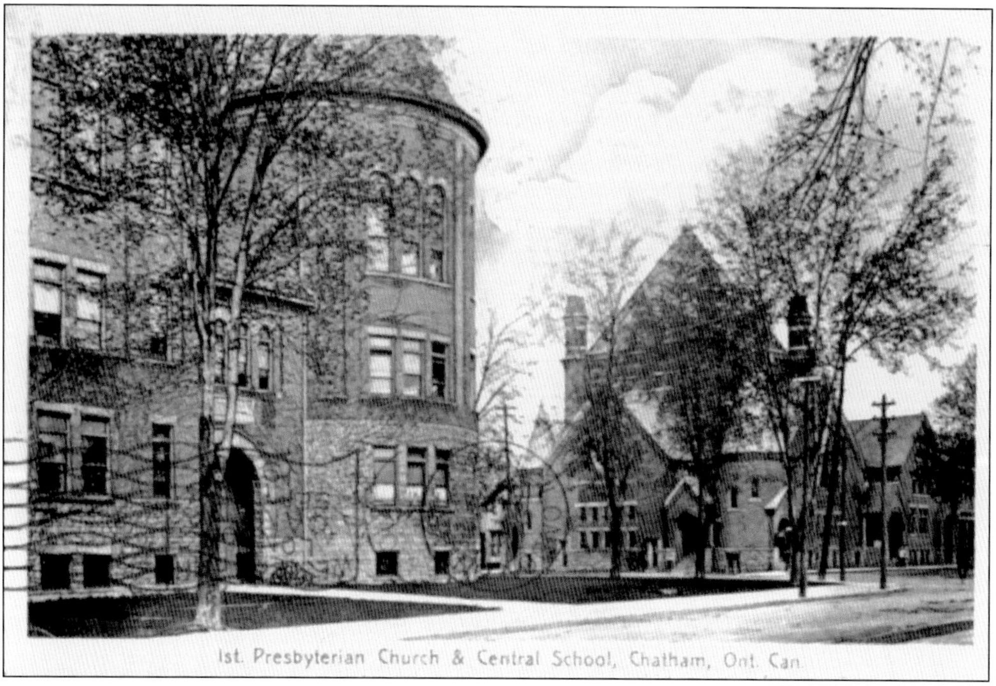

Although the First Presbyterian Church (centre) still stands today, the Central School (left foreground) was torn down in 1954, as the corner became too busy with automobile traffic to make it safe for students to attend. When the new Central School first opened in 1896, with a staff of 24 teachers, it was the largest school in all of Ontario. Its closest rival was the Ryerson School in Toronto with 22 teachers. This picture was taken c. 1912. (Authors' collection.)

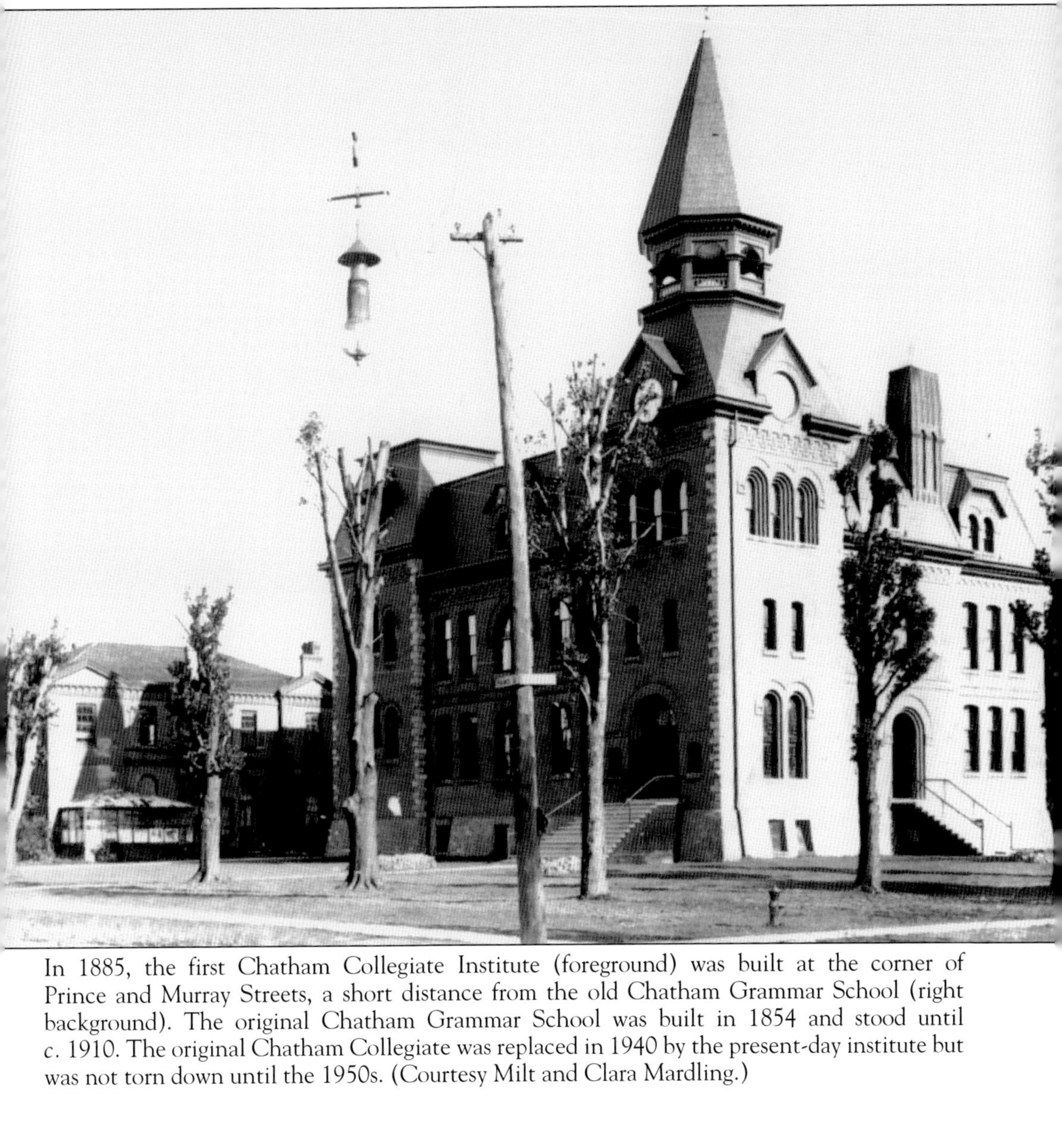

In 1885, the first Chatham Collegiate Institute (foreground) was built at the corner of Prince and Murray Streets, a short distance from the old Chatham Grammar School (right background). The original Chatham Grammar School was built in 1854 and stood until c. 1910. The original Chatham Collegiate was replaced in 1940 by the present-day institute but was not torn down until the 1950s. (Courtesy Milt and Clara Mardling.)

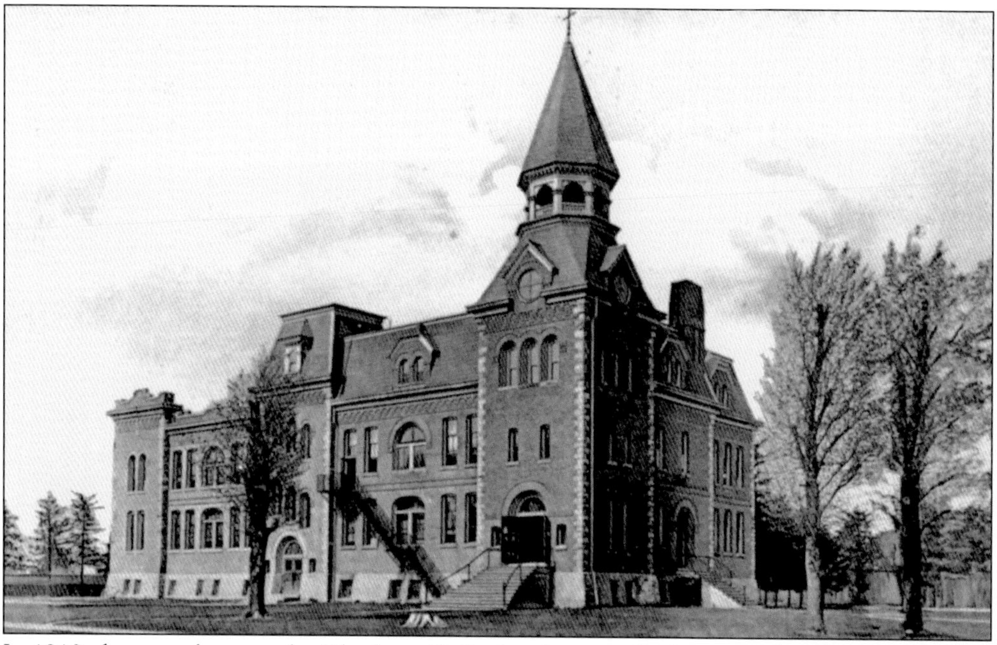

In 1910, the attendance at the Chatham Collegiate Institute had increased so dramatically that an addition had to be put onto the school. The addition, seen here *c.* 1915, was added to the north wing of the original school. Although an architecturally beautiful school, it did not have a terribly long life span. By the 1920s, the upper floor was condemned, and by 1940, a whole new school was built to the north of the old institute. It was used as a hospital for the elderly until the 1950s. (Authors' collection.)

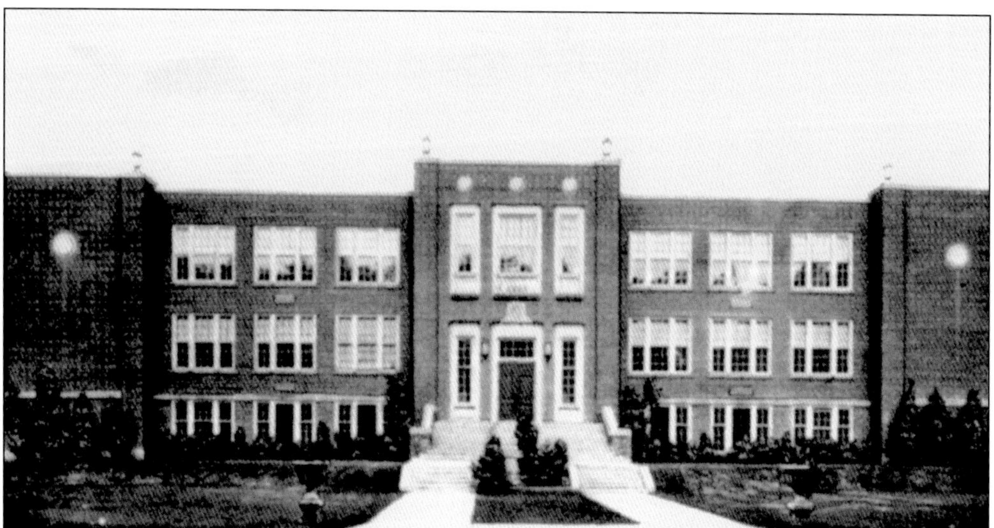

The present-day Chatham Collegiate Institute opened in 1940 after a special bylaw plebiscite in May 1939. The citizens of Chatham voted for the construction of a new $250,000 school on the same site that the Chatham Grammar School and the first Chatham Collegiate Institute had occupied. This photograph was taken *c.* 1940. (Authors' collection.)

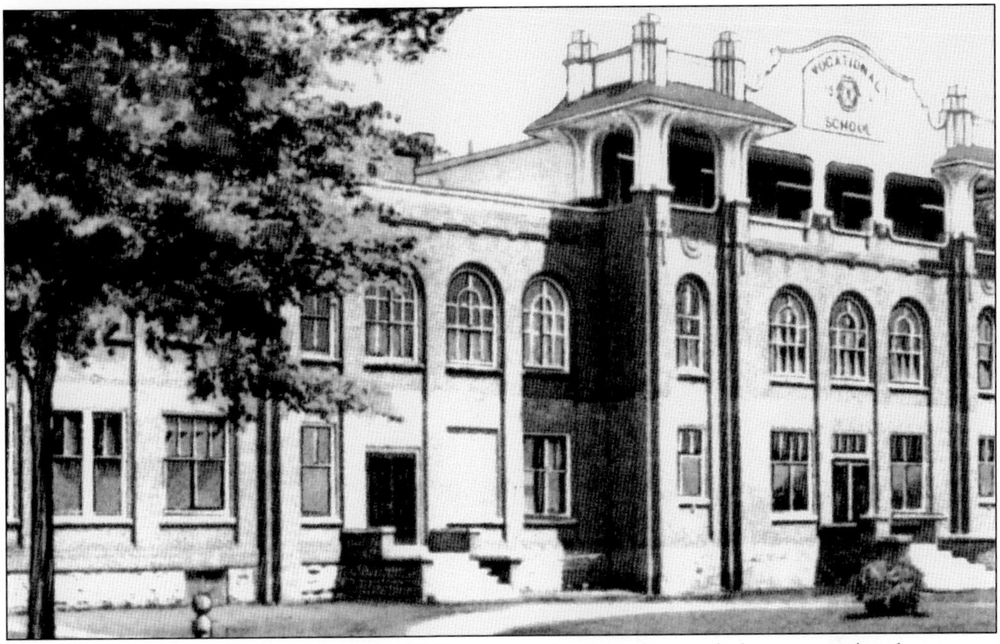

In the 1920s, the Chatham Board of Education desperately needed a new school to meet increased demand. The board purchased the former Hotel Sanita in 1924 and remodelled it into the Chatham Vocational School, seen here *c.* the 1930s. Harry Collins served as its first principal. The school stood until the 1960s, when the Chatham Kent Secondary School was built on the northeast side of the city. The former auditorium of the Chatham Vocational School was kept and transformed into the main stage of the current Chatham Cultural Centre. (Authors' collection.)

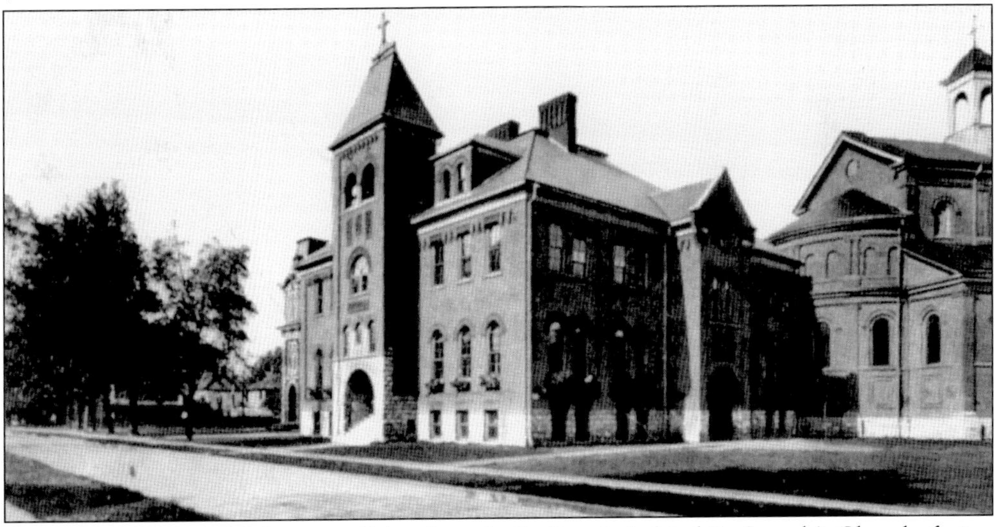

The second St. Joseph's Separate School was built directly behind St. Joseph's Church, facing Cross Street, in 1901. It replaced the original school, which had been built slightly west of this site in 1873. In 1951, under the chairmanship of Harold O'Brien and Mother M. Hildegarde, a Golden Jubilee was held, and a large number of alumni returned to the old school. In the 1960s, the school was torn down and is now the site of a church parking lot. This photograph was taken *c.* 1912. (Courtesy Mollie French.)

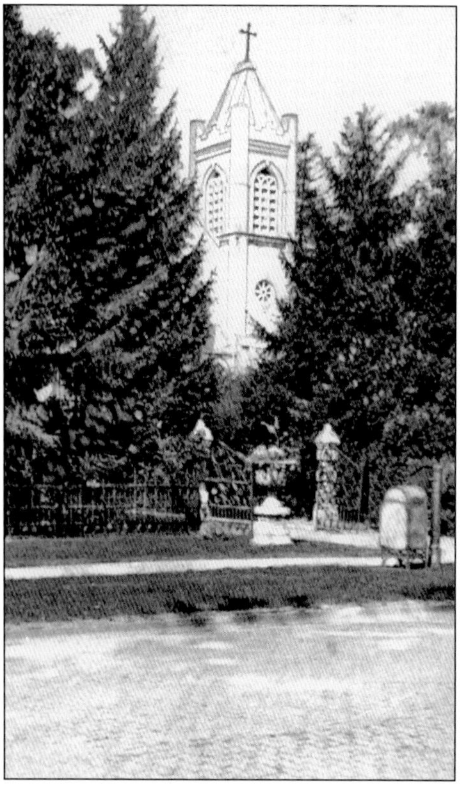

In 1866, Dr. Rowley Pegley sold 12 acres of his estate to the Ursuline Order for the purpose of building a convent and school on Grand Avenue West, which, due to a grove of pine trees on the site, became affectionately known as the Pines. In 1899, a $20,000 contract was signed with the firm of Powell and Carwell for the construction of an addition to the convent and an adjoining chapel. The Pines is shown here *c.* 1915. (Authors' collection.)

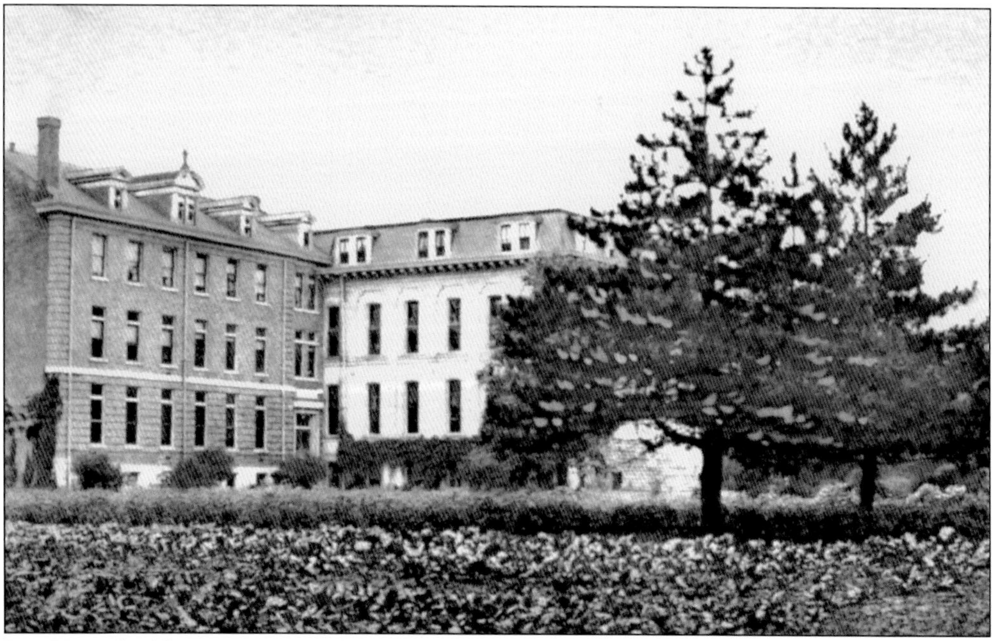

In 1884, a building consisting of a music recital hall on the ground floor and private sleeping quarters and general dormitories on the second and third floors was constructed. The building, shown here *c.* 1915, was completed by fall at a cost of $14,000, allowing the Pines to increase its numbers of boarding students immediately. (Authors' collection.)

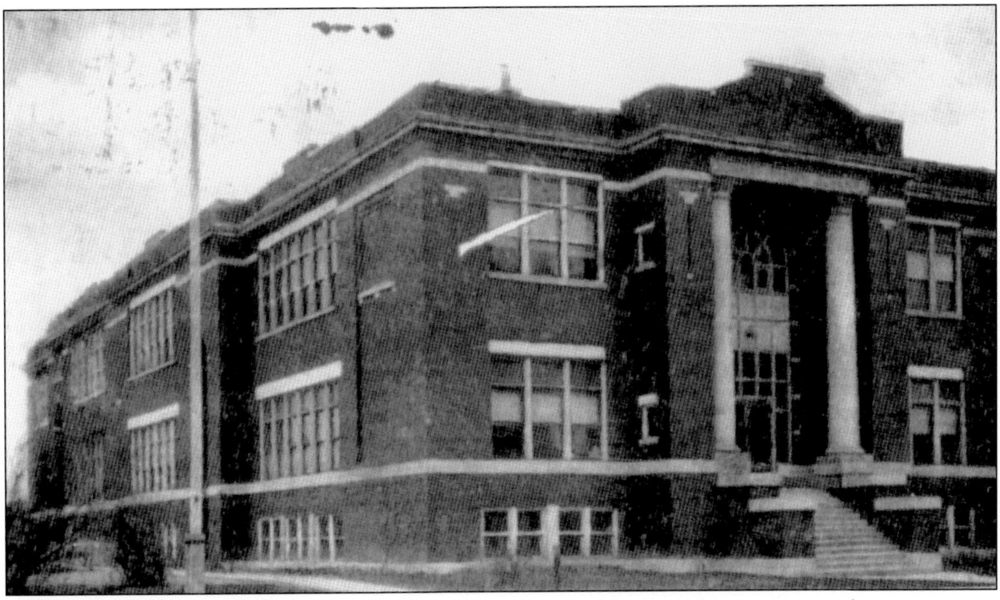

The Queen Mary Public School, built in 1912, was situated at 322 Queen Street, the current site of the Chatham-Kent Public Utilities Commission. The original plan called for eight classrooms and two entrances. The school officially opened on September 18, 1913. This photograph was taken *c.* 1918. (Courtesy Peter Stanojevic.)

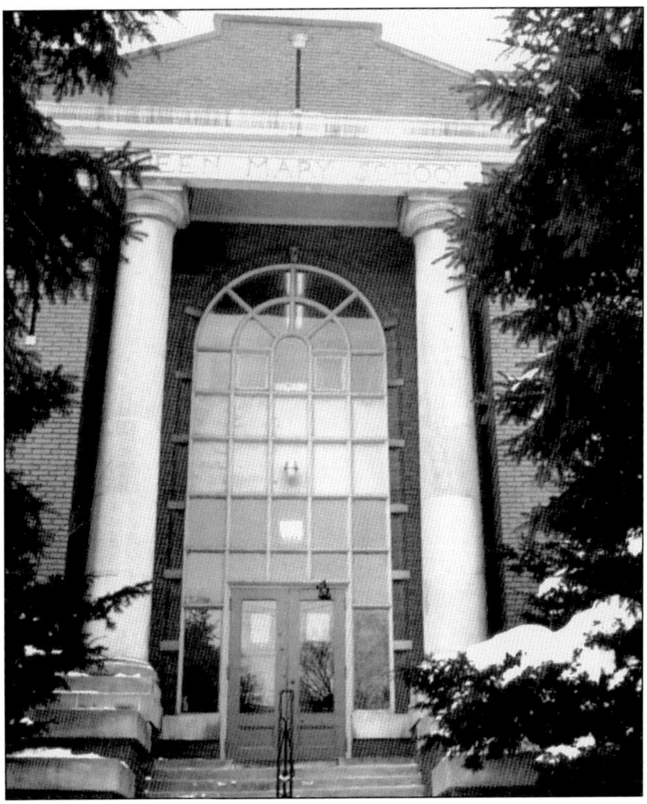

The front entrance of the Queen Mary Public School, seen here *c.* 1912, was particularly beautiful, with its Palladium-style window and Ionic front columns. Due to declining enrollment, the school was closed in 1982 and was subsequently torn down. (Courtesy Peter Stanojevic.)

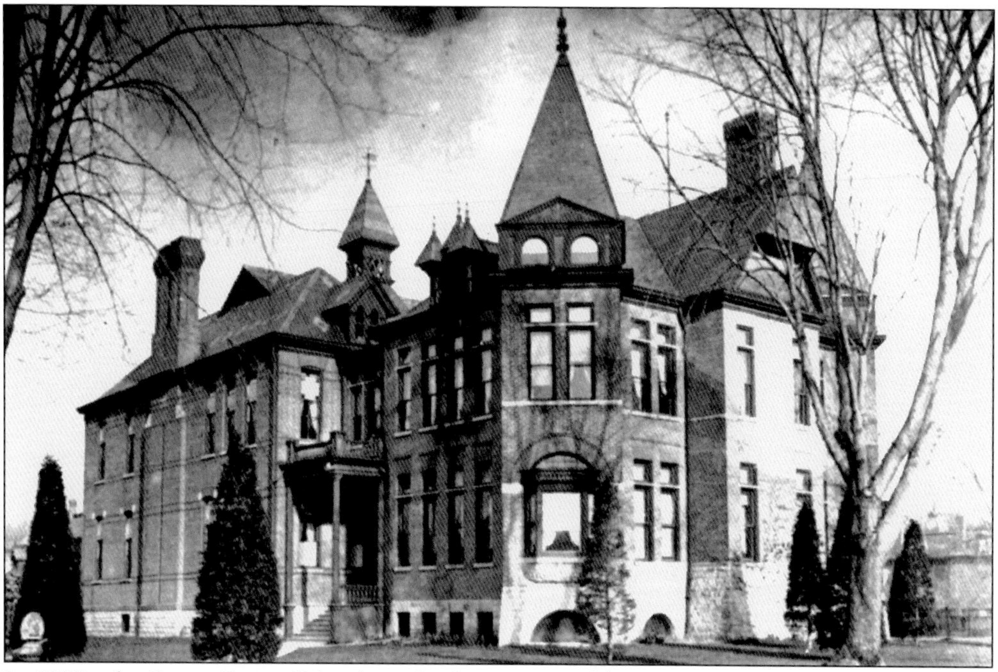

In 1882 , the Forest Street School was built at a cost of $12,000. When William McKeough, longtime chairman of the Chatham Public School Board, died in 1888, the name of the school was changed to McKeough Public School in his honor. It closed its doors as a public school in 2001 after more than 120 years as an elementary school. This picture was taken c. 1915. (Courtesy Chatham Kent Museum.)

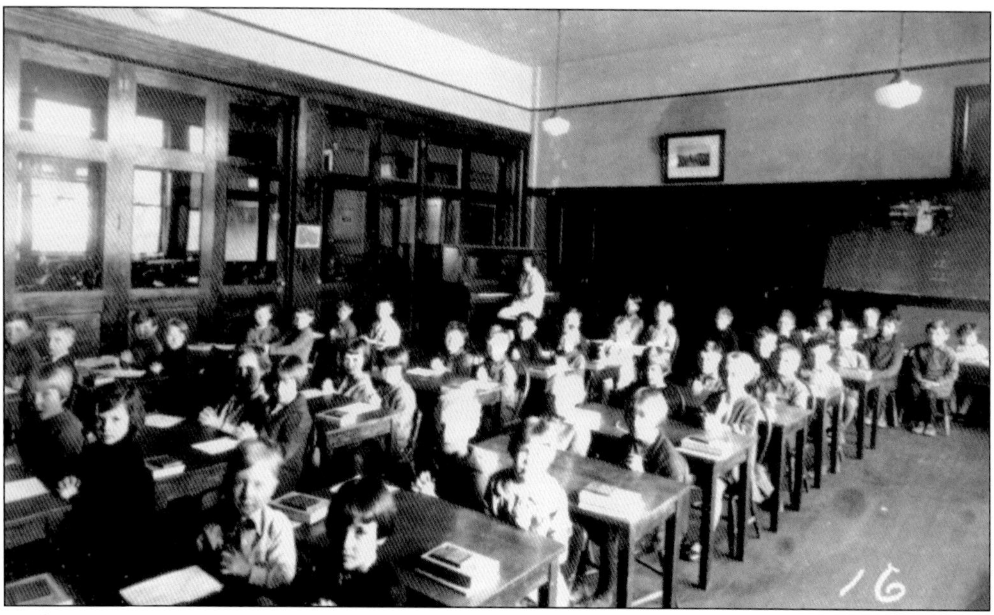

Unfortunately, those pictured here in the early 1900s have not been identified; however, they comprise a McKeough Public School class. Note the desks used by the students as well as the large number of students seemingly under the supervision of only one teacher. (Courtesy Chatham Kent Museum.)

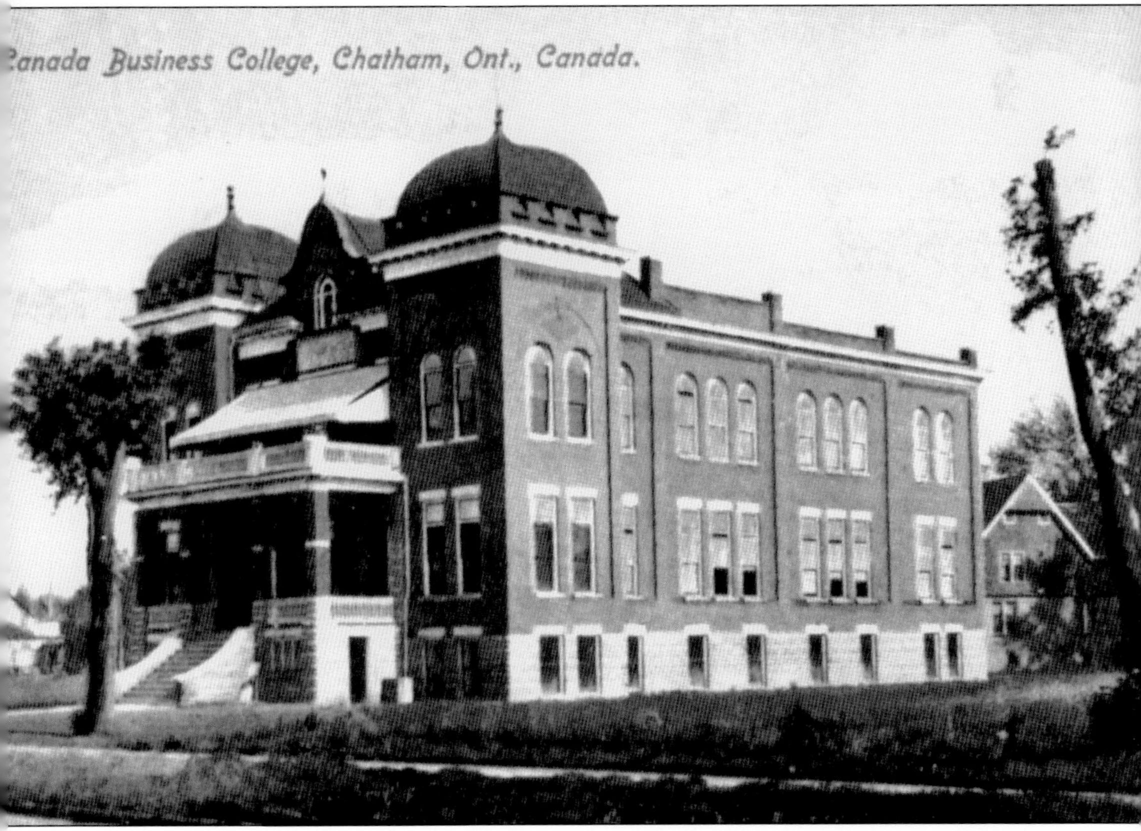

Duncan McLachlan started a branch of the Canada Business College in Chatham in 1876 on King Street West in the Urquhart Block. By the early 1900s, the college was the most successful in Ontario, and this structure, pictured *c.* 1920, was built. In the art of penmanship, as in business instruction, McLachlan was without parallel. The school was closed in 1952 and subsequently became the local Ontario Provincial Police headquarters. In 1998, the building was purchased and made into luxury apartments. (Courtesy Chatham Kent Museum.)

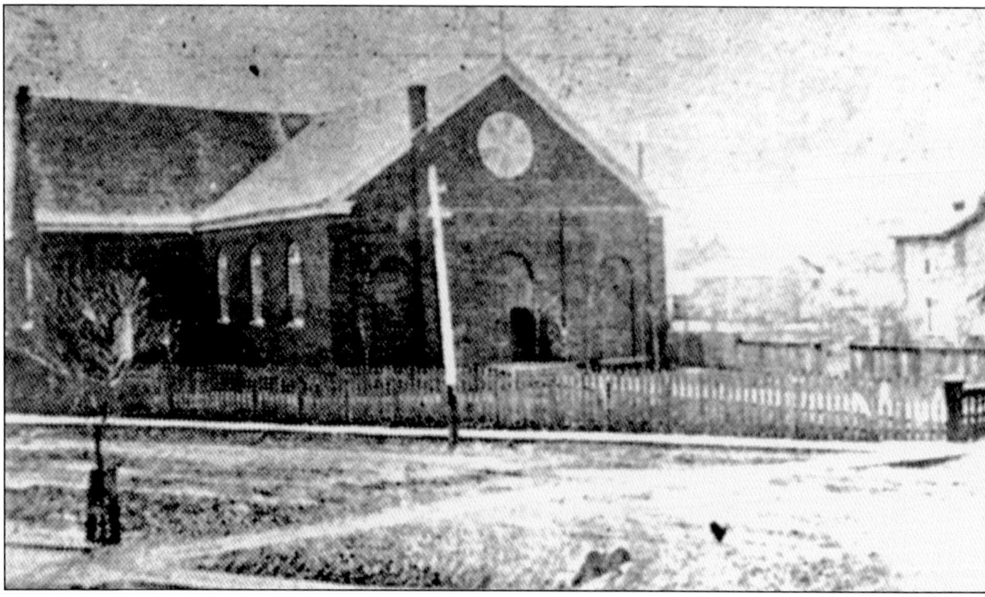

Although the land for the first St. Joseph's Church were received from the government in 1836, a lack of funds prevented the church from being built until 1847 at a cost of $12,000. This photograph was taken *c.* 1880. (Courtesy Chatham Kent Museum.)

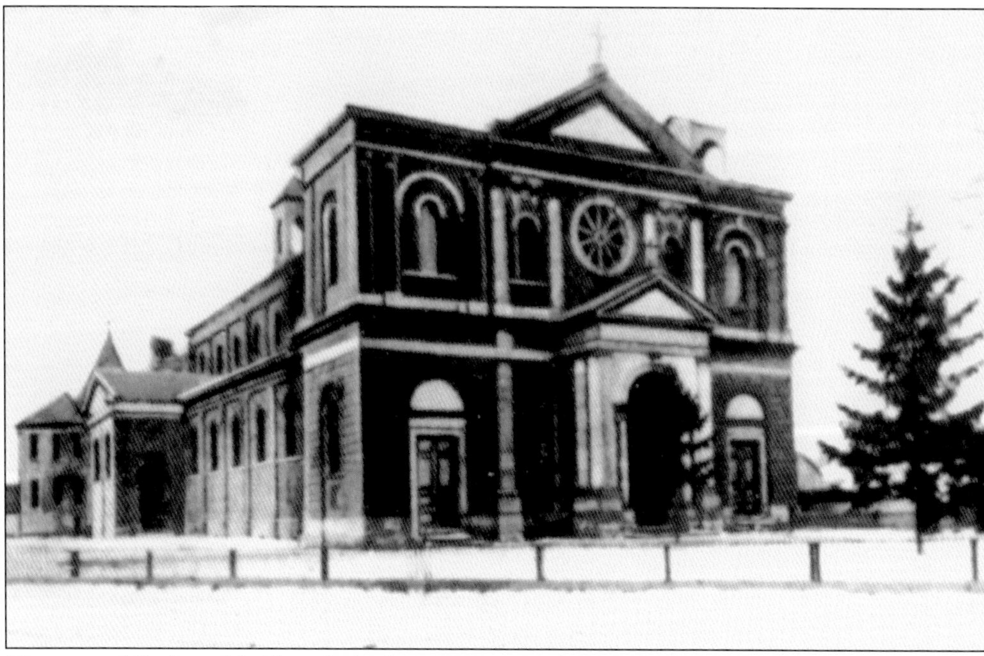

The second St. Joseph's Church, built on the original site, was constructed between 1885 and 1886 but did not include the present-day double steeples. The church was built to be perfectly aligned in the middle of Fourth Street, facing north so that visitors arriving at the Rankin Dock were greeted with an impressive initial view. The rectory, built in 1879, is partially visible on the right in this *c.* 1900 photograph. It was torn down in late 2001. (Courtesy Doug and Dienne Howard.)

The *c*. 1916 addition of the twin steeples was the final dramatic touch to the current St. Joseph's Church, originally built in 1885 and 1886 for $75,000. (Courtesy Doug and Dienne Howard.)

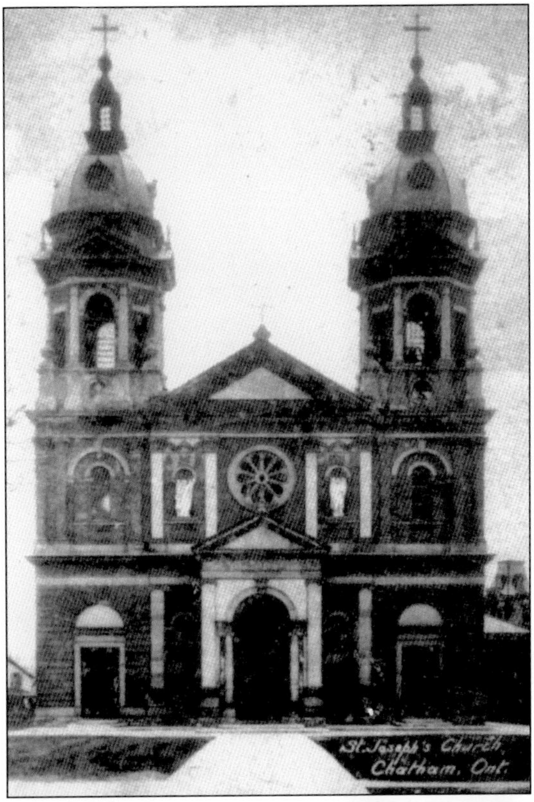

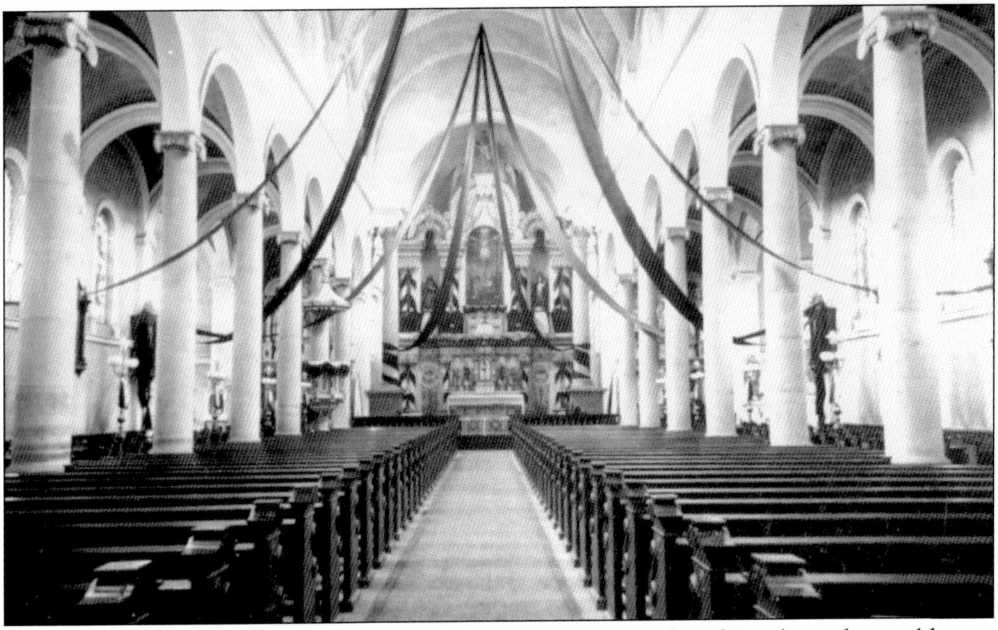

In 1903, Pope Leo XIII died, and many Roman Catholic churches throughout the world went into a state of mourning. Shown here is the interior of St. Joseph's Church as it responded to the death of a beloved pope. This picture was intended to be a souvenir of the memorial service held in his honour. (Courtesy Chatham Kent Museum.)

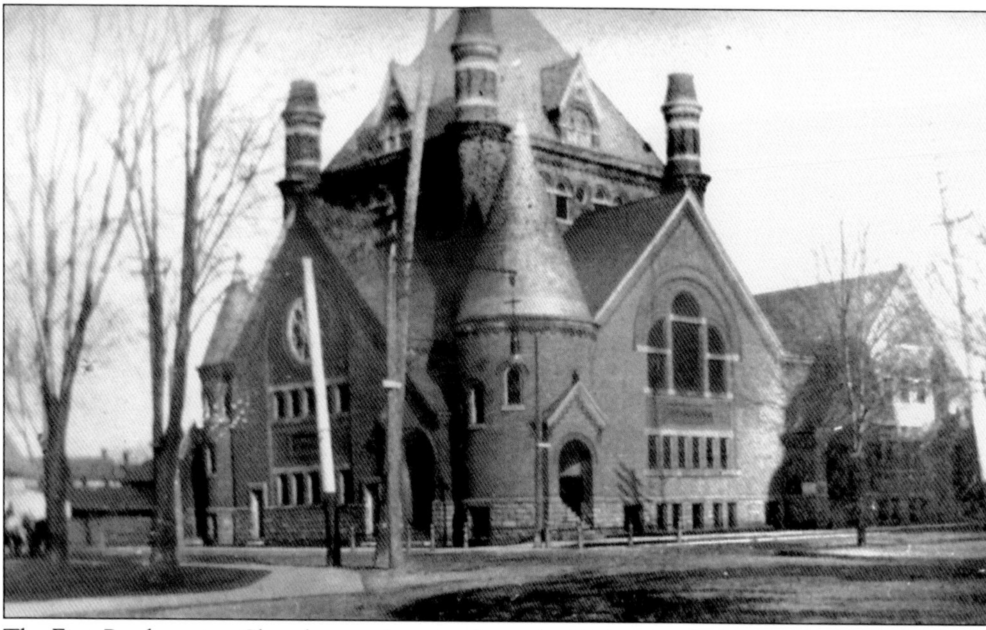

The First Presbyterian Church, seen here in the early 1900s, was the second building to appear in the Richardsonian Romanesque style on the corner of Fifth and Wellington Streets. It was built in 1892 by the joint congregations of St. Andrew's parish and the Wellington Street parish, which later became the site of Smith's Seeds. (Courtesy Chatham Kent Museum.)

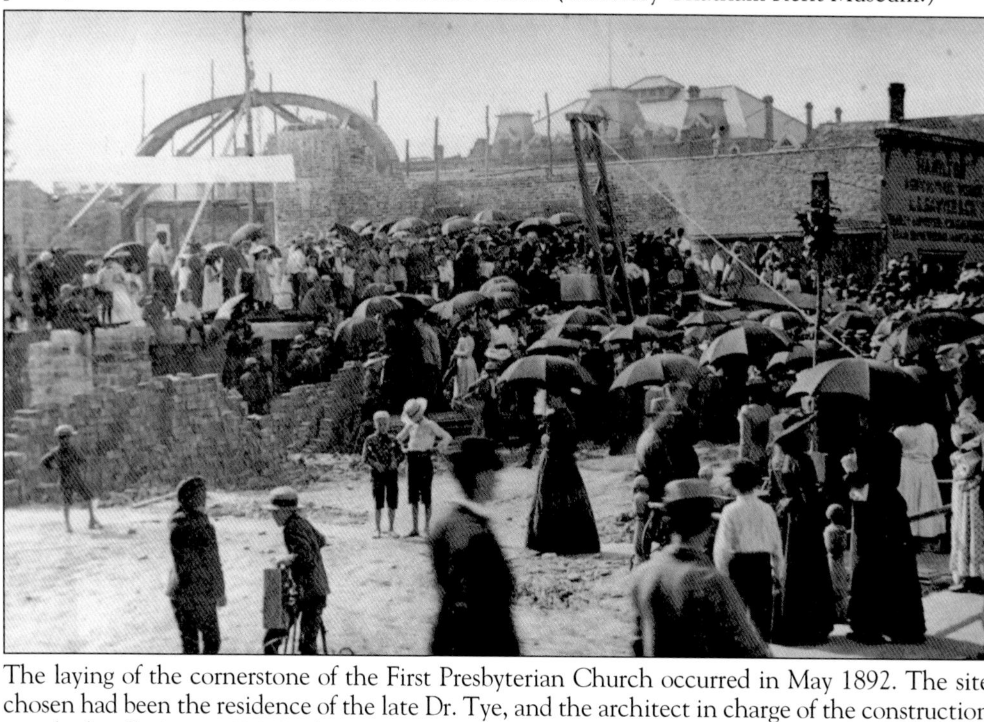

The laying of the cornerstone of the First Presbyterian Church occurred in May 1892. The site chosen had been the residence of the late Dr. Tye, and the architect in charge of the construction was the locally famous T.J. Rutley. The official opening of the First Presbyterian Church occurred on May 24, 1893. In this fascinating photograph, the upper floors of the Chatham Opera House are seen in the background on King Street. (Courtesy First Presbyterian Church.)

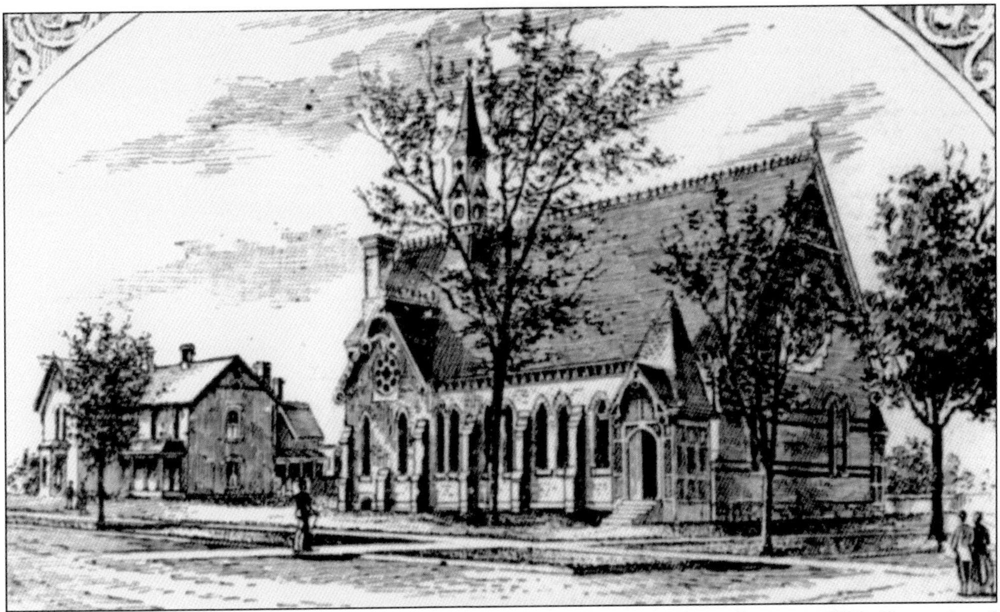

Holy Trinity Church on Victoria Avenue, shown here *c.* 1893, dates from *c.* 1877. From April 1890 to October 1894, Rev. Arthur Murphy served at Holy Trinity and managed to quickly get the church out of debt. In later years, Reverend Murphy's young wife, Emily, became one of Canada's best-known suffragettes. She was a member of the Alberta Five and also played a key role in the landmark Person's Case, which legally made women "persons" in the eyes of the law. (Courtesy Dr. Richard Charteris.)

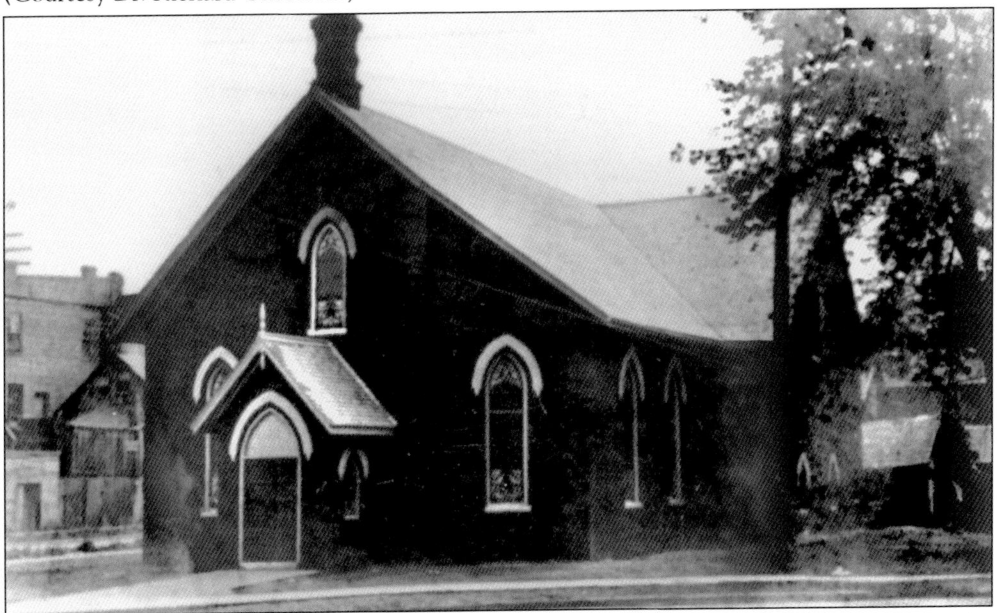

The Central Baptist Church, shown here *c.* 1915, was built in 1867 and was situated at he southeast corner of School, Centre, and Wellington Streets across from the Central School. Rev. Manley Benon was its first minister. Today, it is the site of a small parking lot and is across the street from the federal building, which was built on the former site of the Central School. (Courtesy Doug and Dienne Howard.)

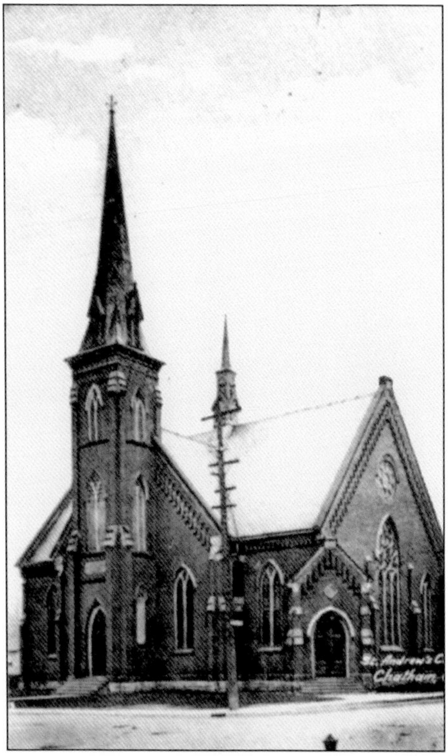

In the autumn of 1834, a number of devout Scotsmen organized themselves into a responsible body to petition the Crown for a grant of land for a church building and a place to bury their dead. The first St. Andrew's Church was built on the southeast corner of William and Wellington Streets in 1841. It was subsequently removed, and the present substantial brick edifice took its place in 1869. The present church, shown here c. 1914, has a seating capacity of 425 and is noted for its many beautiful stained-glass windows. (Courtesy Chatham Kent Museum.)

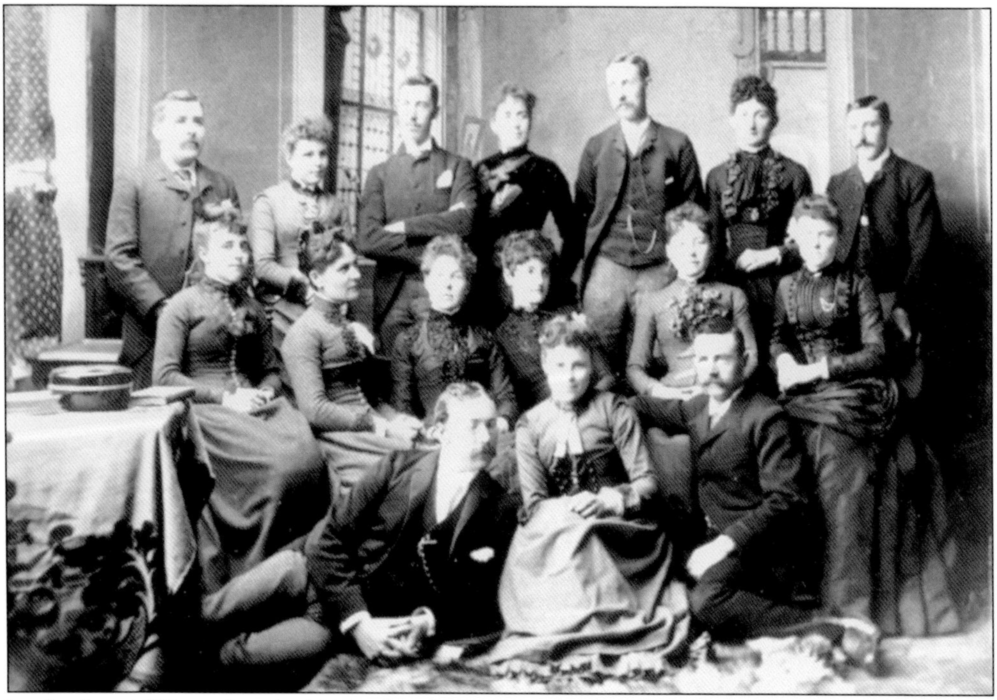

In the late 1890s and early 1900s, the choir at St. Andrew's was locally famous for powerful voices and moving songs. The choir is shown here in the early 1900s. (Courtesy Chatham Kent Museum.)

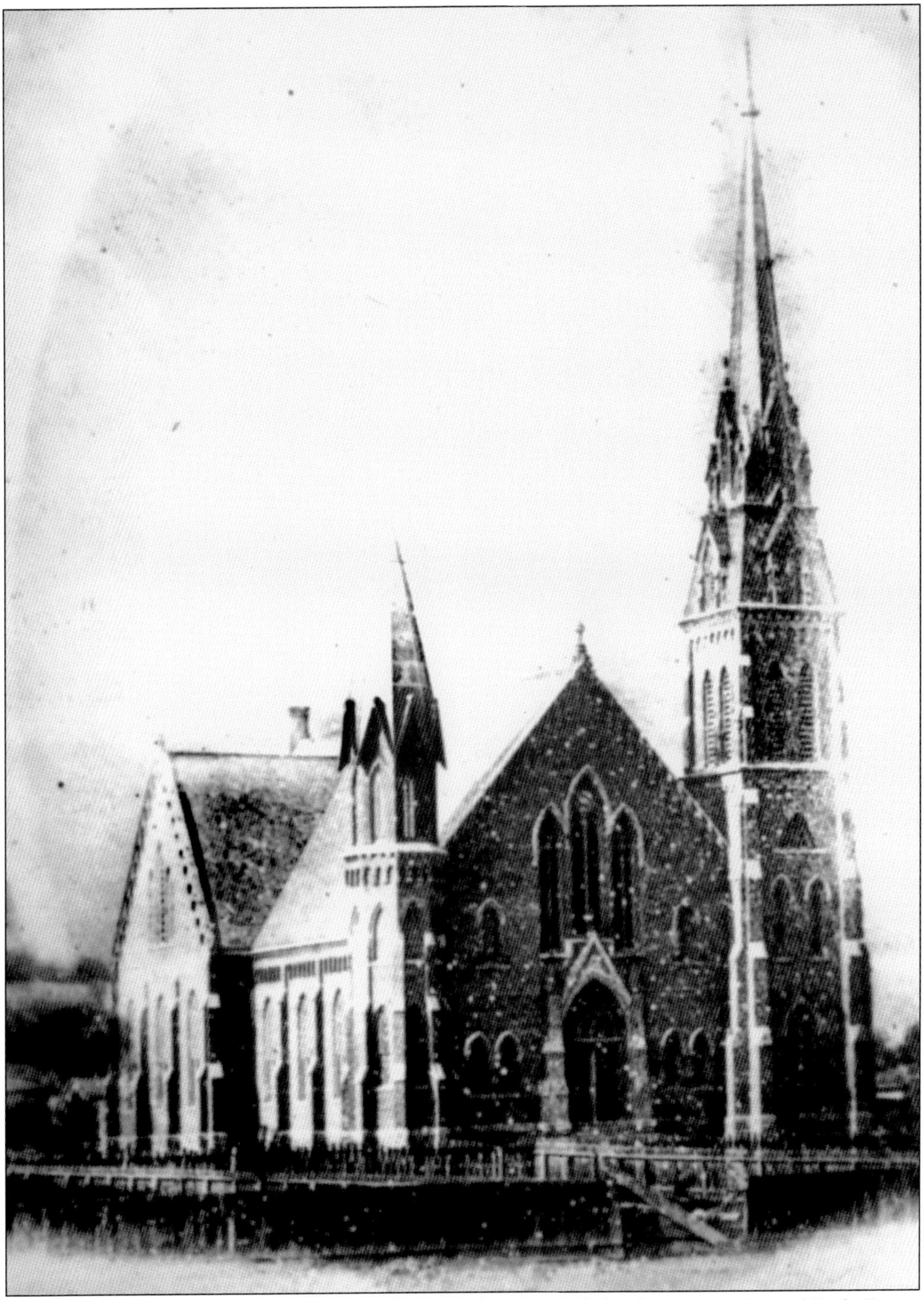

Although in poor shape, this *c.* 1900 photograph is one of the few ever taken of Park Street United Church with its steeple still intact. The steeple was blown off on June 8, 1906, when a powerful tornado touched down in Chatham, damaging almost every structure in Chatham. (Courtesy Chatham Kent Museum.)

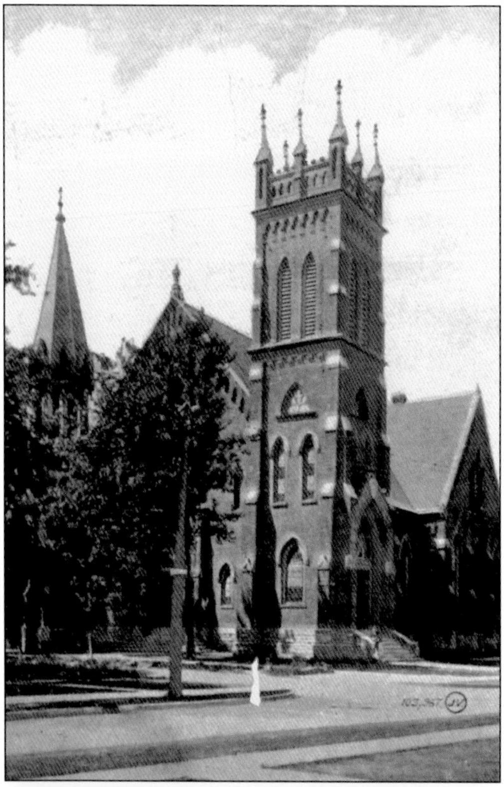

The building of the Park Street Methodist Church at the corner of Park and Dufferin Streets began in 1870 and was completed in the fall of 1873. The official opening of the church occurred on Sunday, October 19. During the years 1911–1914, Prime Minister Lester Pearson's father served as minister, and during the family's stay in Chatham, the future prime minister became very involved in the social and athletic, as well as religious, life of the community. In 1925, this Gothic-style church became the Park Street United Church. This photograph was taken *c.* 1913. (Authors' collection.)

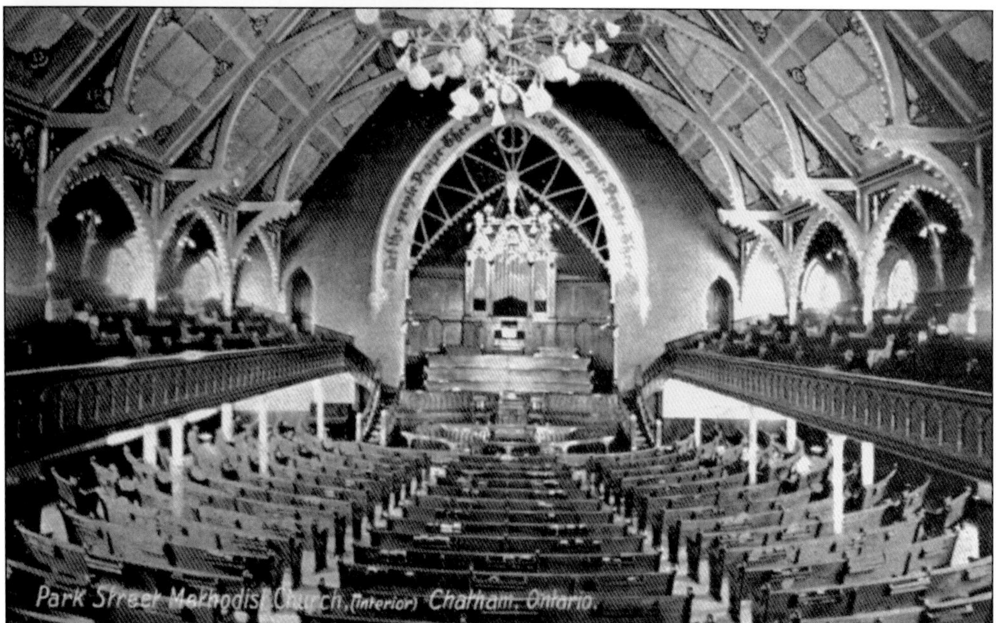

Completed at a cost of $25,000, the Park Street Methodist Church, shown here *c.* 1915, is one of the most beautiful churches in the former city of Chatham. Notable features of the church are the beautiful stained-glass windows, the diamond-shaped slate shingles on the roof, and the impressive organ. (Authors' collection.)

Six

A RIVER RUNS THROUGH IT

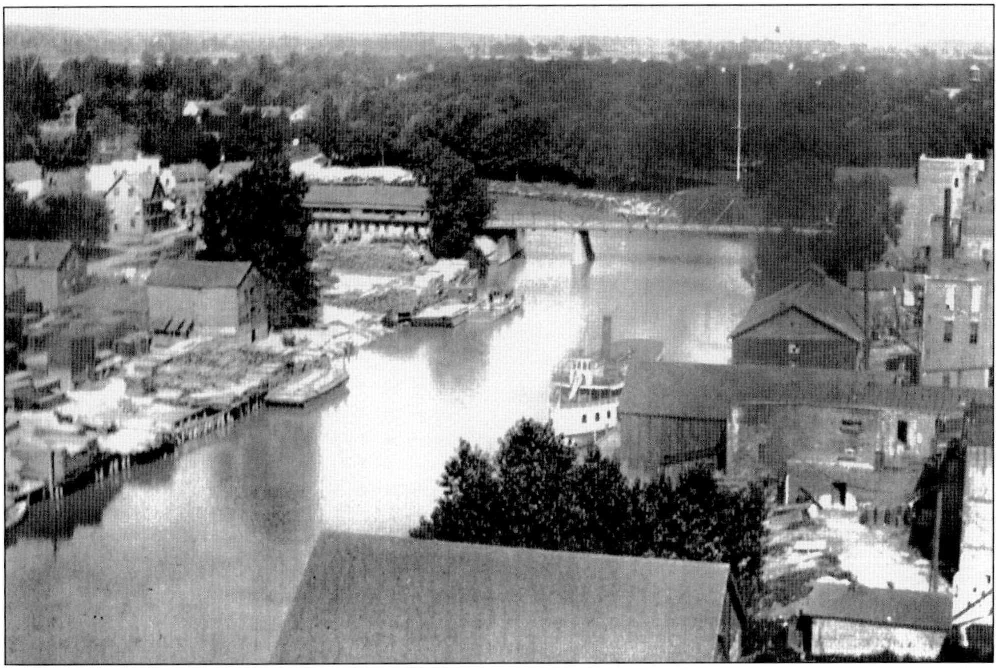

Taken from the chimney of the Chatham, Wallaceburg, and Lake Erie Power House on King Street, this *c.* 1912 photograph shows the back of businesses on King Street and the Hadley Lumber Company on the north side of the river. The Fifth Street Bridge pictured here is the iron bridge constructed in 1884–1885. The excursion steamer docked at the Rankin Dock is identified as the *City of Chatham*. (Courtesy Doug and Dienne Howard.)

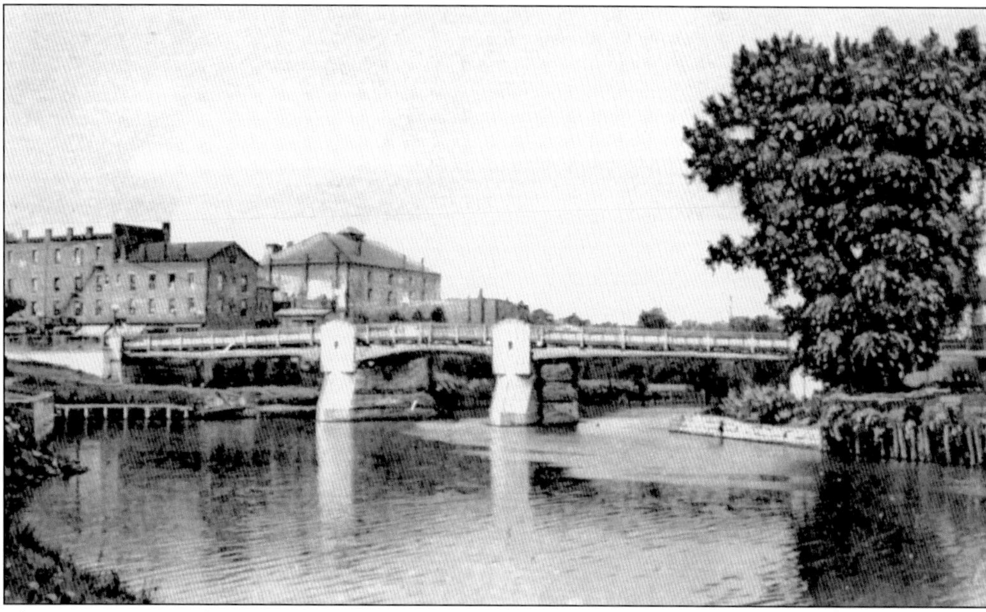

This 1930s postcard view taken from Tecumseh Park shows the latest Fifth Street Bridge, built in 1930 by the Canadian Bridge Company. To the left beyond the bridge is the brick Eberts' Block and Scane's Opera House (the Brisco Hotel). (Authors' collection.)

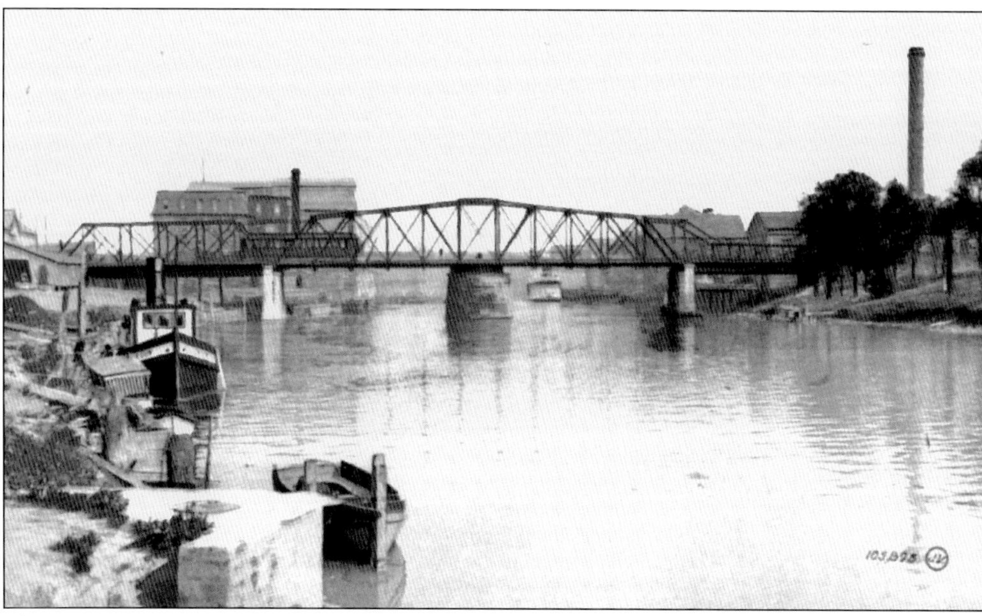

This c. 1911 postcard depicts the second Third Street Bridge, built in 1892, from an area near the former Public General Hospital. On the right is the tall smokestack of the King Street Chatham, Wallaceburg, and Lake Erie Power House. On the left side of the river, beyond the bridge, is the Kent Mill, and docked in the foreground is the steamer tug *Owen*. (Authors' collection.)

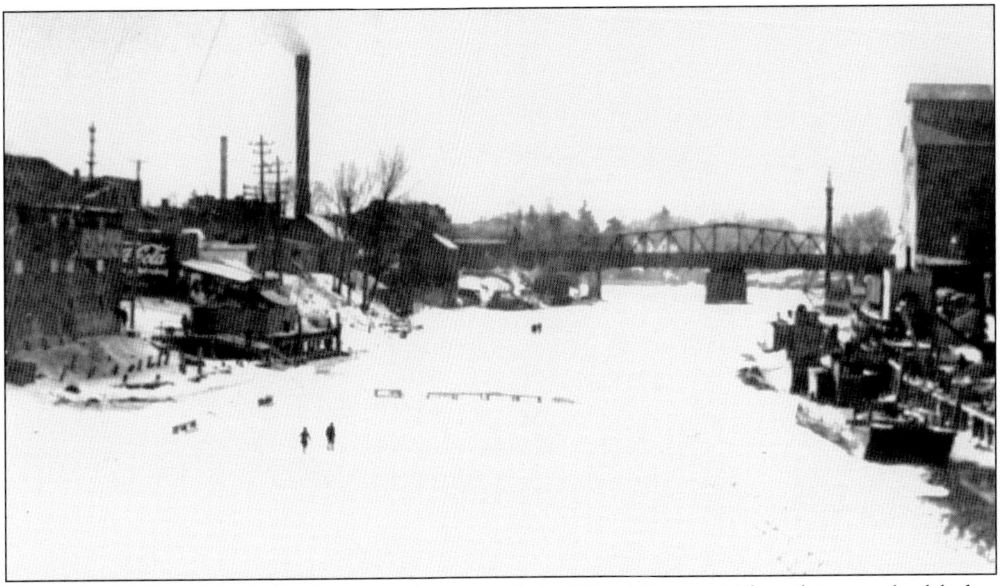

Looking west from the Fifth Street Bridge toward the Third Street Bridge, this view highlights the year-round recreational value of the Thames River. The Rankin Dock is pictured to the left. The smokestack of the Chatham, Wallaceburg, and Lake Erie Power House appears in the left background, while various barges and a sailing ship winter on the north side. (Courtesy Chatham Kent Museum.)

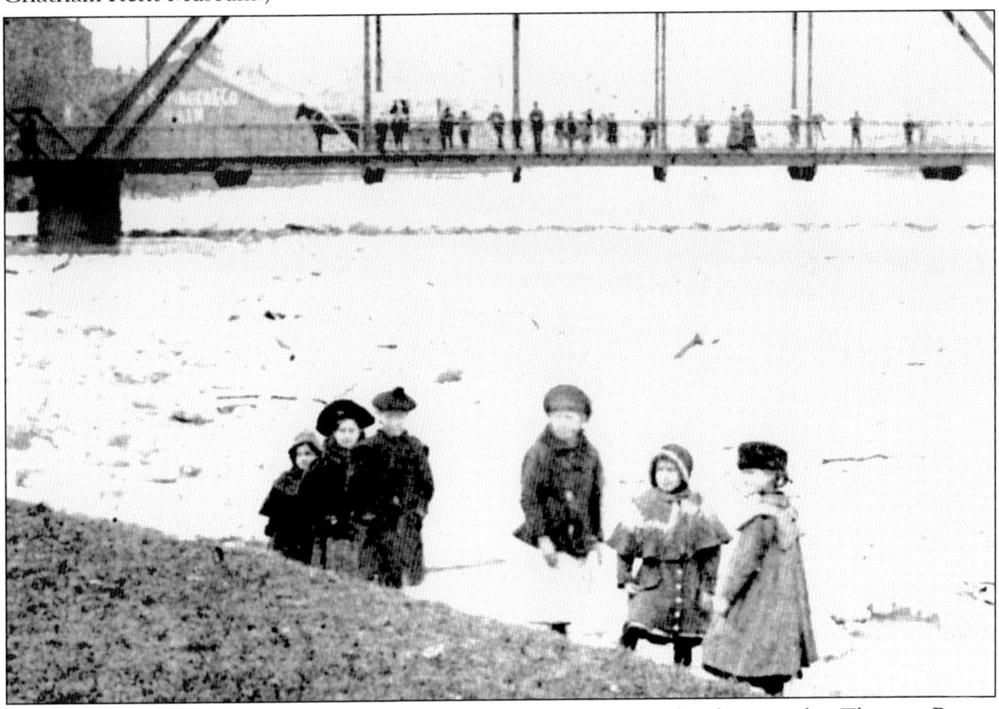

These children stand in Tecumseh Park, appearing dangerously close to the Thames River, during the annual spring breakup c. 1912. The view looks west down the Thames toward the 1885 Fifth Street Bridge. Spring ice jams and flooding were very real dangers to the citizens of Chatham since the earliest of times. (Courtesy Chatham Kent Museum.)

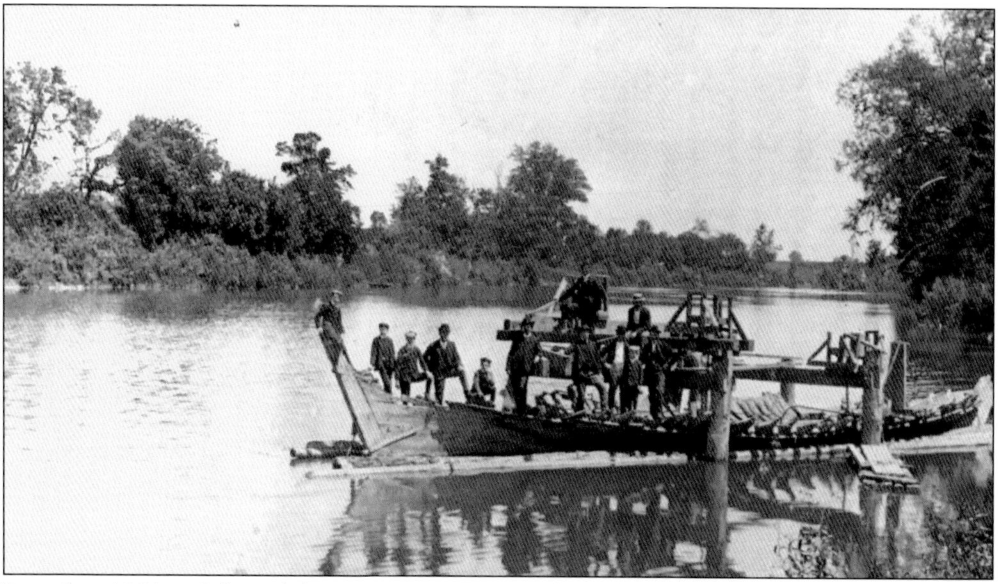

Raised in 1901 and floated downstream to Tecumseh Park, this War of 1812 vessel was long identified as the gunboat *General Myers*, burned by retreating British forces, who were being hotly pursued by the Americans. Recent research has revealed that the vessel was, in all likelihood, the commercial schooner *Miamis*. Pieces of furniture, walking sticks, and other wooden items made from this vessel are scattered throughout homes in Chatham Kent. (Courtesy Chatham Kent Museum.)

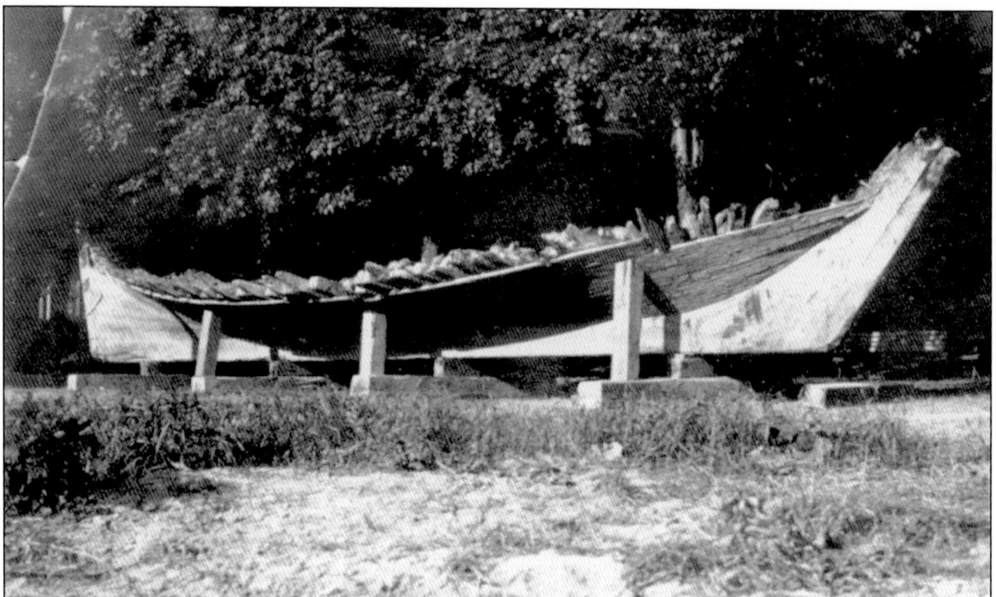

The *Miamis*, or the *General Myers*, seen here *c*. 1901, was floated down the Thames River from a spot near the railroad bridge and set up on the flats in Tecumseh Park. The Tecumseh Historical Society organized to finance the preservation of this War of 1812 cargo schooner. Funds were, unfortunately, not forthcoming, and the craft was eventually dismantled and used by local manufacturer Manson Campbell in the production of gunboat furniture and other smaller items. (Courtesy Doug and Dienne Howard.)

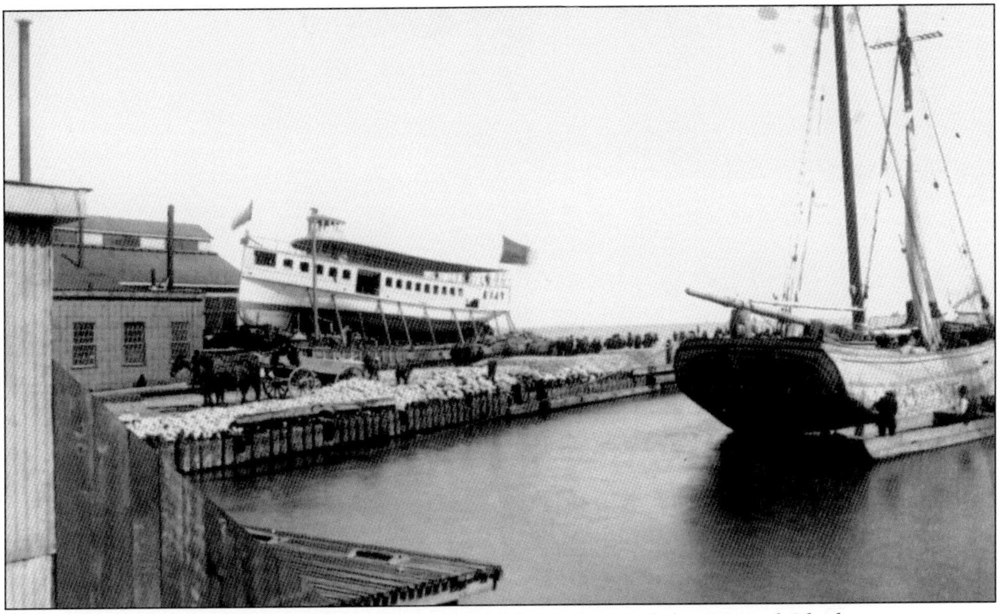

This rare *c.* 1888 photograph shows the actual launching of the *City of Chatham* steamer in Toronto, Ontario, on May 22, 1888. The vessel was built at a cost of $25,000 and was specially designed for excursion traffic. It was 125 feet long, included a 28-foot beam and a 7-foot draft, and could travel at a dizzying 16 miles per hour with 800 passengers on board. (Courtesy National Archives of Canada.)

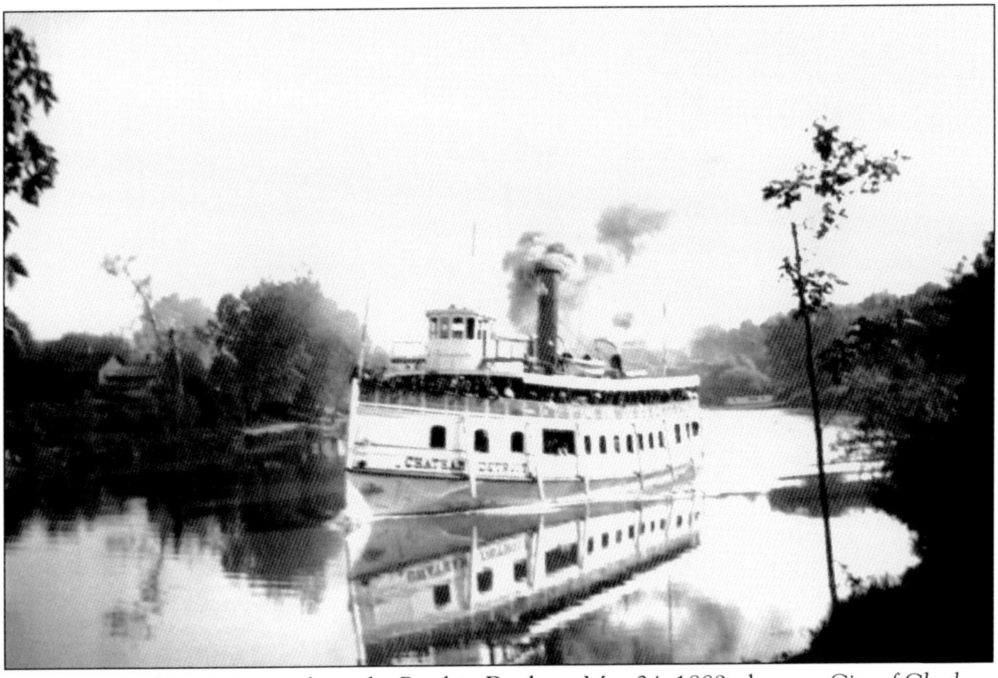

From its very first excursion from the Rankin Dock on May 24, 1889, the new *City of Chatham* steamer, seen here *c.* 1900, became an integral part of the former city of Chatham. According to reports of the day, everybody in the Chatham area sooner or later made the trip to Detroit, the lighthouse, Belle Isle, or Walpole Island on the *City of Chatham*. (Authors' collection.)

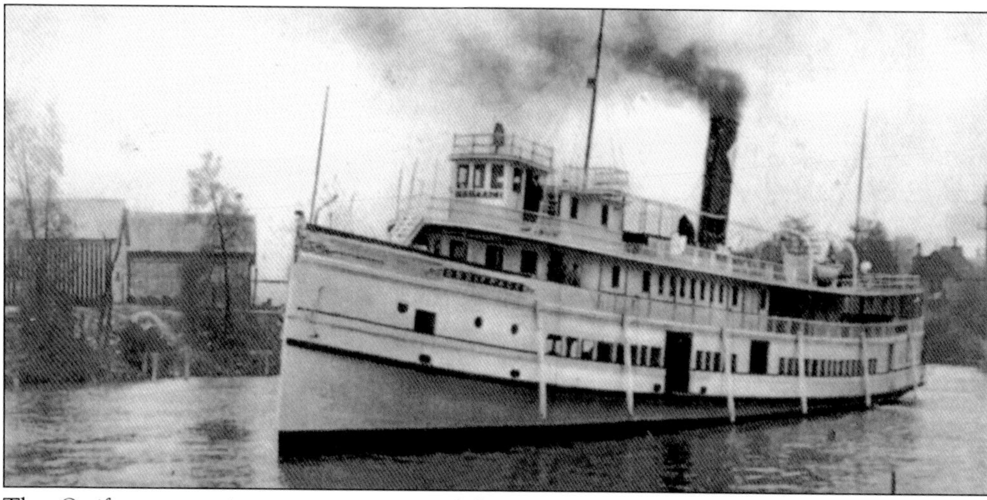

The *Ossifrage* excursion steamer, pictured here *c.* 1910, was purchased by the Chatham Navigation Company in September 1909 to replace the retired *City of Chatham* steamer. The *Fridge*, as it was commonly called, was much larger, more regal, and considerably faster than the *City*. (Courtesy Mr. and Mrs. Jamieson.)

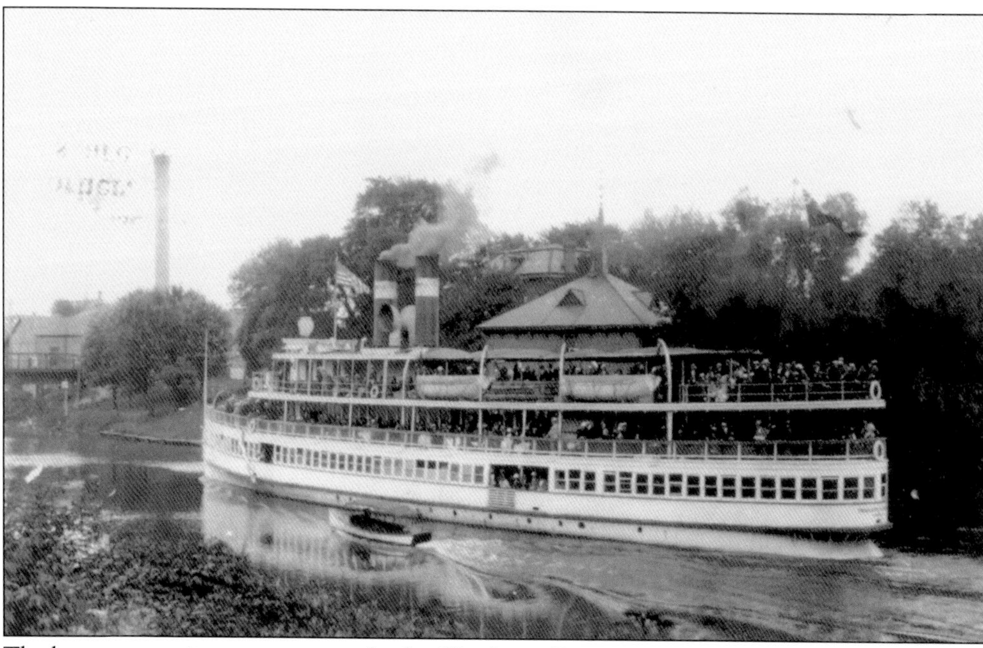

The largest excursion steamer to make the Chatham–Detroit run was a craft called the *Thousand Islander*. This vessel replaced the *Ossifrage c.* 1920. In this *c.* 1925 photograph, the steamer approaches the Third Street Bridge from the west and partially obscures the home of Dr. T.K. Holmes (now the Kent Club). (Courtesy Mollie French.)

Seven

And the Band Played On

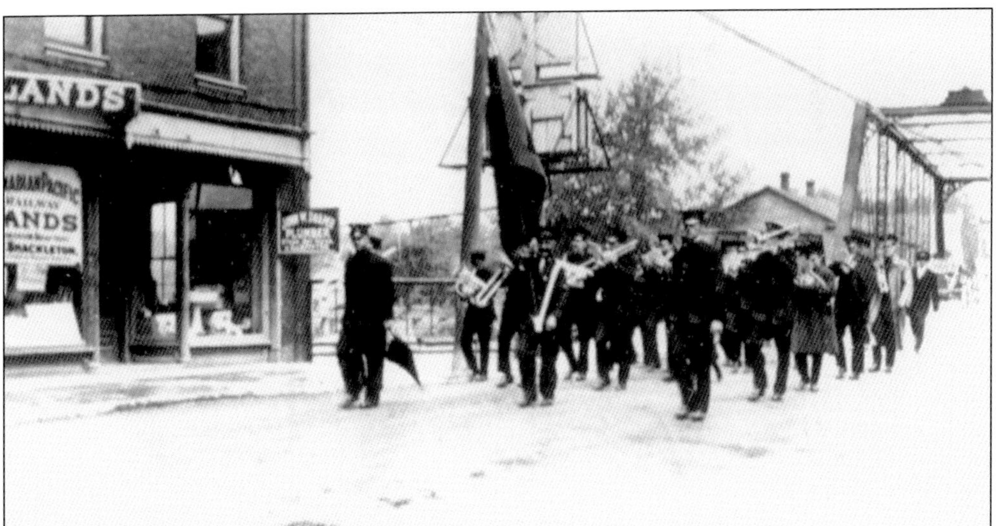

The Salvation Army Band was one of many marching bands that played an important part in Chatham's musical history. Here the band is seen on the south side of the Fifth Street Bridge *c.* 1911. The first store seen to the left of the bandleader was the J.W. Draper Plumbing business situated on the ground level of the Eberts' Block. (Courtesy Chatham Kent Museum.)

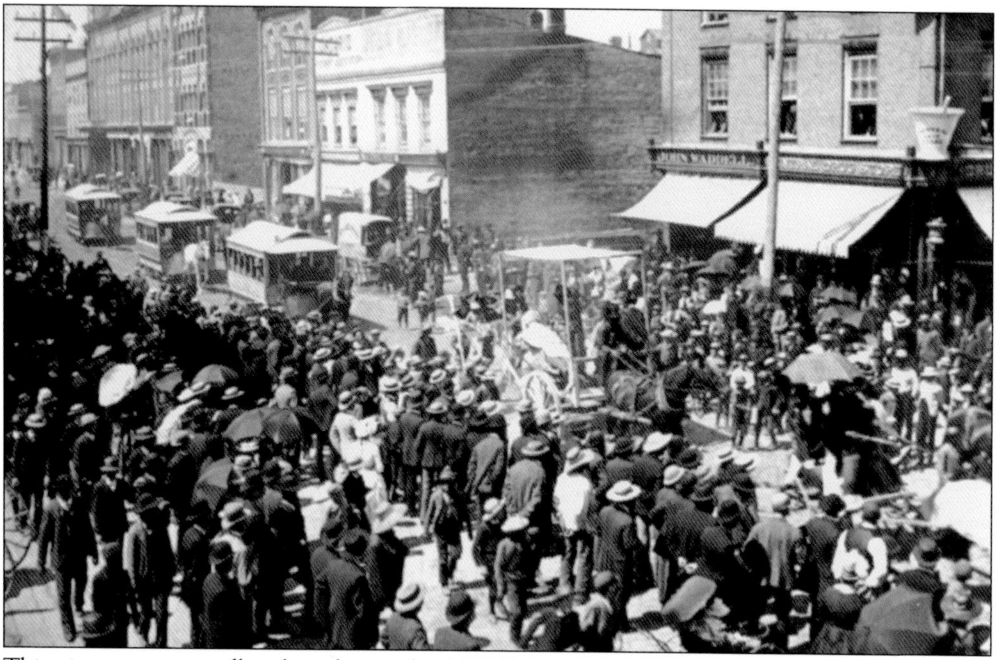

This view was reportedly taken during the 1885 Emancipation Day parade and looks west down King Street from the Fifth Street corner. On the right is the Eberts' Block, which housed the offices of John Waddell and the Central Drug Store. A bit farther down the street, Chatham's impressive opera house appears. In the first horse-drawn carriage pictured here, a rather strange object appearing to be a statue or an Egyptian mummy is paraded. (Courtesy Chatham Kent Museum.)

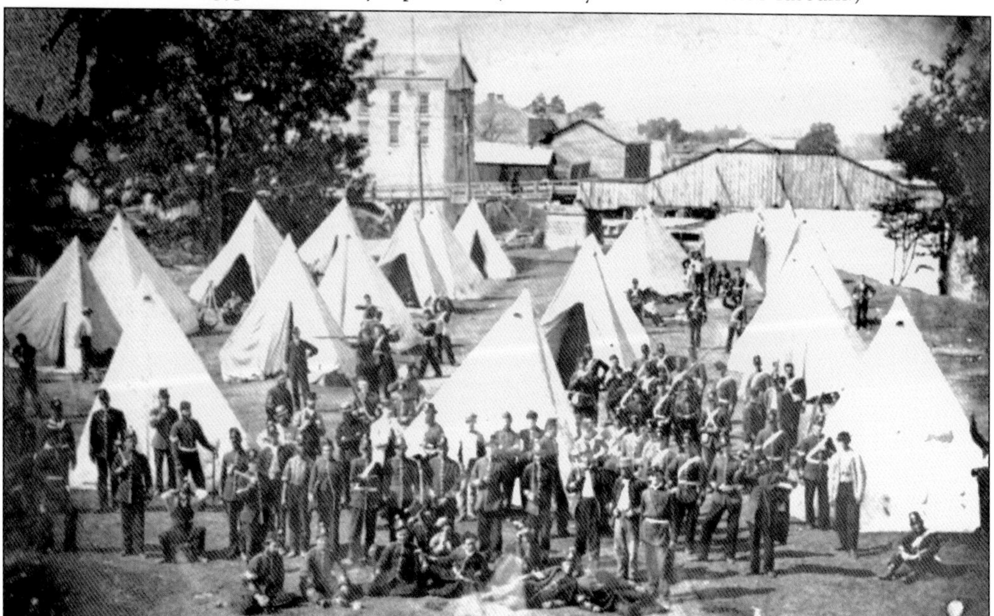

The 24th Battalion is camped at the Point in Tecumseh Park in 1870. This picture is notable for its depiction of the types of military tents popular at the time, Chatham's first wooden Fifth Street Bridge, and to the left of the bridge, the four-storey "Eberts' Skyscraper." (Courtesy Chatham Kent Museum.)

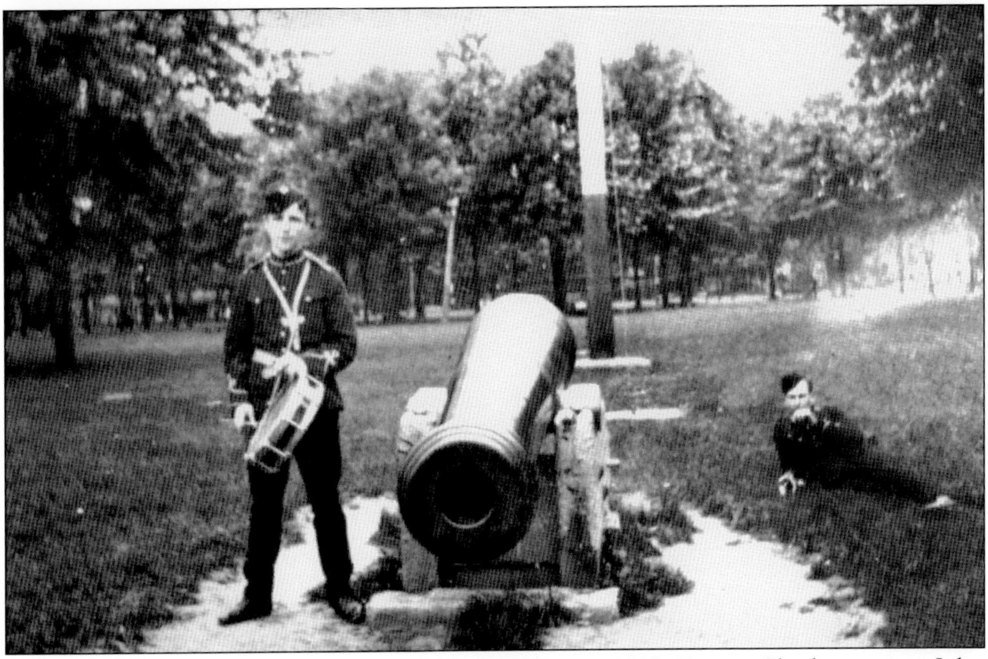

The cannon at the Point in Tecumseh Park dates from *c.* 1902. Former Chatham mayor John Carpenter and John A. Walker formed a committee and obtained the cannon from the town of Point Edward, where three such cannons were half buried in the mud. In this *c.* 1915 photograph, two members of the Bugle Boy Corporation pose beside the cannon. (Courtesy Chatham Kent Museum.)

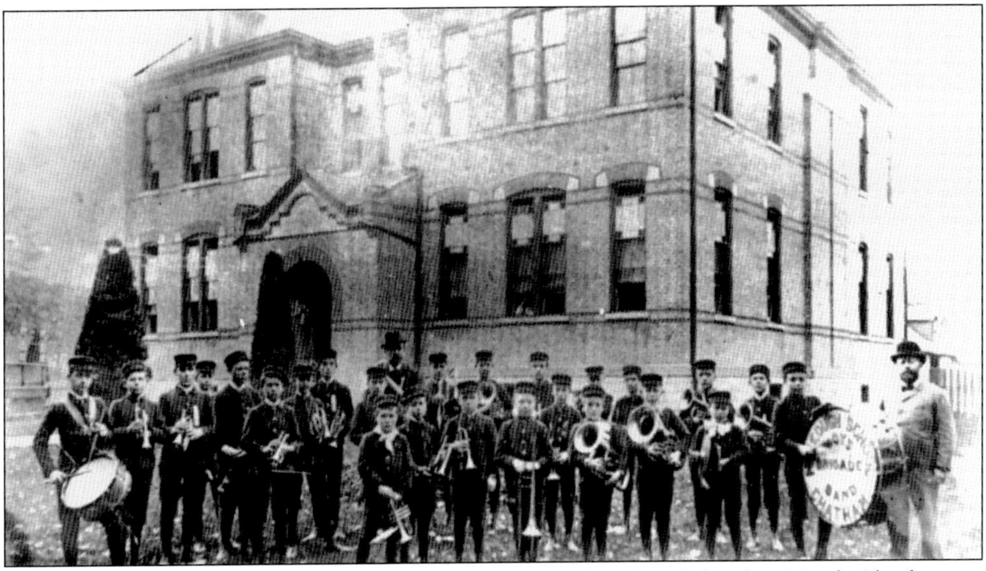

When James Brackin became principal of the McKeough Public School in North Chatham in 1883, he made music a cornerstone of the school's curriculum. Under Brackin's guidance, the McKeough School and Boy's Brigade Band gained fame well beyond Chatham. Notable chorus members in the early years of McKeough's music program were future Canadian novelist and poet Arthur Stringer and future silent movie star Marie Dressler. This photograph was taken *c.* the 1890s. (Courtesy Chatham Kent Museum.)

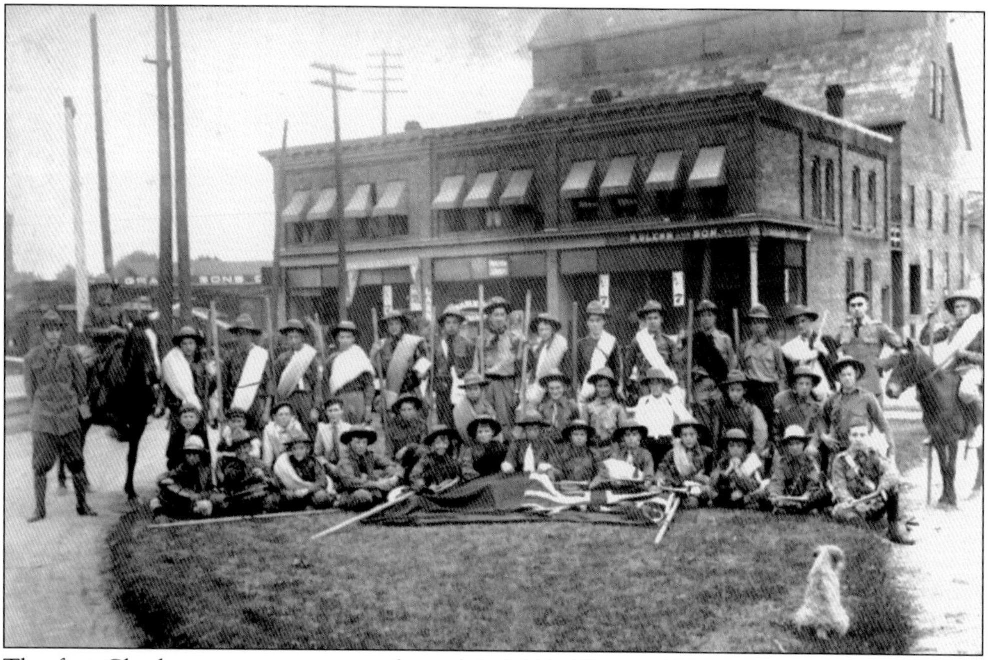

The first Chatham scout troop was formed in 1912. This *c.* 1912 picture was taken at the Canadian Pacific station as the troop prepared to embark on a camping adventure. The buildings behind the scout troop are those recently renovated buildings on William Street at the corner of Jahnke Street. (Courtesy Chatham Kent Museum.)

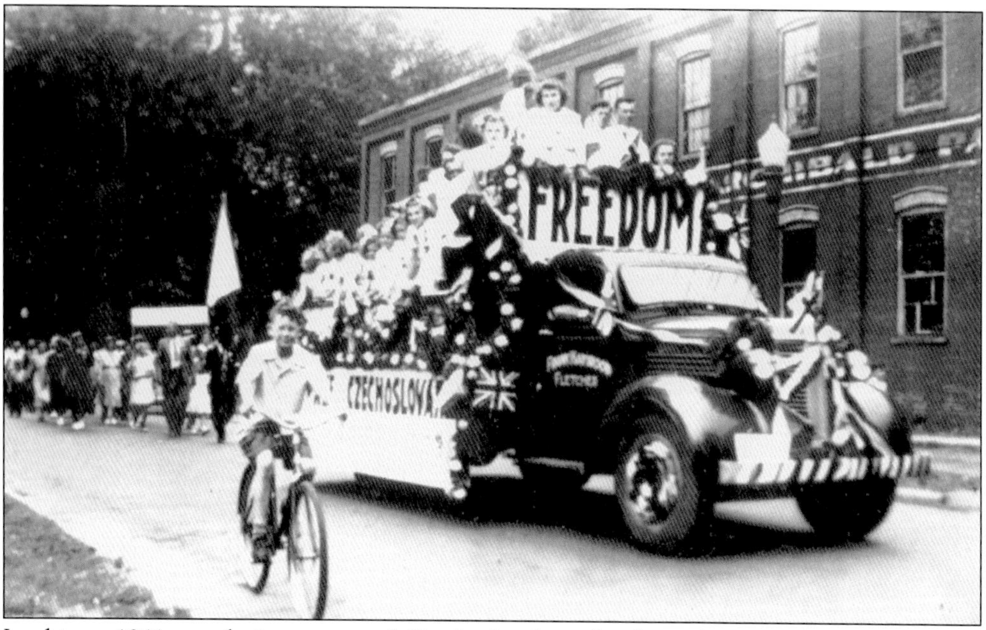

In this *c.* 1941 parade in support of Czechoslovakian freedom, the route headed south on William Street and passed in front of the Park Brothers Foundry. This is the site of the present-day Terrace Forty Apartments. (Courtesy Joe and Jean Uher.)

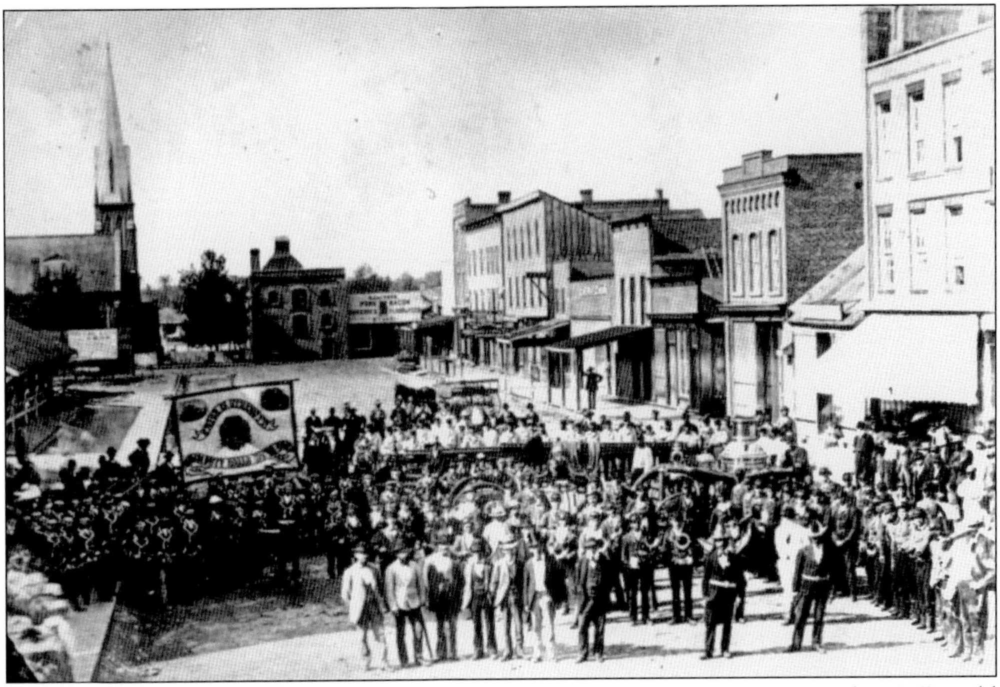

The Chatham Volunteer Fire Department Brigade is pictured here with its prized 1869 Ronald and Hyslop steam engine. The brigade is preparing for a review on Market Street West in 1876. The first paid Chatham Fire Department was formed in 1880 and took up residence in Fire Hall No. 1 on Sixth Street in 1881. (Courtesy Chatham Kent Museum.)

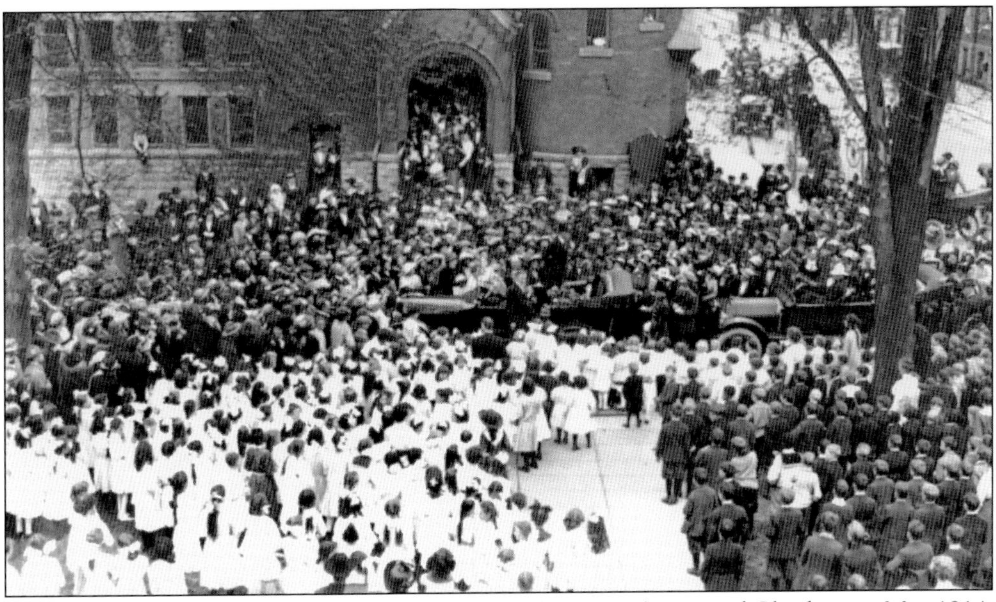

When the governor general of Canada, the Duke of Connaught, visited Chatham in May 1914, he agreed to spend a grand total of five minutes at each Chatham school. In the center of this picture, the governor general appears in his car, greeting appropriately dressed girls (left) and boys (right foreground) at Central School. (Courtesy Dr. Dick Charteris.)

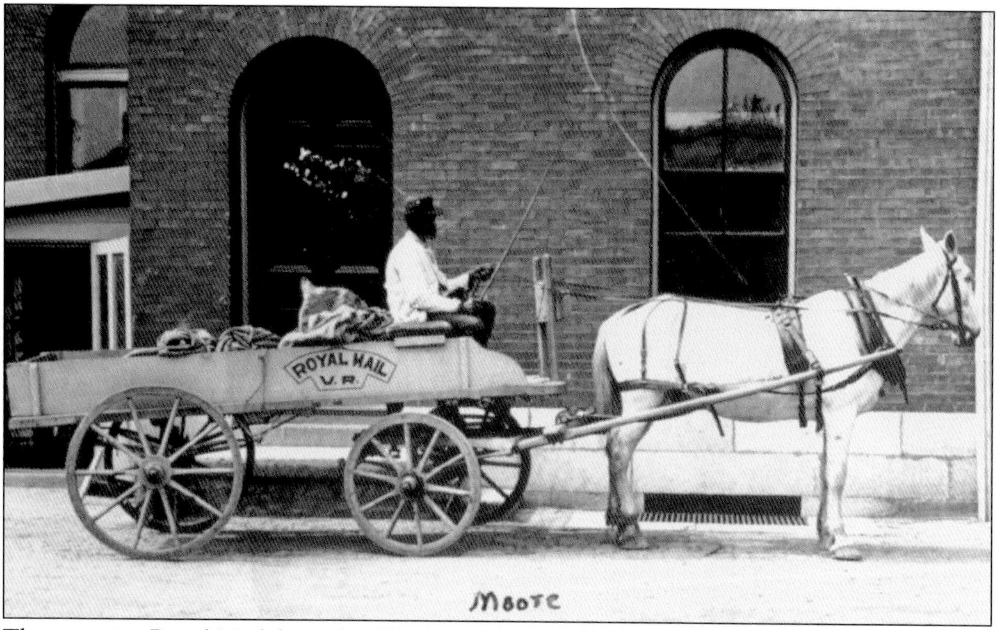

The outgoing Royal Mail from the Chatham Post Office on the southwest corner of King and Fourth Streets was taken to the railway station to be shipped, while the incoming mail was picked up there. In addition, mail was carted around town in such early conveyances as is pictured here. This *c.* 1900 photograph was taken on Fourth Street to the side of the Chatham Post Office. (Courtesy Chatham Kent Museum.)

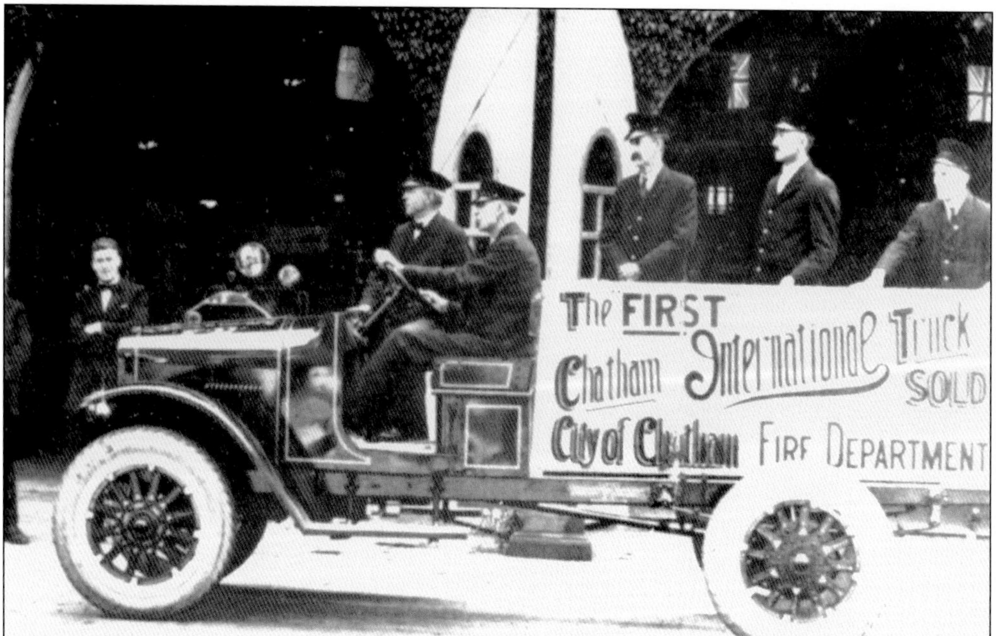

In 1910, Daniel Ross Van Allen's Grand Avenue wagon works business was purchased and greatly expanded to encompass the International Harvester Company of Canada. The first truck manufactured at the Grand Avenue plant, pictured here, was purchased by the Chatham Fire Department on May 13, 1921, for $2,100. (Courtesy Chatham Kent Museum.)

Eight

Moving On down the Road

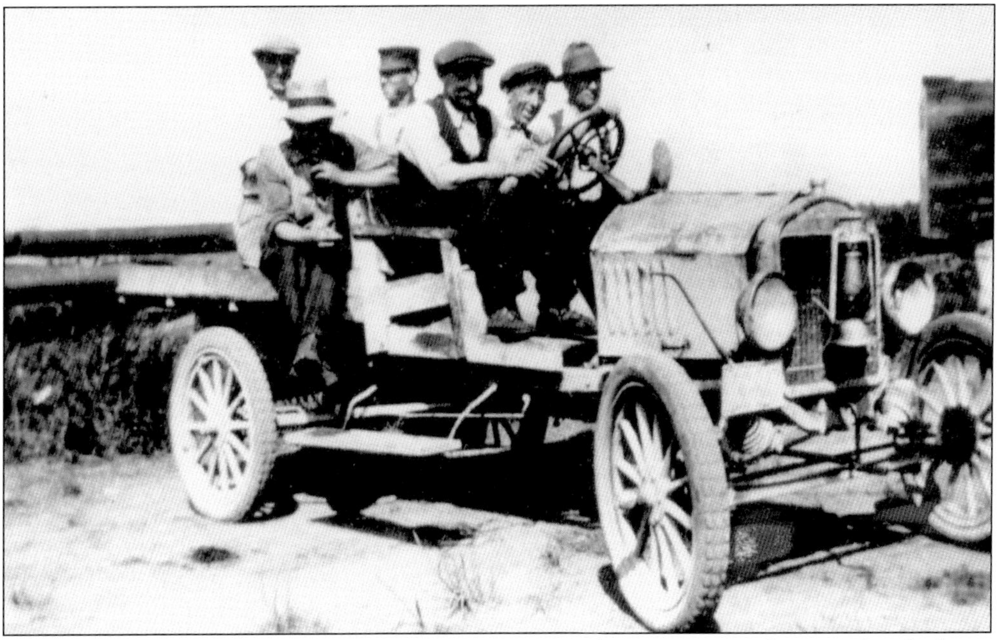

This 1920 Model T Ford was converted from an E.E. Steels touring car and was used as the latest thing in trucks by the Union Natural Gas Company. Pictured here, from left to right, are Shorty Bellinger, W.D. Tudgope, George Peltier, Alex Archibald, Harry Kress, and Charlie Barnhart. Note the lantern out front that was used just in case the headlights failed. (Courtesy Union Gas Archives.)

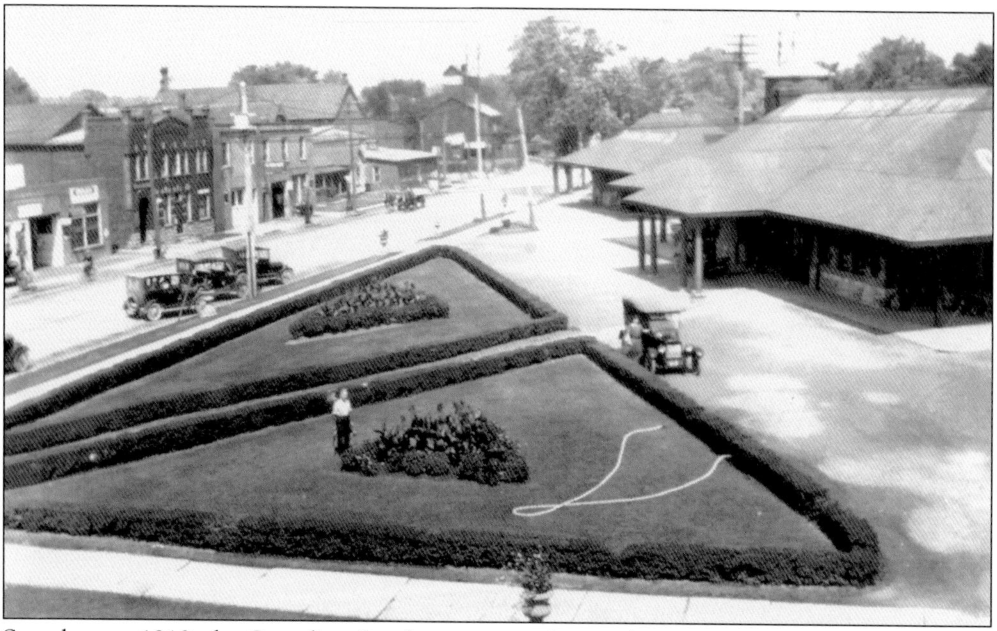

Seen here *c*. 1910, the Canadian Pacific station at the southwest corner of King and William Streets was a rather impressive entry point for travelers coming to Chatham by train. Today, the area pictured is a large parking lot, and the station has been moved, brick by brick, to a new location on the northeast side of town, becoming the home of Fred's Nursery. (Courtesy Doug and Dienne Howard.)

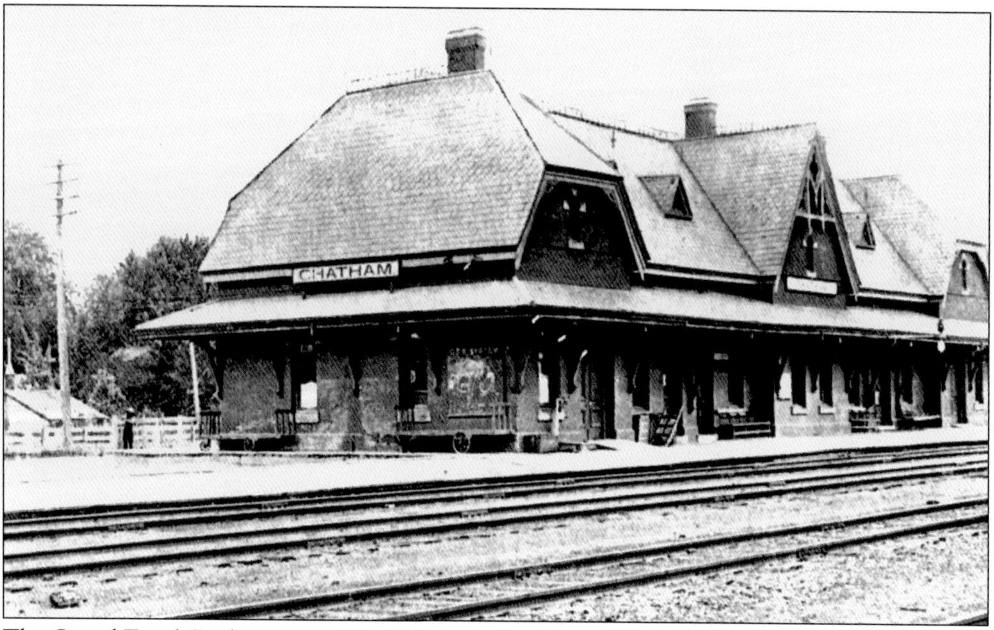

The Grand Trunk Railway station on Queen Street, pictured *c*. 1900, was built in 1879 at a cost of $10,000. It advertised itself in the late 1880s as offering "cheap rail and steamship tickets to any part of the world." W.E. Rispin was a longtime agent for the Grand Trunk Railway. This station remains today as the VIA station for passenger service to and from Chatham. (Courtesy Mollie French.)

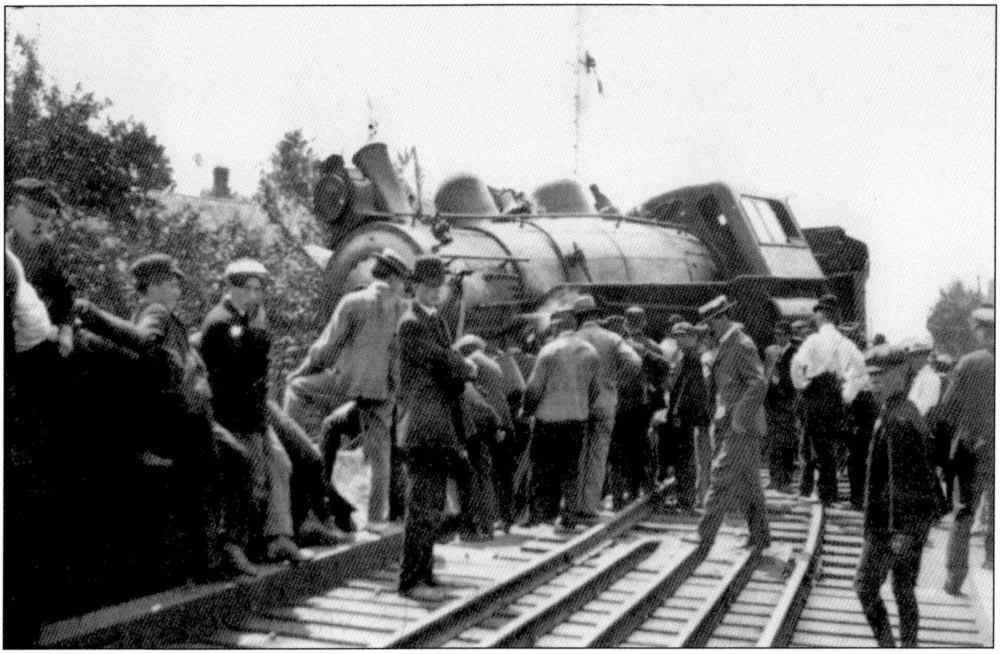

This Powell and Davis postcard shows a locomotive that had just gone off the track a short distance from King Street East, near the railroad bridge over McGregor's Creek. In the early days of train travel, derailments of major and minor consequence were not uncommon events. This particular one, a minor mishap, occurred on August 14, 1906. (Courtesy Doug and Dienne Howard.)

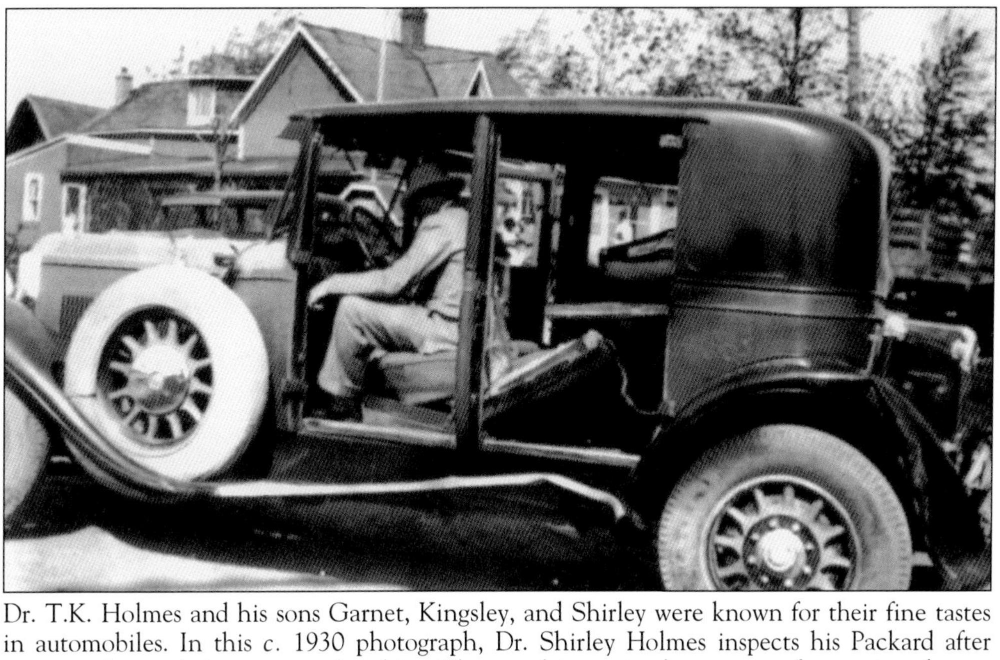

Dr. T.K. Holmes and his sons Garnet, Kingsley, and Shirley were known for their fine tastes in automobiles. In this *c.* 1930 photograph, Dr. Shirley Holmes inspects his Packard after it was stolen and then returned to him. The car thieves, in the process of removing the car from Holmes's garage, unceremoniously ripped off both doors on the driver's side. (Courtesy Bill Coltart.)

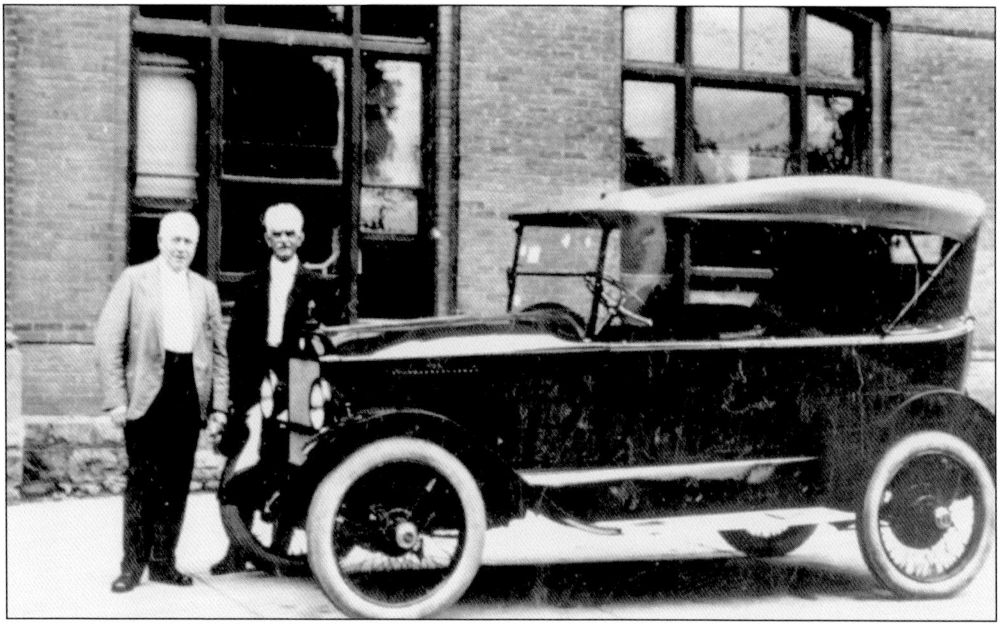

The Gray-Dort automobile, produced in Chatham at William and Wellington Streets from 1915 to 1924, had a short but illustrious life. Described as "the class of the light car field," it was a very popular car in its time. The two industrialists who created this car are pictured here beside a 1919 Gray-Dort Ace. Robert Gray stands on the left, and Dallas Dort of Flint, Michigan, is on the right. (Courtesy Chatham Kent Museum.)

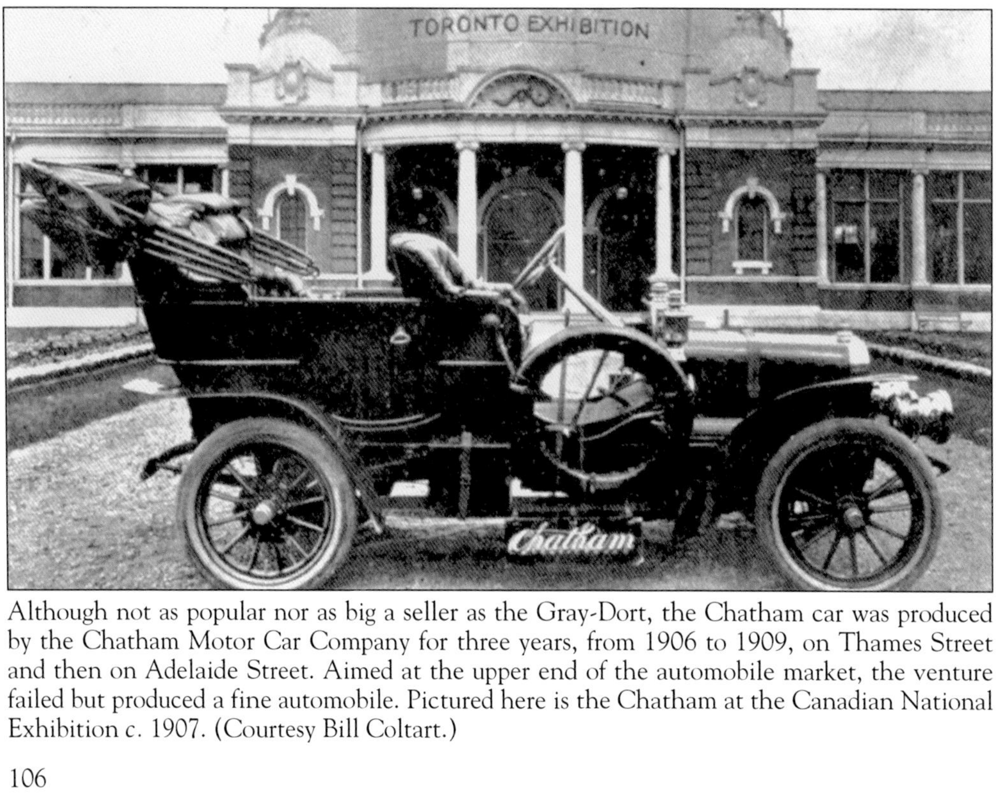

Although not as popular nor as big a seller as the Gray-Dort, the Chatham car was produced by the Chatham Motor Car Company for three years, from 1906 to 1909, on Thames Street and then on Adelaide Street. Aimed at the upper end of the automobile market, the venture failed but produced a fine automobile. Pictured here is the Chatham at the Canadian National Exhibition c. 1907. (Courtesy Bill Coltart.)

Nine

PLACES, FACES, AND SPACES

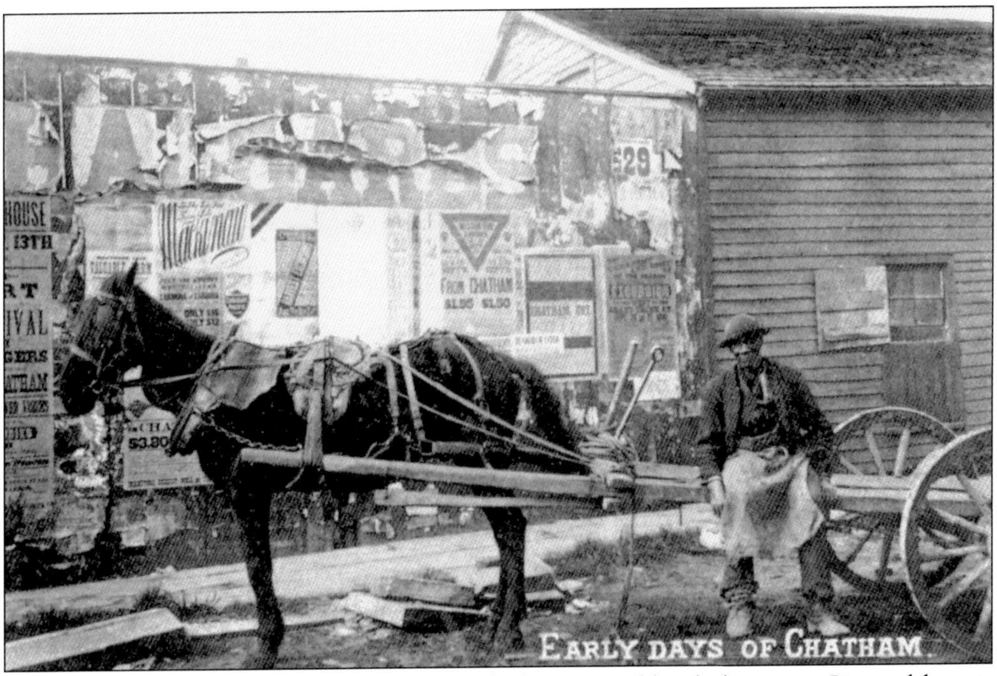

Chatham, like any other town in the 1880s, had its cast of local characters. Pictured here is one of these unidentified characters. This postcard, which is valued highly by local collectors, is interesting not only for the horse-drawn cart and its operator but for the many posters of the time plastered on the background wall. These posters advertise such things as the Western Fair in London, Grand Trunk Railway excursions, and various other local events. (Authors' collection.)

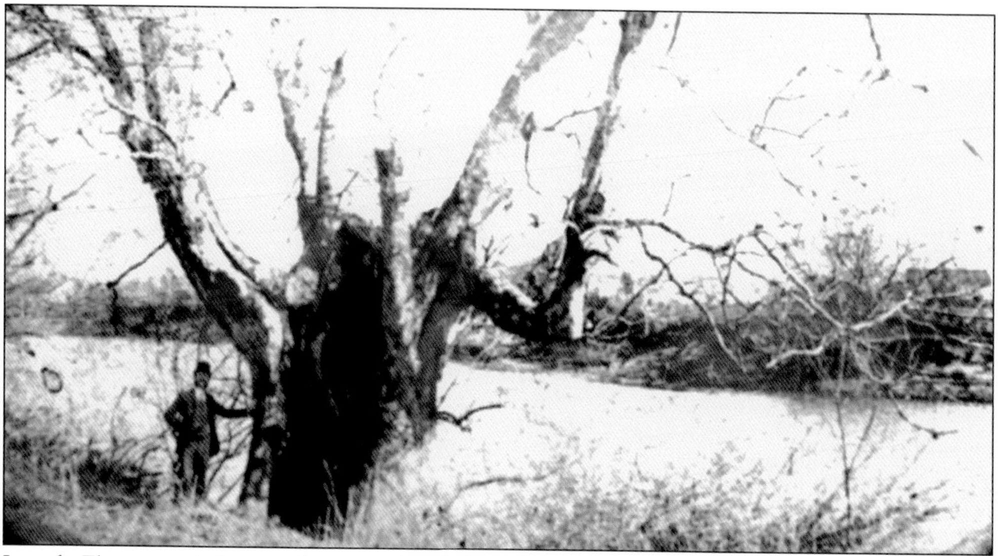

Joseph Eberts settled on a farm north of the Thames River in 1816 at the site of the old Chatham Waterworks on Grand Avenue East. He soon opened a store, kept a tavern, rented boats, and ran a ferry service. The tree pictured here *c.* 1900 survived until the 1900s and was rumoured to have stored in its trunk cannon balls, swords, muskets, and pistols from the War of 1812 that had been gleaned from the Thames River over the years. (Courtesy Chatham Kent Museum.)

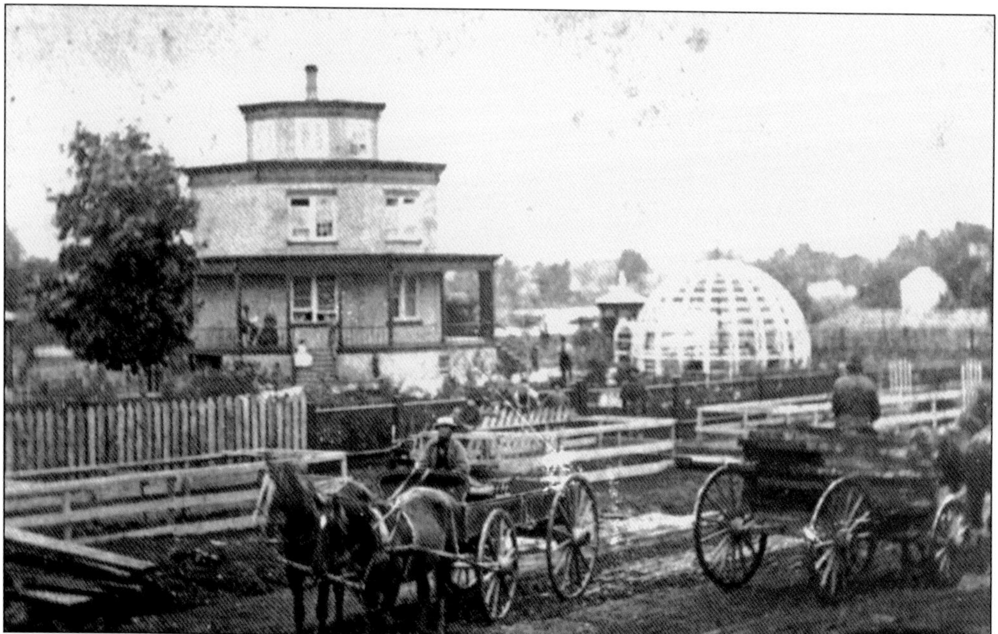

One of Chatham's most distinctive homes was built *c.* 1850s by Daniel Ross Van Allen on Head Street (Grand Avenue East). Van Allen was one of Chatham's earliest businessmen who came to Chatham in 1833. Described at various times as the Wedding Cake House, the home had expansive gardens, gazebos, and a greenhouse. Its grandiose features befitted a man who owned sawmills employing 70 men and had an annual output of more than $100,000 in the late 1850s. This photograph was taken *c.* the 1890s. (Courtesy Chatham Kent Museum.)

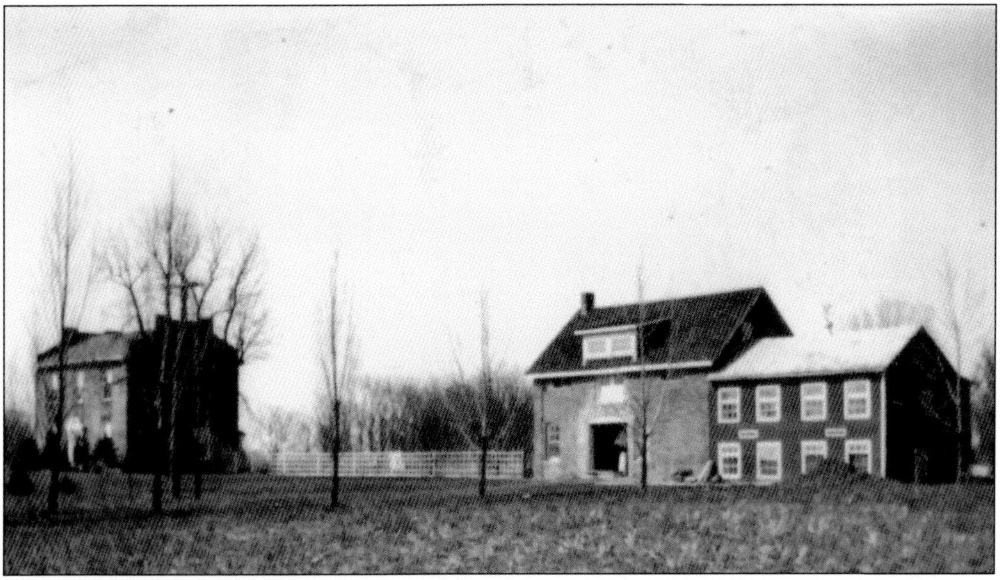

Built in the early 1800s, one of the earliest homes in the area, pictured on the left in the mid-1900s, still stands today on Colborne Street Extension near Colonial Nurseries. The outbuildings, on the right, also exist today, though in an altered form, as a home on the grounds of Colonial Nursery. (Courtesy Doug and Dienne Howard.)

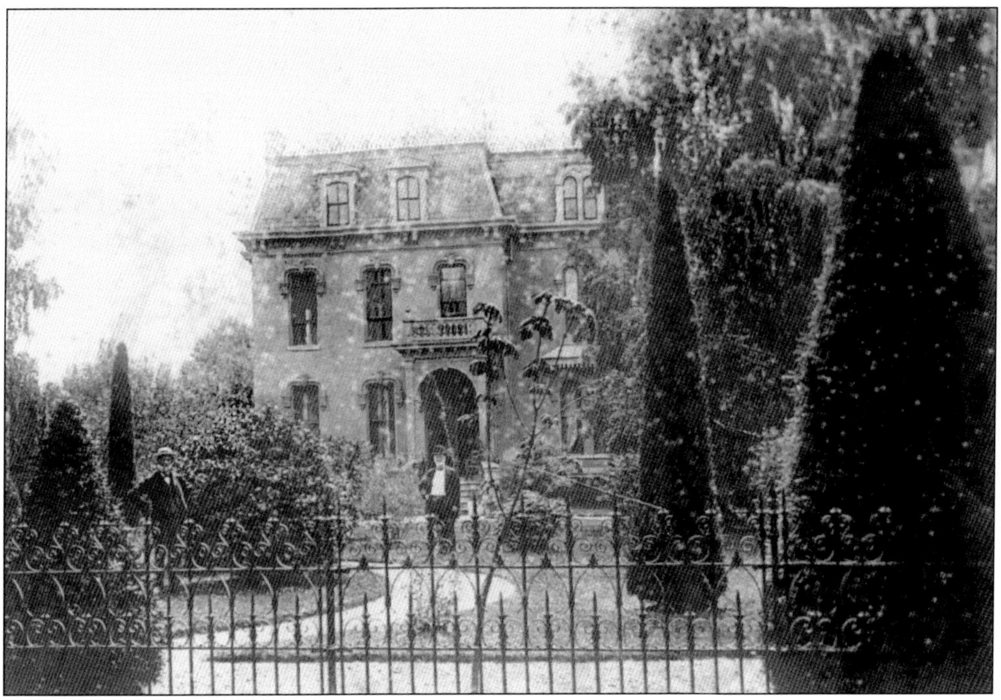

Spencer Stone was the son of King Street's early dry goods businessman Thomas Stone. Carrying on his father's very successful business, Spencer Stone eventually bought this impressive home at 210 Victoria Avenue from Samuel Sutherland, the original owner. Although the house has long since disappeared, the iron fence seen here still exists outside the two newer homes built on the site. (Courtesy Bill Glassco.)

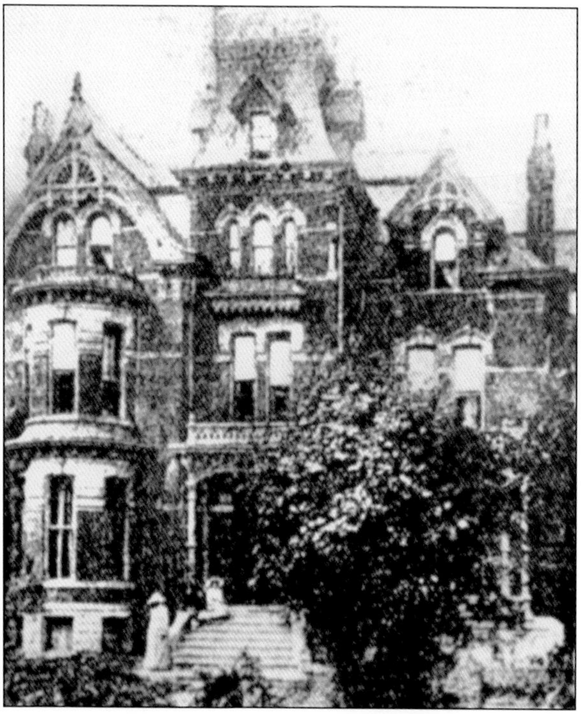

E.W. Scane not only owned Chatham's opulent opera house and music hall on King Street but also built one of Chatham's most palatial homes. Spenser Villa, seen here *c.* 1880, stood on Queen Street where the Chatham Hydro and Utilities Commission Office is today. After this home was torn down, the Queen Mary Public School was constructed on the site. (Courtesy Chatham Kent Museum.)

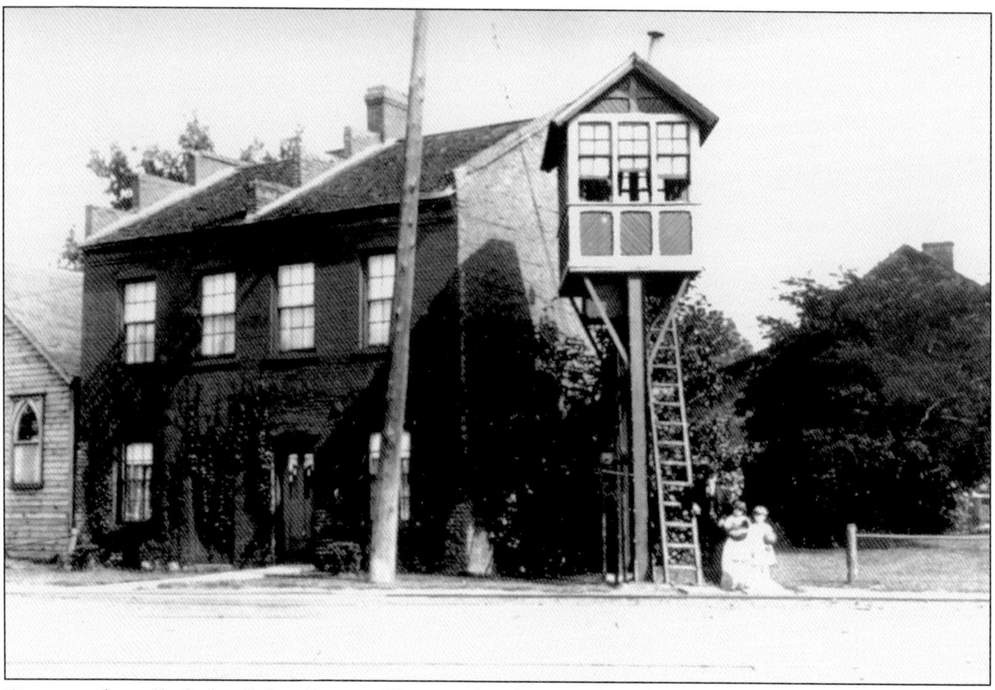

Commonly called the John Brown House, this home played host to a few of the Chatham Convention meetings that led to John Brown's ill-fated raid on Harper's Ferry. However, its real significance lies in the fact that the very influential black newspaper, the *Provincial Freeman*, was edited here by Mary Shadd Cary in the late 1850s. Unfortunately, the house was torn down in the 1950s. This photograph was taken *c.* 1915. (Courtesy Chatham Kent Museum.)

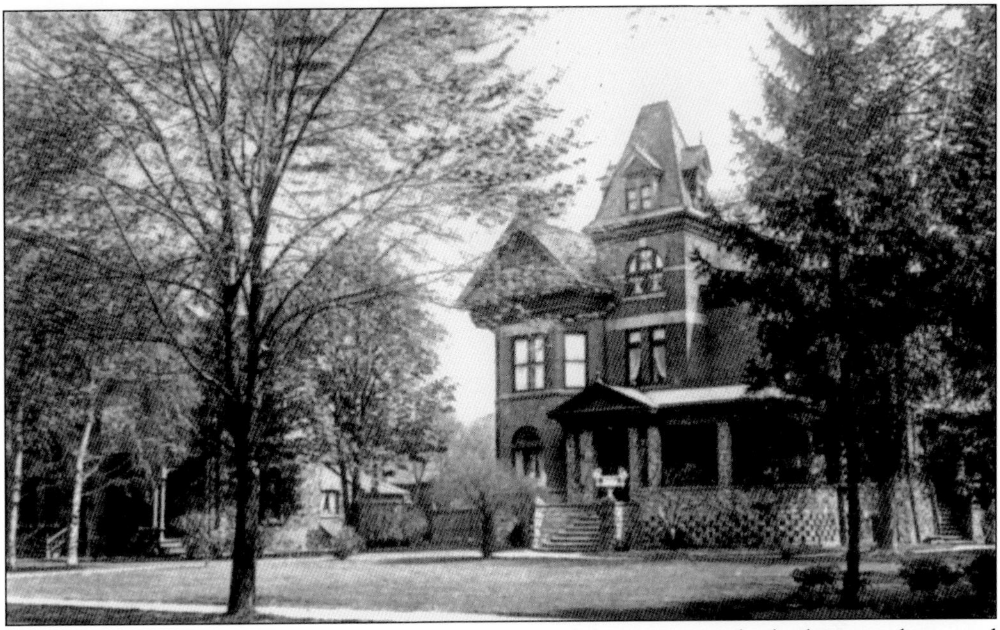

Robert Gray, the founder of the Gray-Dort Automobile Company, built this very large and impressive home, Avenal, at 141 William Street South in the 1880s. It remains today, after extensive and painstaking restorations, one of the city's most beautiful homes. The home is seen here in the mid-1900s. (Courtesy Doug and Dienne Howard.)

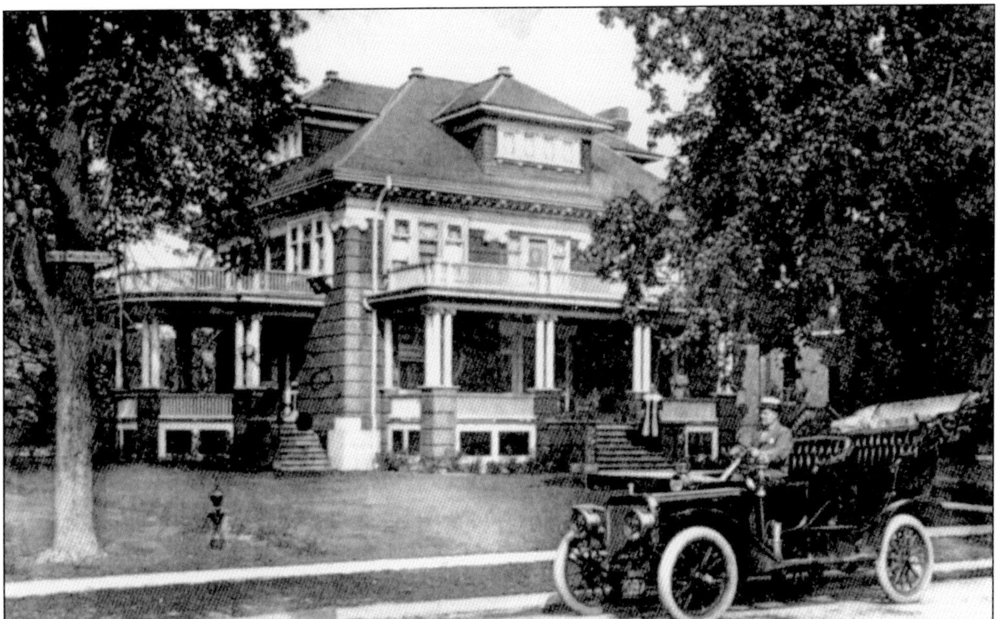

This home on Wellington Street was built by O.L. Lewis, who had been city solicitor for Chatham c. 1909 and had played a major role in the formation of the city manager system. In this picture, Lewis sits in his Chatham car outside his home in the early 1900s. (Courtesy Mollie French.)

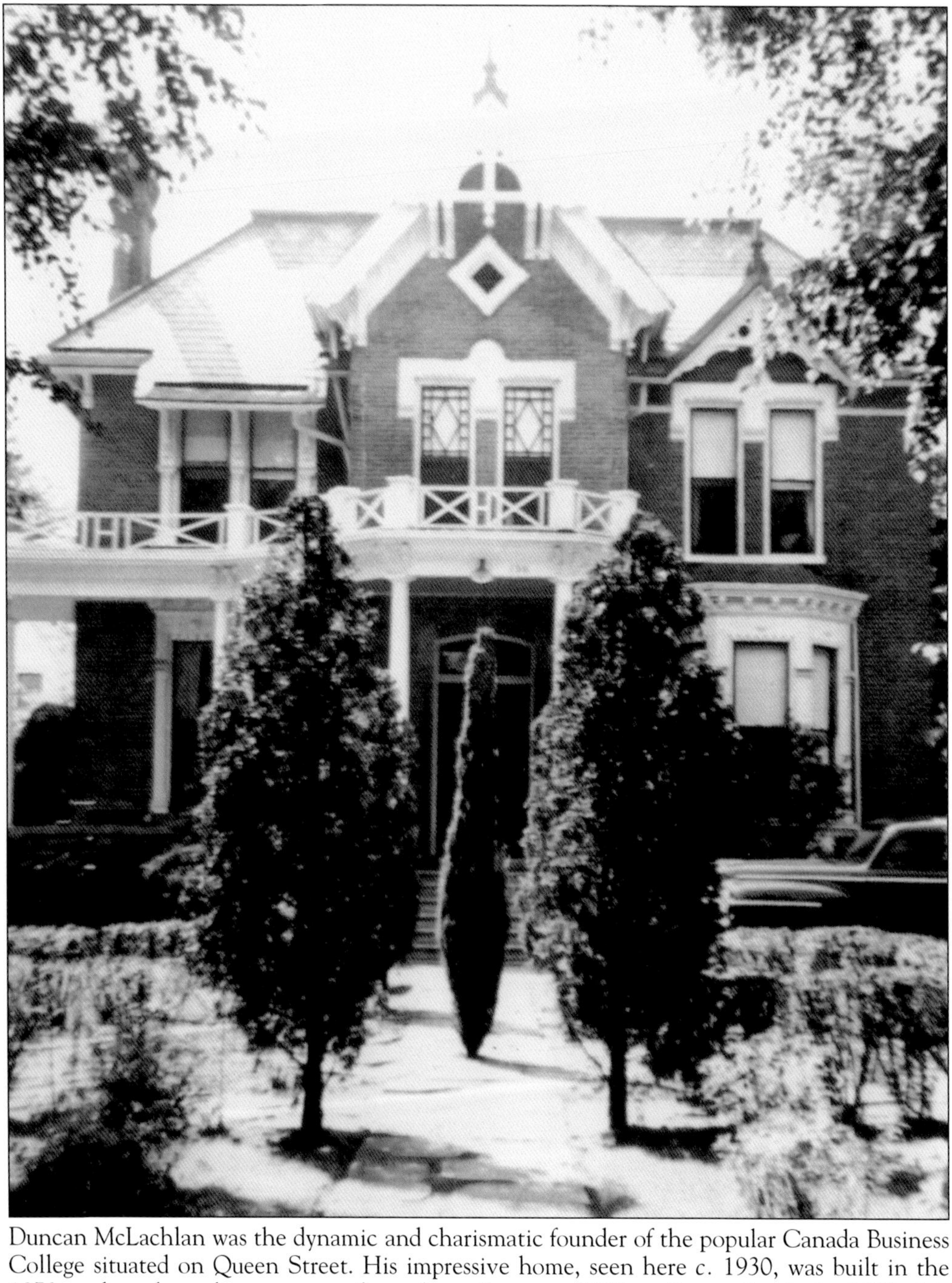

Duncan McLachlan was the dynamic and charismatic founder of the popular Canada Business College situated on Queen Street. His impressive home, seen here *c.* 1930, was built in the 1870s only a short distance away from the college, on William Street South. In 1932, this building became the Hinnegan Funeral Home (now the Hinnegan-Peseski Funeral Home). (Courtesy Doug and Dienne Howard.)

Shown here *c.* the 1940s, Kent McLachlan, son of Canada Business College owner Duncan McLachlan, left Chatham in the 1930s and eventually settled in Hollywood. He arrived just after the transition to talkies, and his rich voice and rugged good looks made him a popular Western movie actor between 1930 and 1972. He later adopted the stage name Keene Duncan. He often visited Chatham and sometimes promoted his latest movie at local movie houses or at the Chatham Drive-In. His last movies were with the legendary Ed Wood. Kent McLachlan died in Hollywood in February 1972. (Authors' collection.)

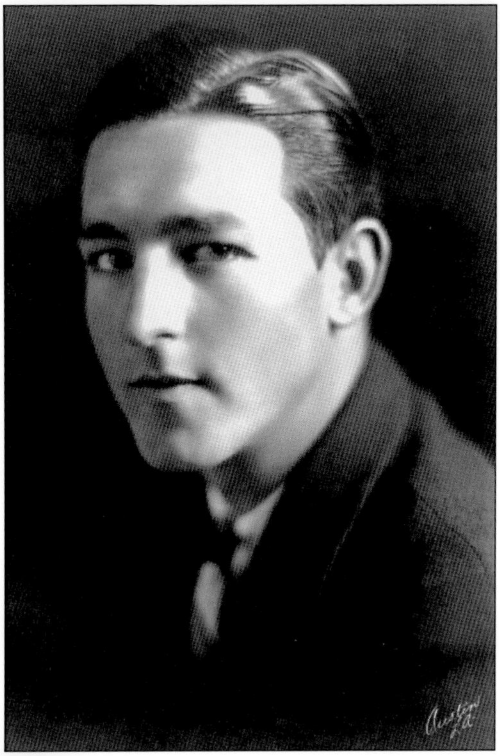

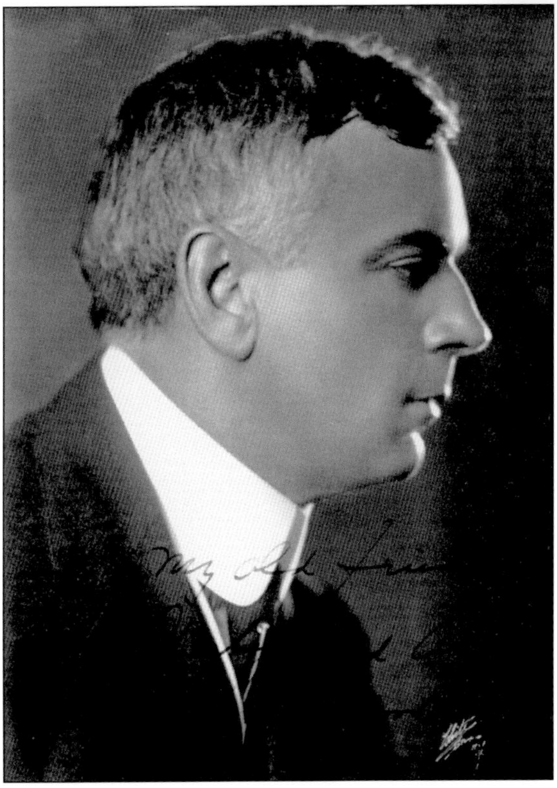

Arthur Stringer (1874–1950) was born in Chatham on Colborne Street and grew up to be one of North America's most prolific writers of the time. He wrote more than 40 novels, hundreds of magazine articles, and more than two dozen books of poetry. Although Stringer left Canada for New York, he often returned to Chatham, where he kept a home on Wellington Street and a home on Lake Erie near Cedar Springs. This photograph was taken *c.* 1916. (Authors' collection.)

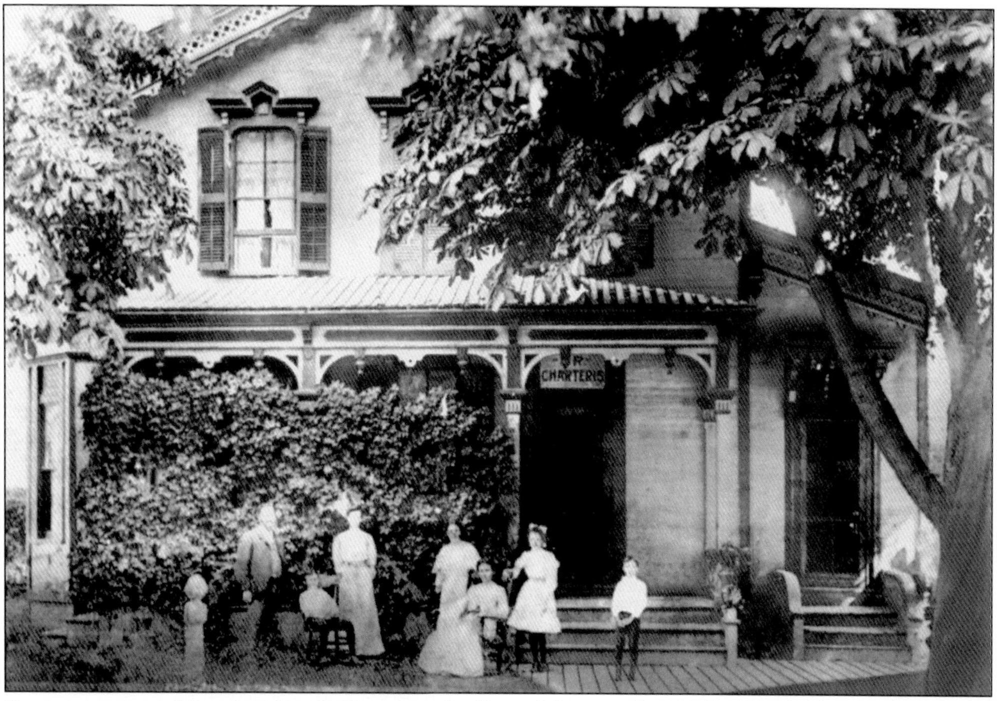

For many years, this existed as the home and office of the popular Dr. Richard Charteris, who was the first of three successive doctors by that name in Chatham. The building was situated on Sixth Street directly across from Harrison Hall. Dr. Charteris, his wife, and his children stand in front of their home in this picture dating from the early 1900s. (Courtesy Dr. Dick Charteris.)

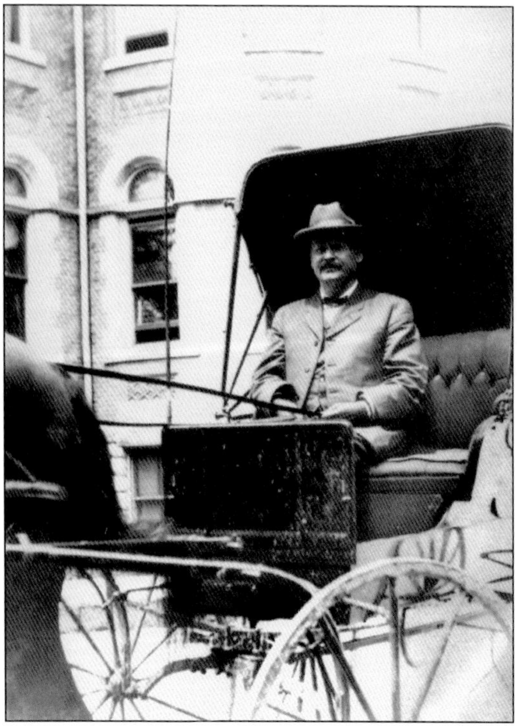

The first of three doctors practicing medicine in Chatham with the name of Charteris rides in his horse and buggy on Sixth Street in front of Harrison Hall, across the street from his home and office, c. 1905. (Courtesy Dr. Dick Charteris.)

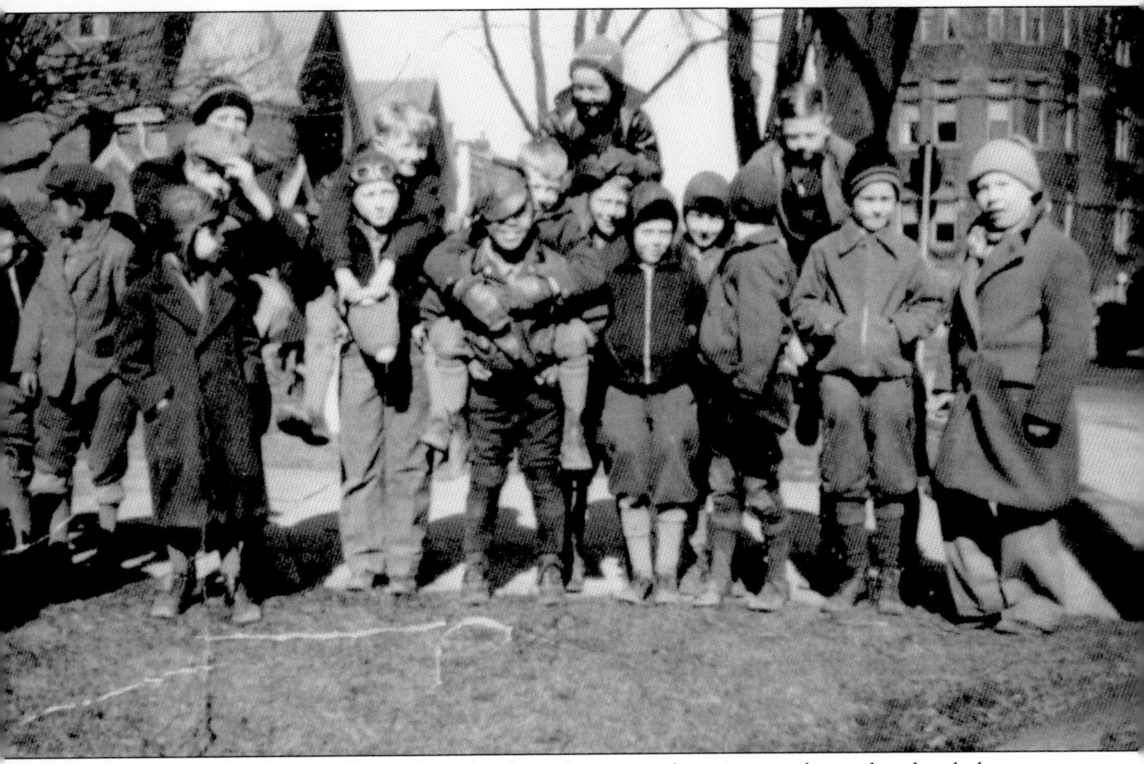

Charming smiles, with just a hint of mischief, predominate this picture of a grade school class at Chatham's Central School in 1938. In the background, the First Presbyterian Church appears on the left, and Harrison Hall is on the right. This photograph was taken near the eastern entrance to Central School. (Courtesy Glen Wood.)

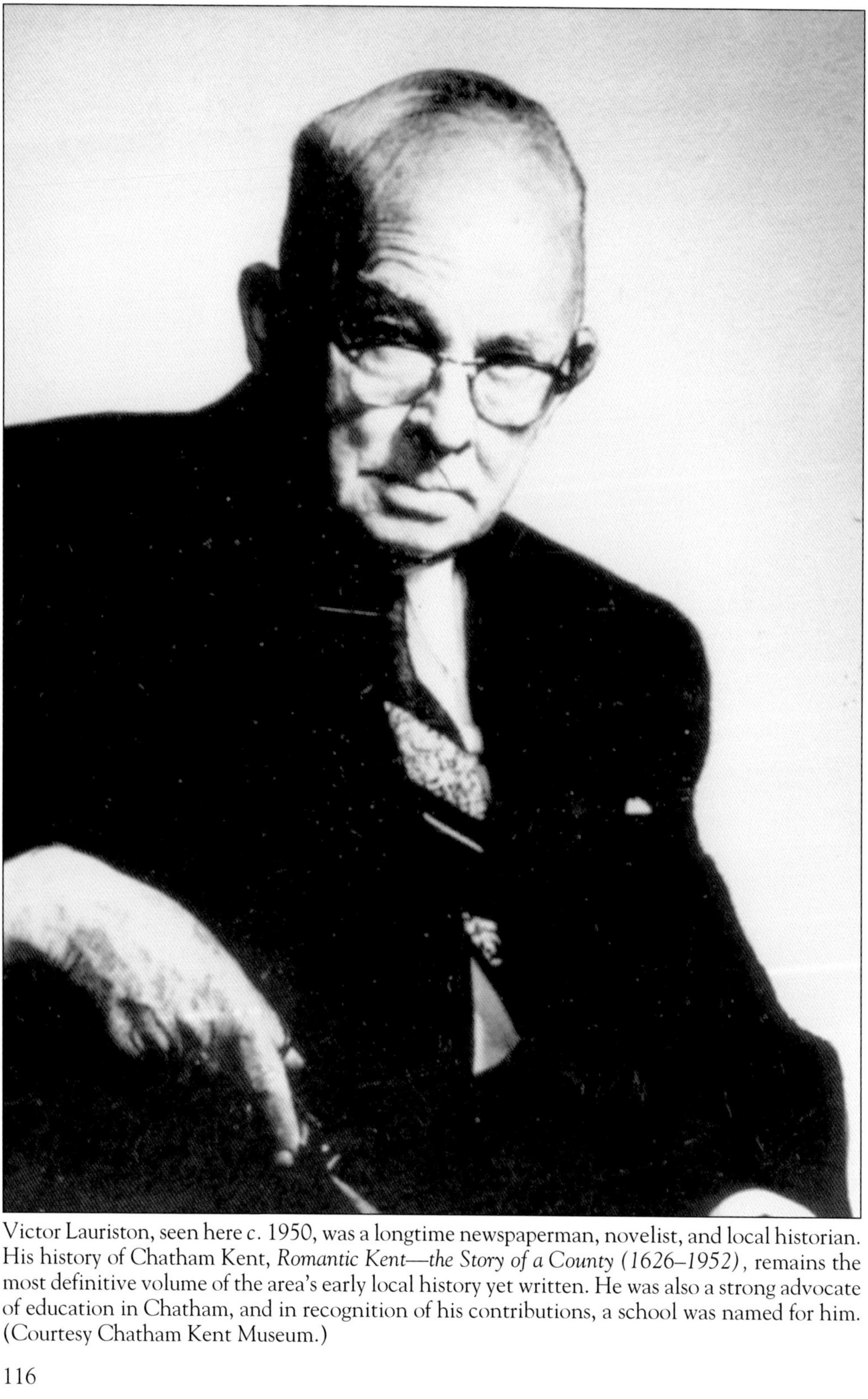

Victor Lauriston, seen here *c*. 1950, was a longtime newspaperman, novelist, and local historian. His history of Chatham Kent, *Romantic Kent—the Story of a County (1626–1952)*, remains the most definitive volume of the area's early local history yet written. He was also a strong advocate of education in Chatham, and in recognition of his contributions, a school was named for him. (Courtesy Chatham Kent Museum.)

Ten

Delivering the Goods

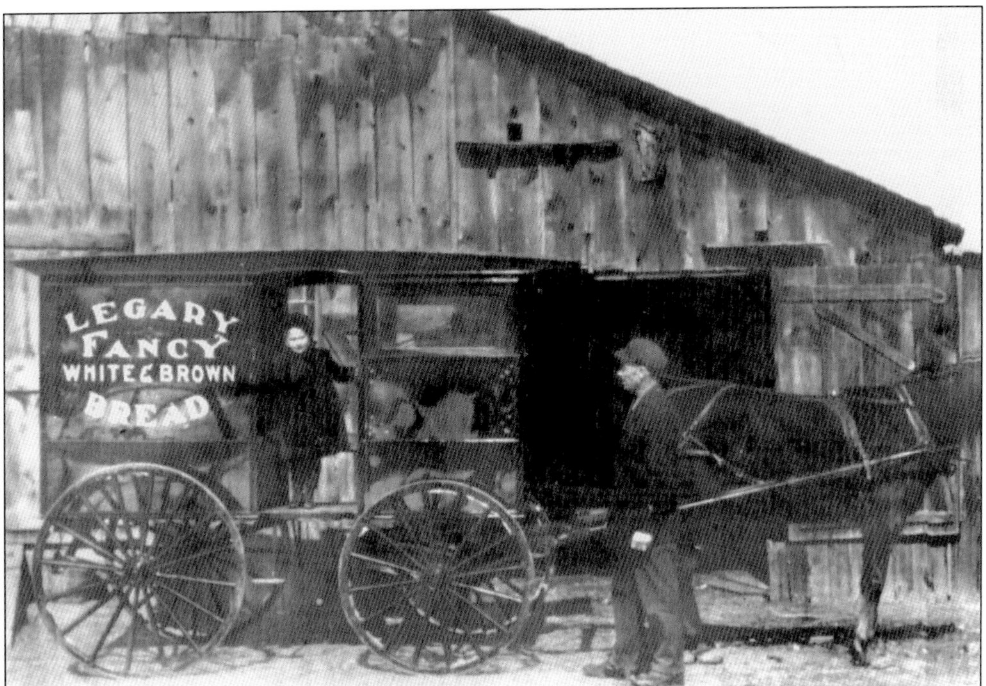

The Legary Bakery was situated on Park Avenue East and employed five expert bakers. It quickly grew in popularity, and Legary was soon known in newspaper advertisements as "the only baker in the city to label his bread so that his customers knew that they were getting quality." His delivery wagon, pictured here *c.* 1920, was a familiar sight on Chatham streets. (Courtesy Dale Legary.)

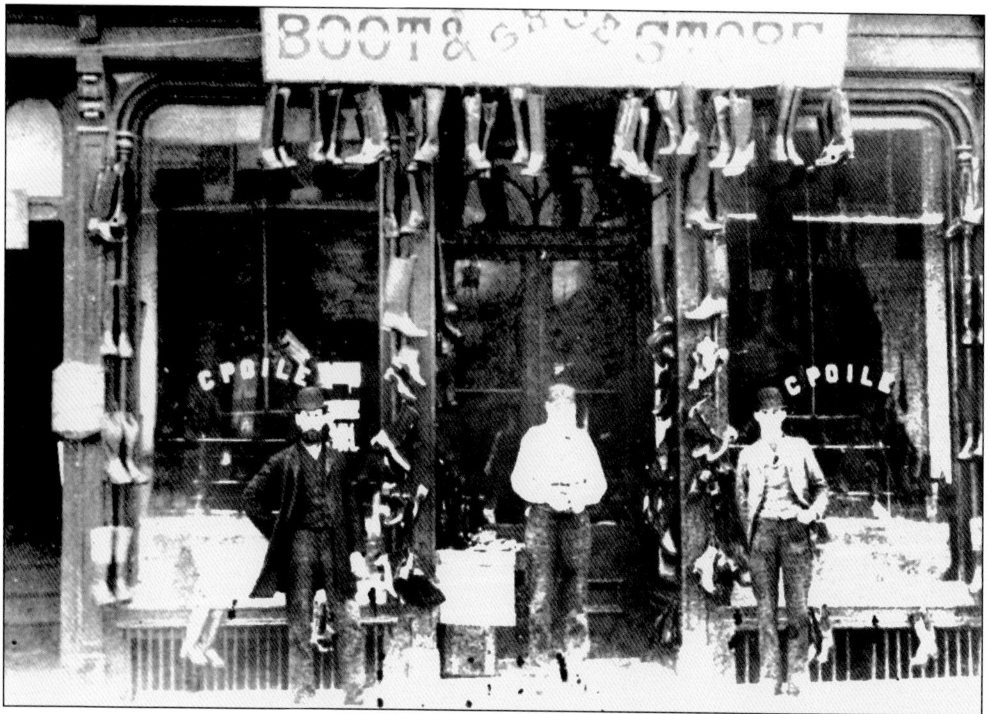

In the 1885 Chatham directory, Charles Poile is listed as an "importer, manufacturer and dealer in Boots and Shoes." As can be seen in this *c.* 1890 photograph, he had a large stock of leather boots and shoes, and according to his advertisement, he "paid special attention to Custom Work and Repairing." His shop was situated at 52 King Street West. (Courtesy Chatham Kent Museum.)

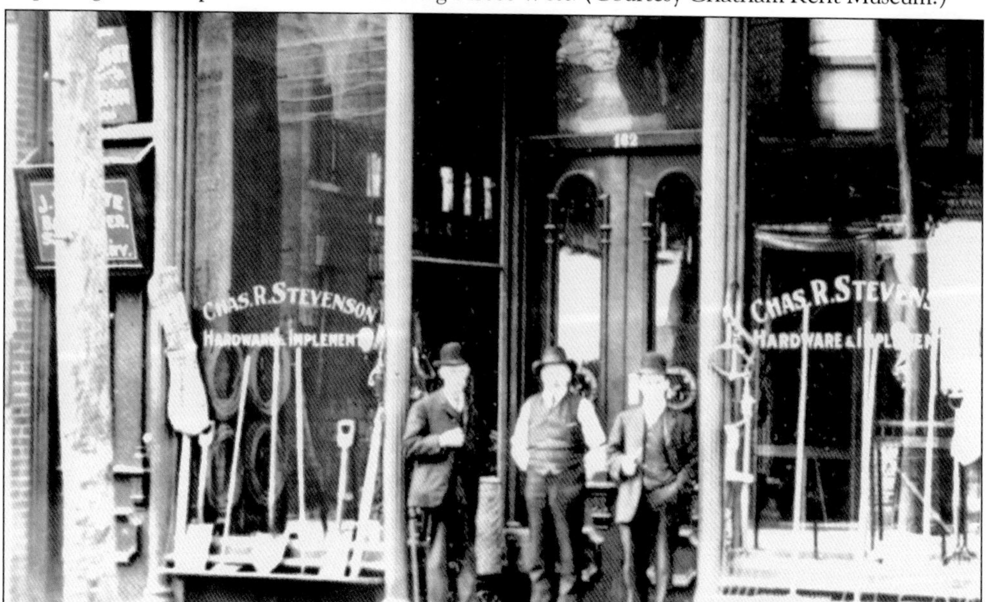

The Charles R. Stevenson hardware store, shown here *c.* 1909, opened for business at 162 King Street West in 1908. A unique feature of this store was its "automobile delivery service" for the "speedy and economical" delivery of hardware purchases. (Courtesy Chatham Kent Museum.)

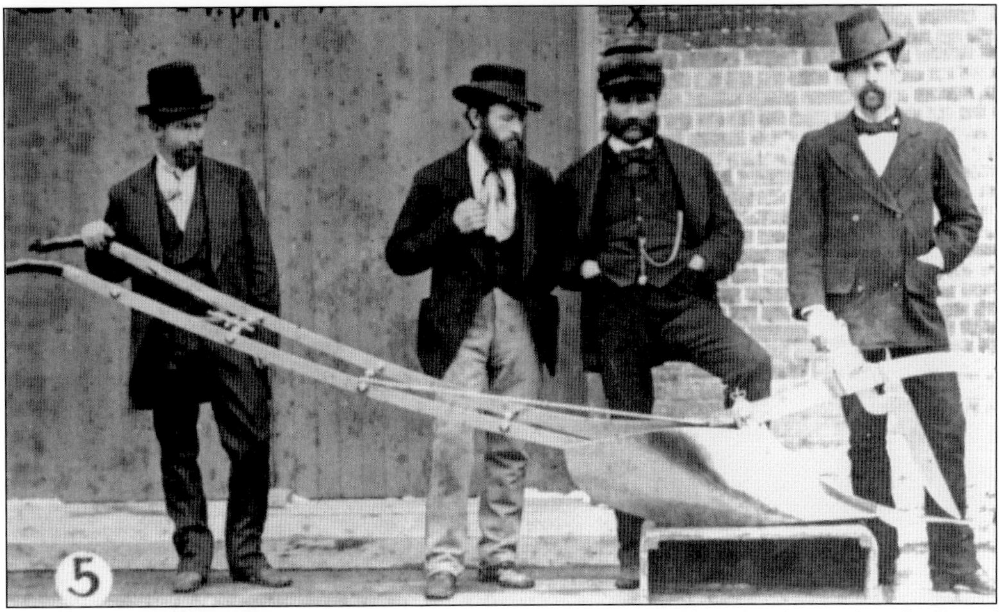

Located on Colborne Street behind the Taylor Mills, the Ross Plow Works produced some of the finest agricultural implements of its day. The Ross plow, pictured here *c.* 1900, was shown at the 1896 Colombian Exposition. Seen from left to right are R. Duncan Grey, Albert Mann, George Ross, and an unidentified man. (Courtesy Chatham Kent Museum.)

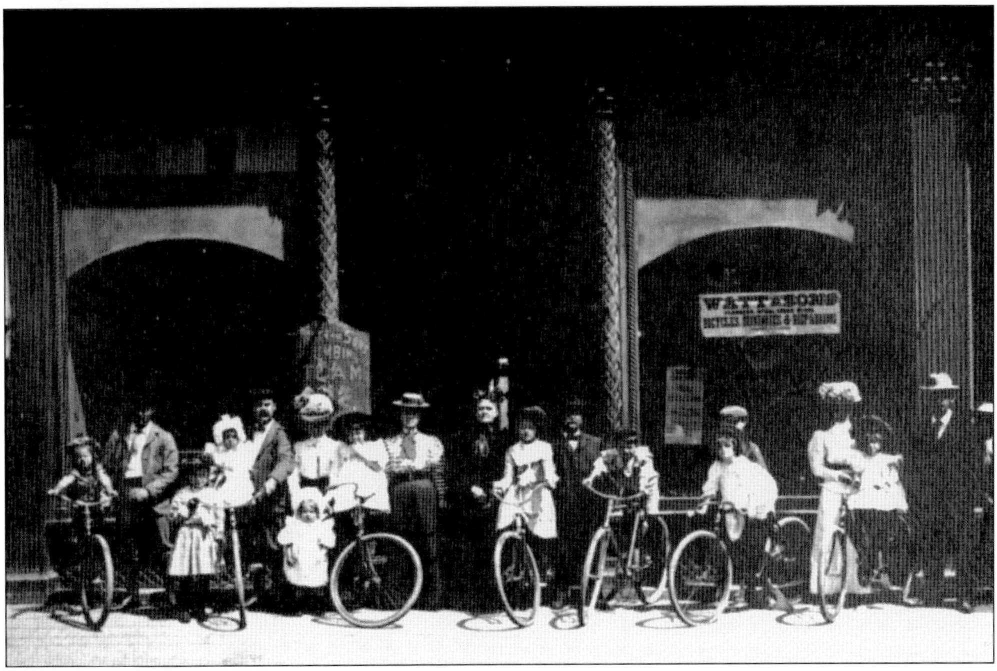

Taken in the late 1890s, this picture purportedly shows members of the Watt family standing outside of their business on King Street West. The store's official name was Watt and Sons Bicycles, Sundries, and Repairing; however, it was also known as the Plumbing Team. The various types of clothing depicted here provide valuable insights into local styles of the time. (Courtesy Chatham Kent Museum.)

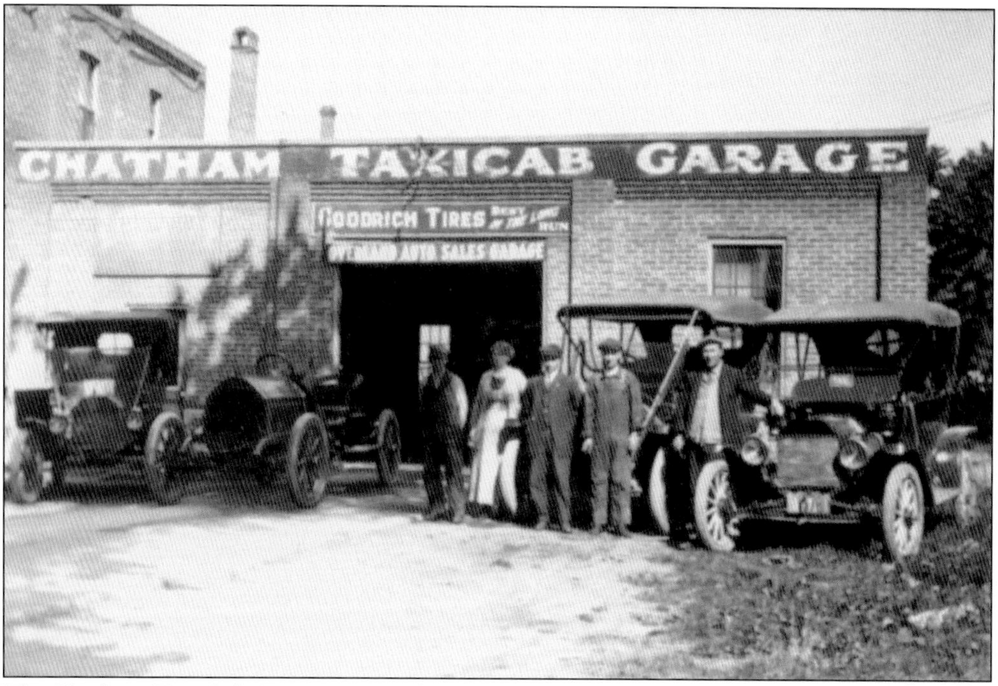

The Chatham Taxi Cab Company, seen here *c.* 1908, was a prosperous car dealership in the early 1900s, operating out of the rear of the Hotel Sanita on William Street. Its serious competitors were the Gray-Campbell Agency on William Street and Martin Buggy Works on Adelaide Street. (Authors' collection.)

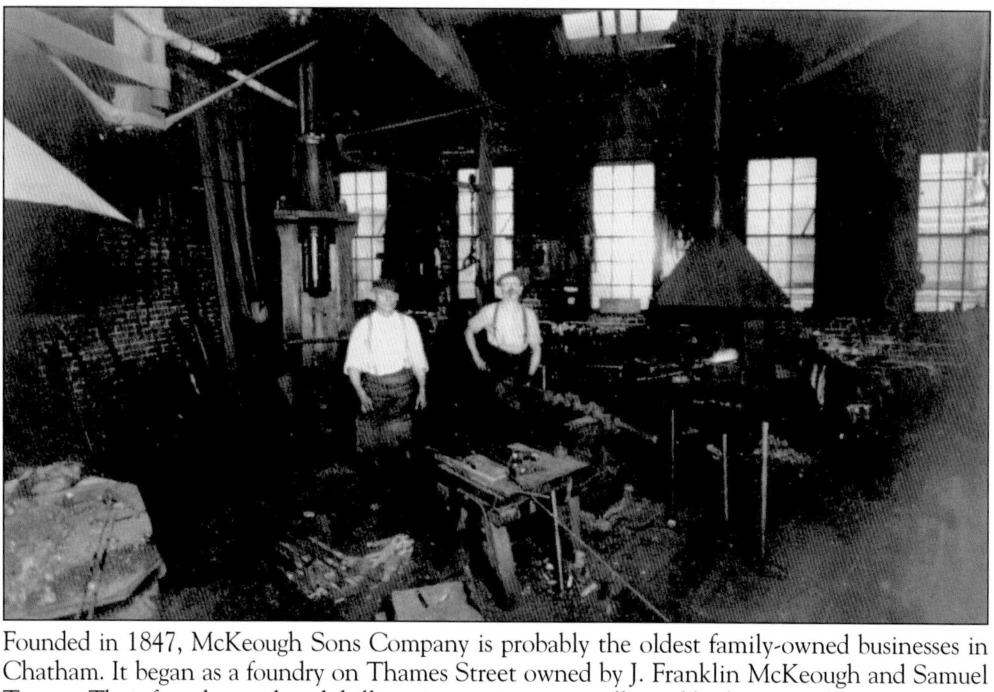

Founded in 1847, McKeough Sons Company is probably the oldest family-owned businesses in Chatham. It began as a foundry on Thames Street owned by J. Franklin McKeough and Samuel Trotter. Their foundry produced drilling rigs, engines, sawmills, and boilers, as well as many other products. Two unidentified foundry workers are shown here at the Dover Street plant *c.* 1890.

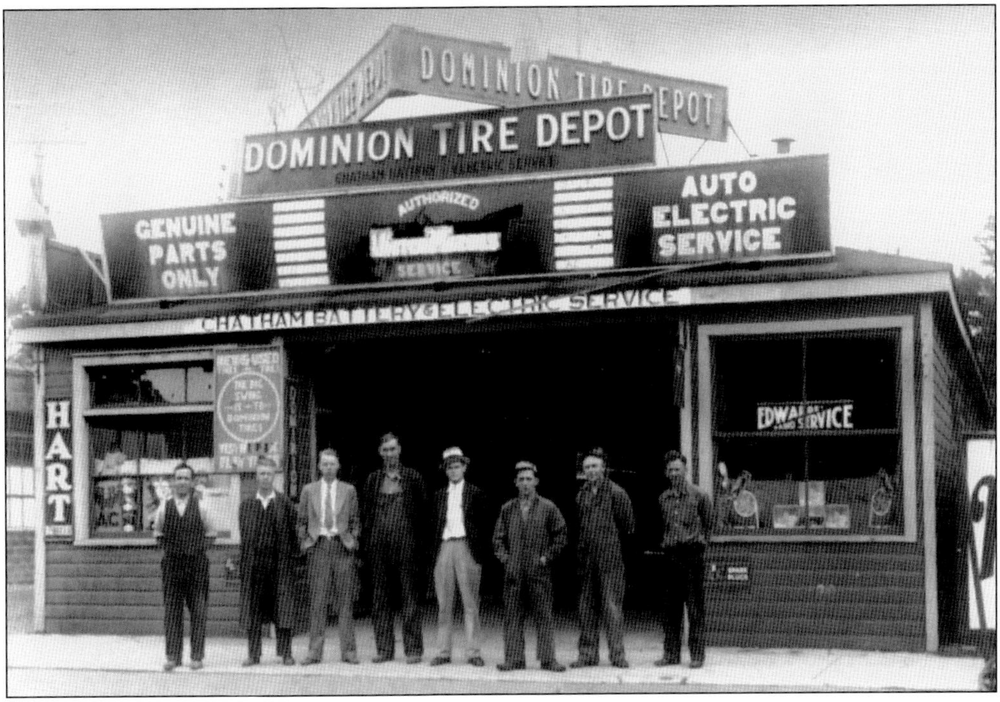

The onset of automobiles in Chatham allowed a number of new business enterprises to come into existence. These new businesses sold batteries, tires, spark plugs, tires, and other items. One such business was the Dominion Tire Depot on the east side of Queen Street near Harvey Street. This photograph was taken *c.* the 1920s. (Courtesy Chatham Kent Museum.)

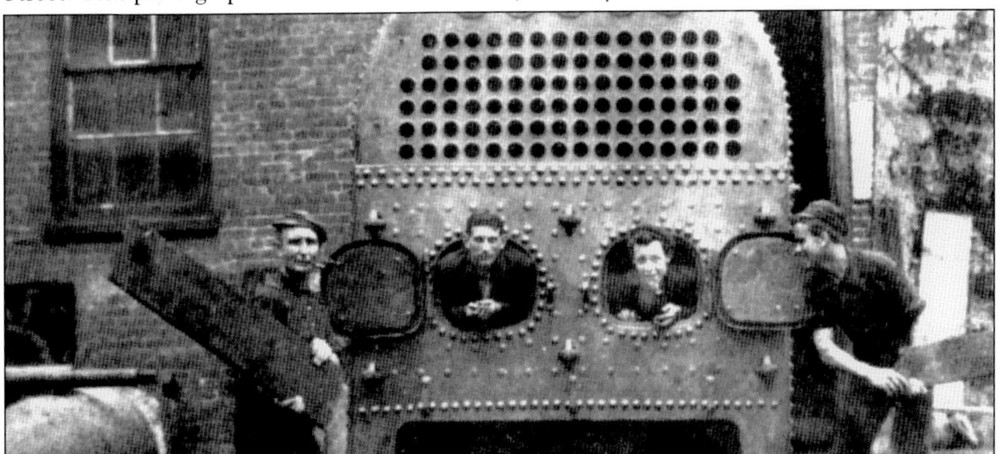

Seen here *c.* 1880, the Park Brothers Foundry, located on William Street where the Terrace Forty Apartments are currently located, was a frenetic and creative place in the mid-1880s. The foundry was busy making steam boilers and pumping machinery for the many drainage projects going on in Kent County. (Courtesy Bill Glassco.)

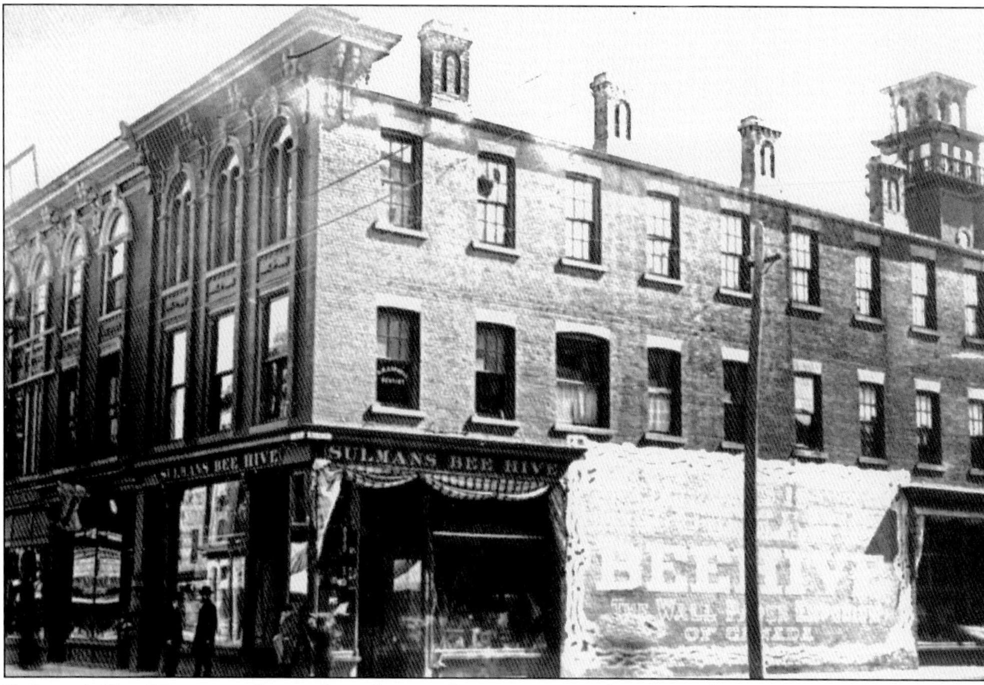

Sulman's Bee Hive was located at the southeast corner of King and Sixth Streets next to Fire Hall No. 1 on Sixth Street. Founded by George W. Sulman in 1888, the store sold wallpaper, stationery, and fancy goods. Sulman also served as alderman and mayor for Chatham, as well as MPP for West Kent. This photograph was taken c. 1908. (Courtesy Chatham Kent Museum.)

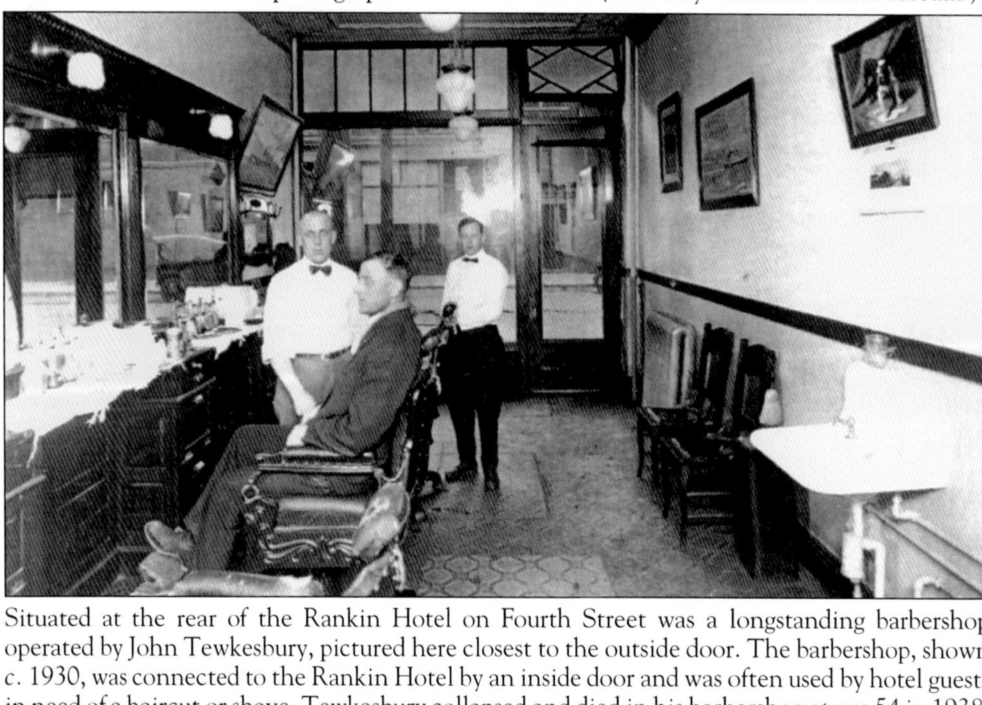

Situated at the rear of the Rankin Hotel on Fourth Street was a longstanding barbershop operated by John Tewkesbury, pictured here closest to the outside door. The barbershop, shown c. 1930, was connected to the Rankin Hotel by an inside door and was often used by hotel guests in need of a haircut or shave. Tewkesbury collapsed and died in his barbershop at age 54 in 1938. (Courtesy Joanne Gail Sewell.)

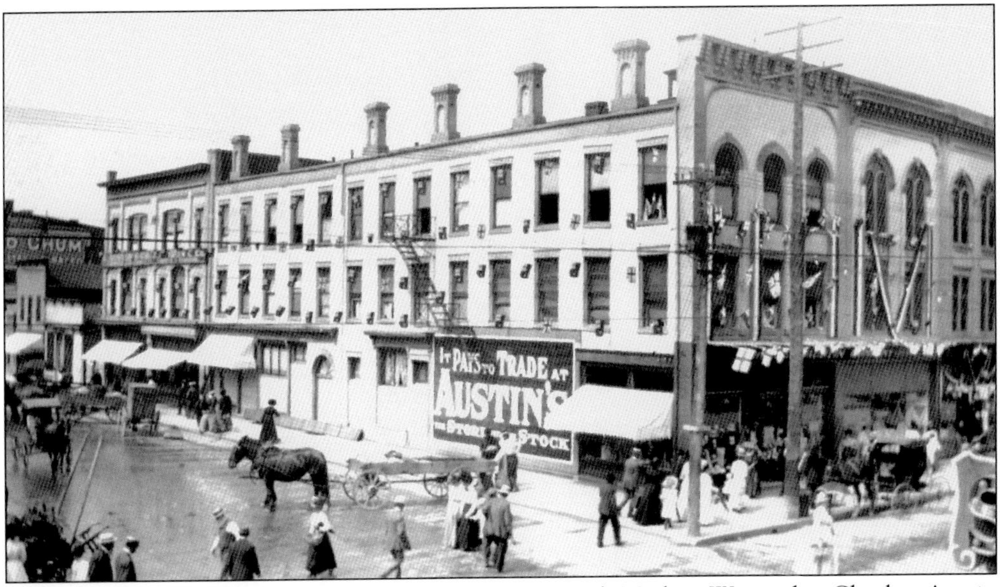

Located on the southwest corner of King Street and Market West, the Charles Austin Department Store was an important and thriving centre of commercial activity for many years. When Austin sold his store, it became the Canadian Department Store, and still later it became the T. Eaton Department Store. It was torn down in the 1980s to make way for the Chatham Downtown Centre. In this *c.* 1905 picture, the Austin Department Store is decked out with flags in anticipation of a parade coming down King Street. (Courtesy Austin Wright.)

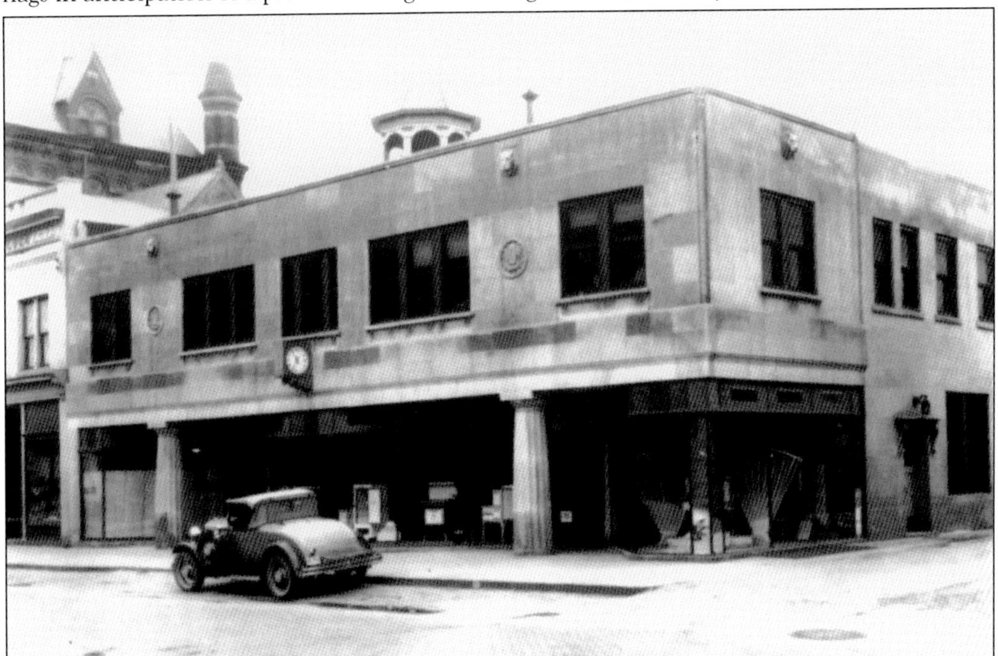

Union Gas, Canada's second-largest natural gas utility, was incorporated in 1911. In 1928, after a period of rapid growth, a new head office was built on the west side of Fifth Street. It remained the company's head office until a new structure was built on Keil Drive in 1966. This photograph was taken *c.* 1928. (Courtesy Union Gas Archives.)

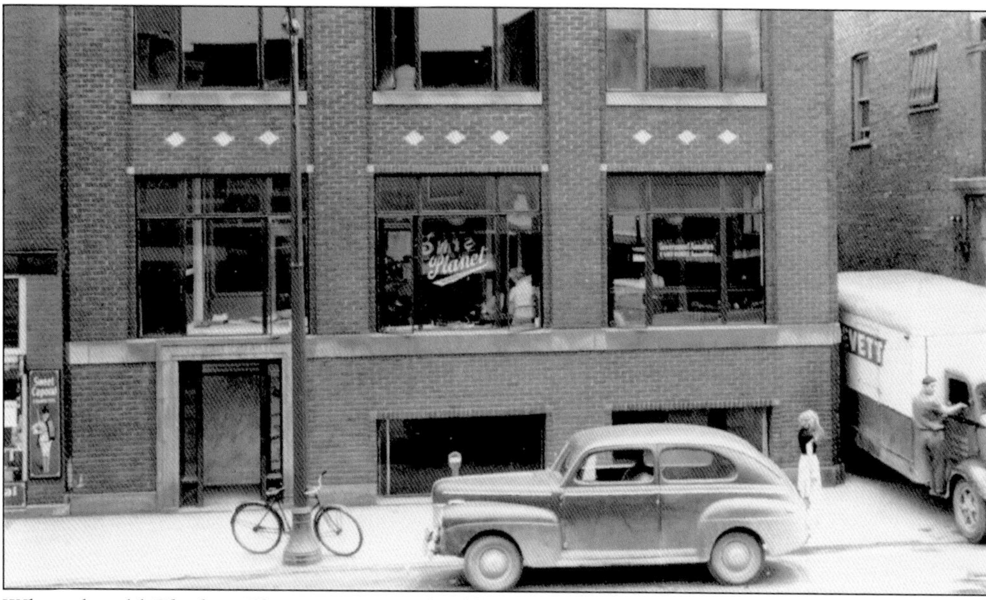

When the old *Chatham Planet* newspaper building burned down in 1913, owner Syd Stephenson wasted little time in constructing a new one using poured cement, which was the newest in building techniques. The new structure, seen here *c.* 1940, still stands today at 202 King Street West. (Courtesy Doug and Dienne Howard.)

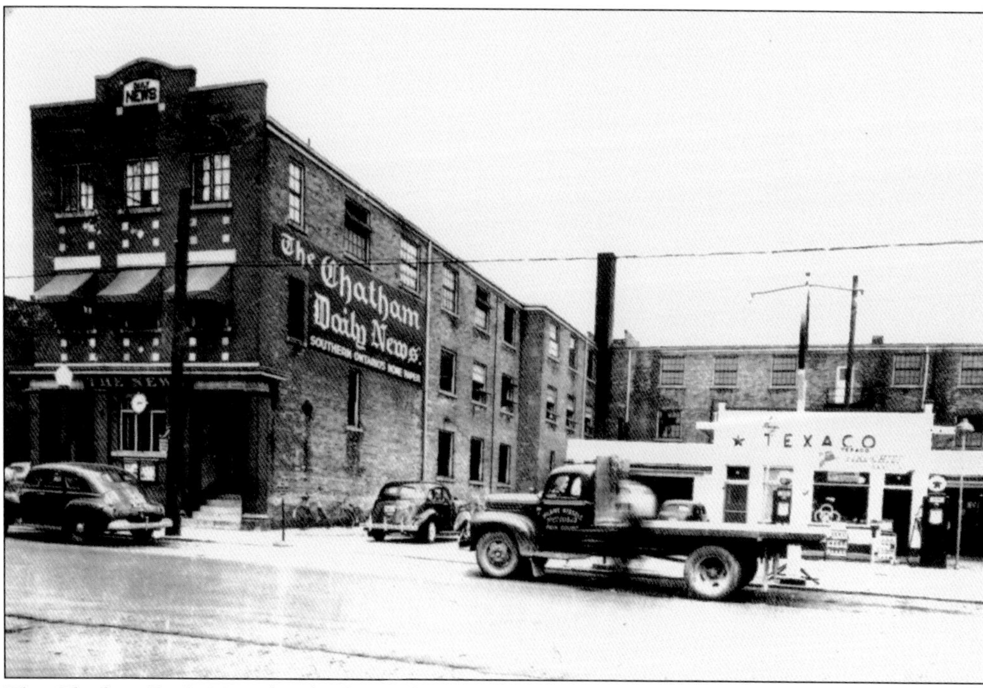

The *Chatham Daily News* has had an office on Fourth Street for several years and has remained largely the same, with only a few alterations (for example, the removal of a floor) since it was built. The Texaco gas station was situated beside the *Chatham Daily News* for many years; the area is now a parking lot for newspaper workers. This photograph was taken *c.* 1940. (Courtesy Doug and Dienne Howard.)

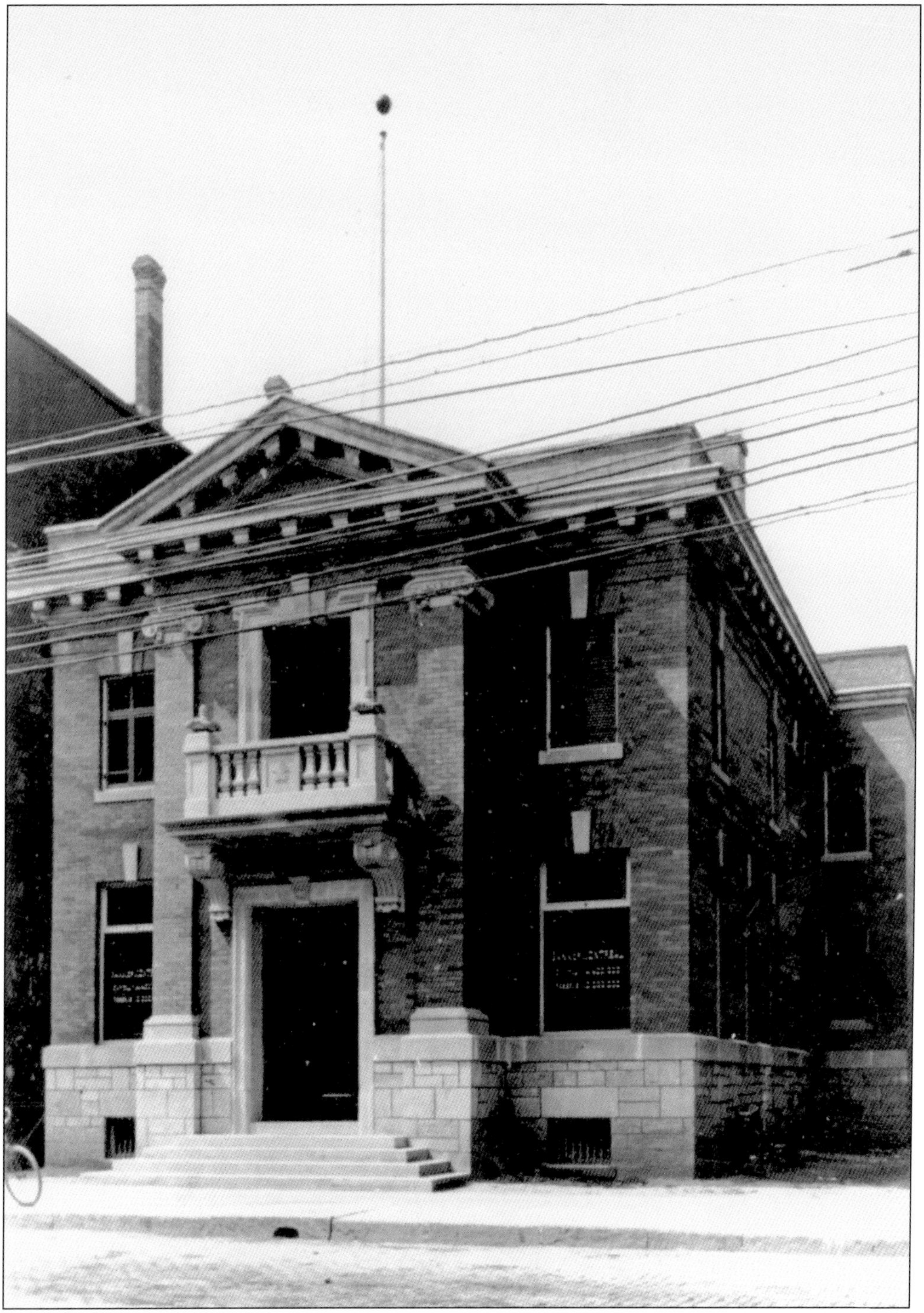

Just east of Scane's Opera House and set back from King Street was the classically designed Bank of Montreal. In later years, the Bank of Montreal moved to new quarters at the northeast corner of King and Fifth Streets. The beautiful structure, seen *c.* 1910, was eventually torn down like so many others on King Street. (Courtesy Mollie French.)

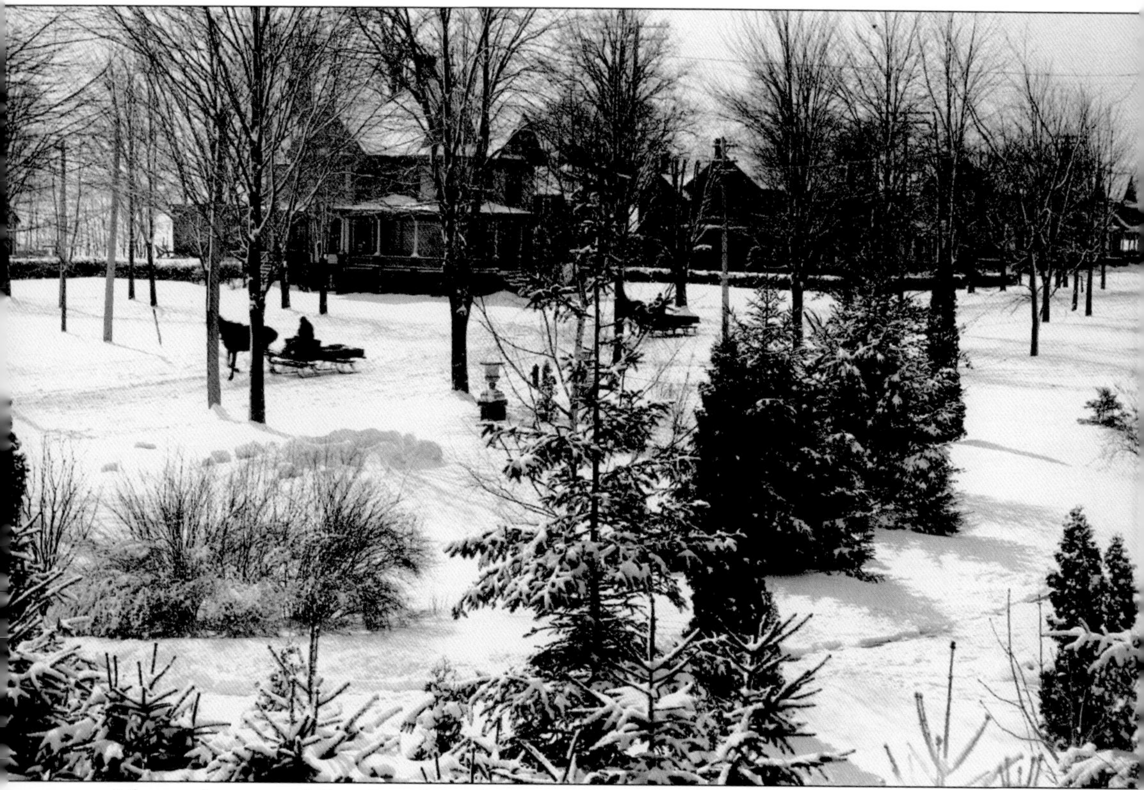

After early automobiles arrived on the scene, they often had major difficulties navigating even the best of roads in the snow and ice of a Chatham winter. When winter arrived in the early 1900s, many people stored their cars and returned to the horse and sled to deliver the goods and to simply get around town. This view, taken by Mrs. Charles Austin *c.* 1905 from her home on King Street West, looks southwest toward the corner of King Street and Inshes Avenue. (Courtesy Austin Wright.)

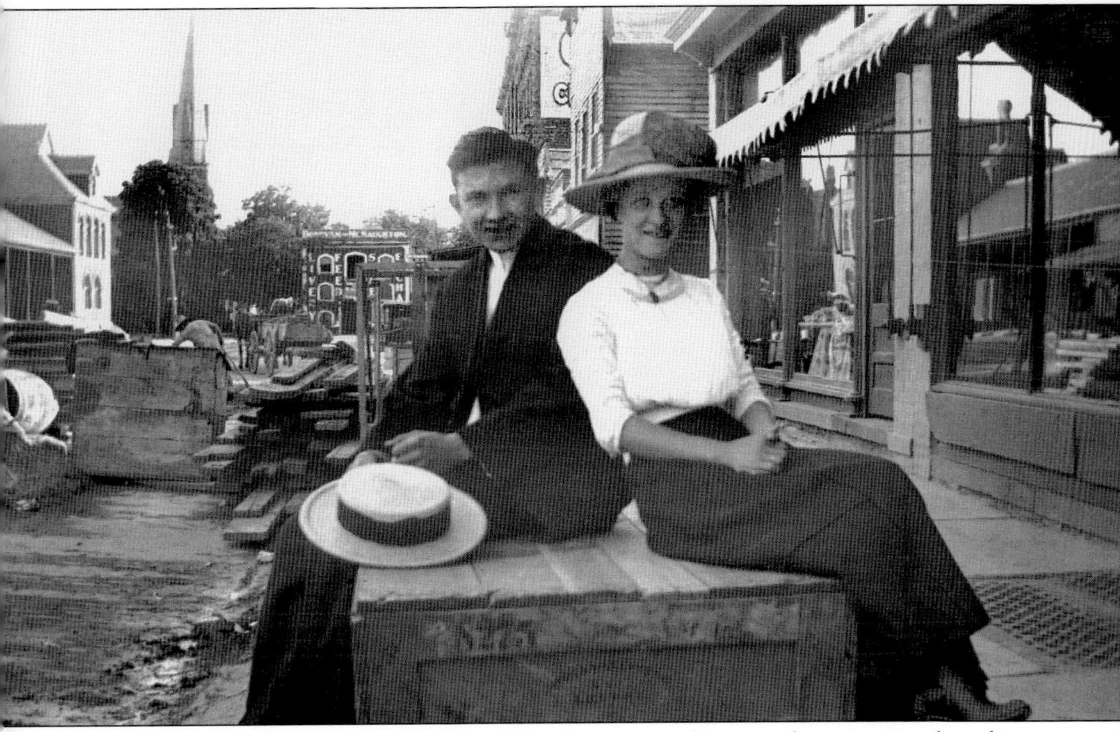

It is not evident whether these people are attempting to move this crate, have just purchased its contents at the nearby Charles Austin Department Store, or are simply using it as a convenient place of rest. Whatever the reason, this charming photograph from the early 1900s depicts a view looking south down Market Street West. The Market Building appears to the left, with the Chatham Police Station at its most southerly end. The steeple in the background belongs to Christ Church, and the business at the end of the street is the livery stable of Donovan and McNaughton. (Courtesy Austin Wright.)

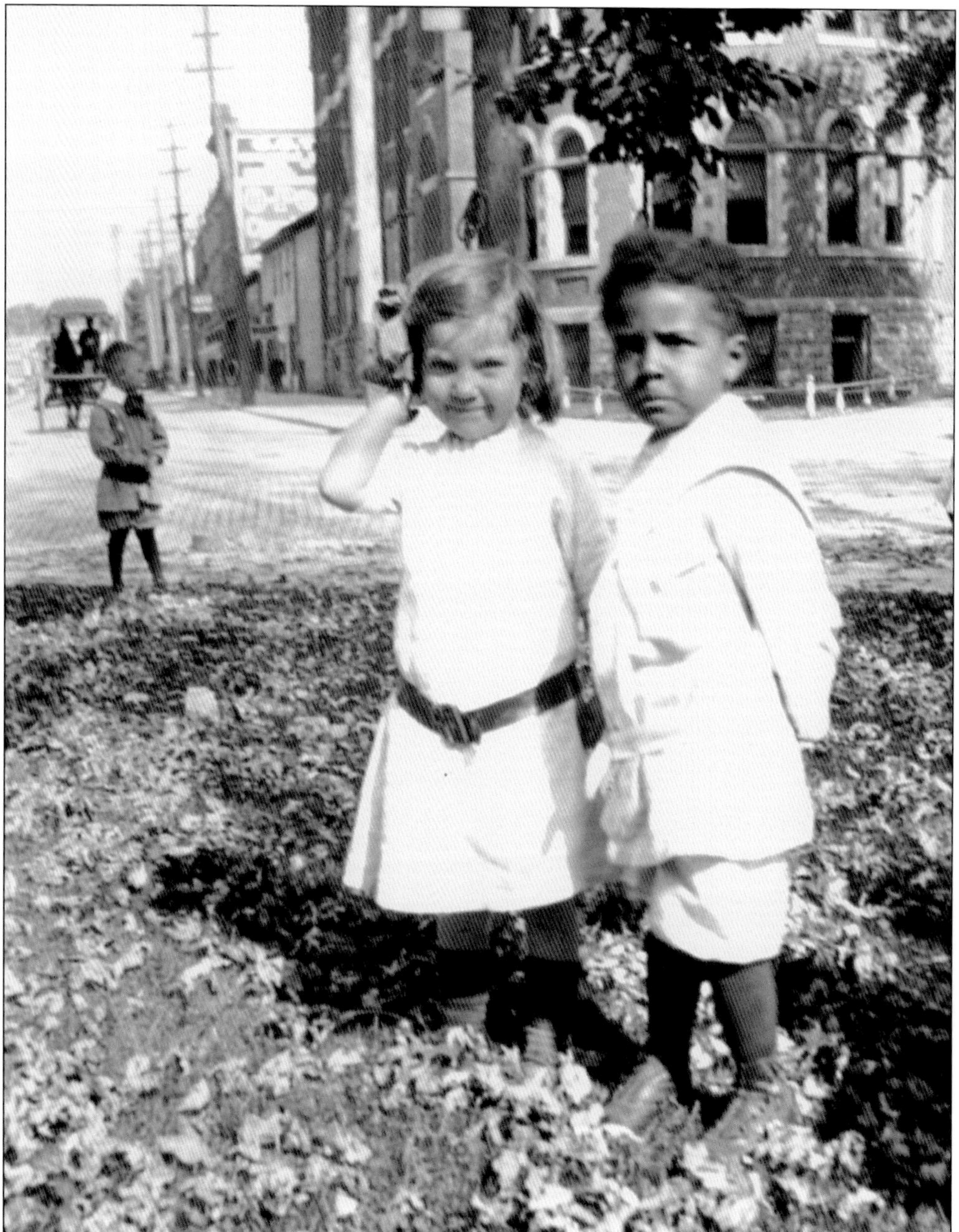

Although these two smartly dressed elementary school students from Chatham Central School did not know it in 1905, they were about to embark on lives that would witness many things. Two world wars, a horrible influenza epidemic, the invention of the jet plane, the television, and the atomic bomb would dramatically change the world in which they lived. From a local perspective, they would also live to see the changes in their own city of Chatham that would elicit great joy as well as utter despair. In reality, however, they were no different from any other students standing in any other schoolyard in any other place and time, cautiously looking forward to the future and innocently pondering the past in much the same way that this book has attempted to do. (Courtesy Austin Wright.)